*saved by beauty*

Roger Housden

ADVENTURES OF AN AMERICAN ROMANTIC IN IRAN

*saved by beauty*

BROADWAY BOOKS / NEW YORK

Library of Congress Cataloging-in-Publication Data

Housden, Roger.
Saved by beauty : adventures of an American romantic in Iran / Roger
Housden. — 1st ed.
1. Iran—Description and travel. 2. Housden, Roger—Travel—Iran.
3. Americans—Travel—Iran. 4. Iran—Social life and customs.
5. Jalal al-Din Rumi, Maulana, 1207–1273. 6. Hafiz, 14th cent.
7. Iran—Intellectual life. 8. Iran—Biography. I. Title.
DS259.2.H68 2011
955—dc22
2011003323

ISBN 978-0-307-58773-2
eISBN 978-0-307-58775-6

Printed in the United States of America

BOOK DESIGN BY ELINA NUDELMAN
MAP BY MAPPING SPECIALISTS, LTD
JACKET DESIGN BY THOMAS BECK STVAN
JACKET PHOTOGRAPH: JALAL SEPEHR
AUTHOR PHOTOGRAPH: DAVIDMULLERPHOTOGRAPHY.COM

10  9  8  7  6  5  4  3  2  1

First Edition

This book is dedicated to the humanity, the dignity,
and the spirit of the Iranian people,
all of whom continue to shine
even in their current time of darkness.

# CONTENTS

## Contents

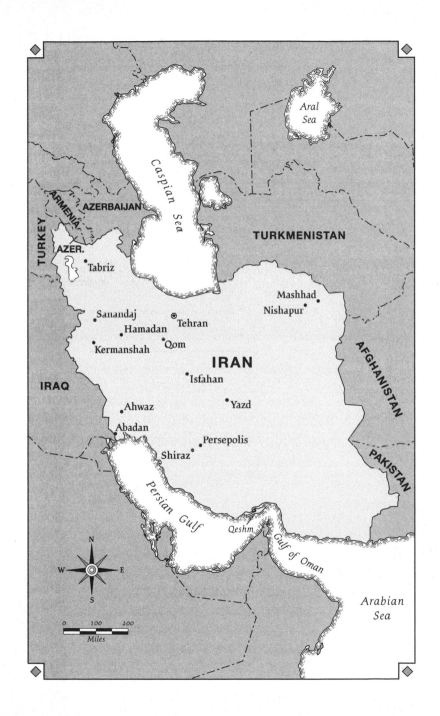

ARMENIA

AZERBAIJAN

AZER.

TURKEY

TURKMENISTAN

Aral
Sea

Caspian Sea

Tabriz

Sanandaj

Mashhad

Nishapur

Hamadan

⊗ Tehran

Kermanshah

Qom

IRAN

AFGHANISTAN

IRAQ

Isfahan

Ahwaz

Yazd

Abadan

PAKISTAN

Persepolis

Shiraz

Persian Gulf

Qeshm

Gulf of Oman

N

W        E

S

Arabian
Sea

0    100   200
Miles

"Why did you come to Iran, Mr. Roger?"

The chair I am sitting in faces three men. One of them wears reflecting wraparound sunglasses. He is a small, almost winsome presence. Harmless, you would think. Impassive as stone. Another fiddles with a pen behind a desk; he barely looks up. He is small, too, though more rotund, with grayish jowls and thin strands of hair brushed up from the side in a vain attempt to hide premature baldness. He is the one who has just spoken. A third man, younger and more dapper, with an intelligent gaze, sits to one side. He wears a checked sports jacket over a blue shirt.

"I am your translator," says the dapper one. "Please, just be calm and try not to get angry. I told them I didn't want to do this. I am just a translator. I am too emotional for this kind of work, but they said I had to help them. So please, cooperate, tell them the truth and make it as easy as possible for both of us."

"*Tell us, Mr. Roger, why did you come to Iran?*" *The man behind the desk repeats his question without looking up, his words sounding as casual as if he were asking about the weather.*

"*I came to write a book to show people in the West that Iran is not what they think. I came to find the soul of Iran, the truth and beauty of its past and also its present.*"

"*And what else?*" *Baldy asks, his gaze still studying the grain of his desk.*

"*Nothing else. That's it.*"

*Shades shakes his head slowly from side to side. Baldy clucks and lightly stabs the desk with his pen. Translator glances first at them and then at me.*

"*Please,*" *he says.* "*Please, give them the right answers. It will be better for all of us.*"

"*We do not believe your answer, Mr. Roger,*" *Baldy is saying, in heavily accented English, scrutinizing his desk all the while.* "*Please, listen to me. We understand you have a problem. We want to help you solve your problem and leave Iran on your flight. But you need to cooperate with us. Now, please, tell us why you came to Iran.*"

*I register that Baldy is eerily, almost condescendingly, polite.*

"*By the way,*" *Translator pipes up in a jaunty voice,* "*Peter from Scotland says hi.*"

*Peter from Scotland says hi? I am instantly, entirely, present, as when an inevitable crash looms on the freeway. They have hacked into my e-mail account. They must know everyone I have seen and everything I have said on e-mail.*

"*Who are you working for, Mr. Roger?*" *Baldy lets fly his question like a bullet.*

"*I've already told you. I work for myself, and I'm working on a book. It's commissioned by Random House in New York. If you look back at my e-mails you will see my correspondence with them."*

*"We know about the book. We are not interested. Many people come here under the cover of artistic or journalistic activities in order to hide their true motives. Nonprofits come here—ones like the Soros Foundation and the Aspen Institute—to spread their liberal agenda and to act as covers for Western intelligence. Now listen to me, Mr. Roger. Do you want to leave Iran?"* Baldy is speaking softly now. *"You are not helping us to solve your problem. You need to tell us the truth. We want to know why you were always changing hotels. We want to know why you wanted to meet Mr. Abbas Kiarostami. We want to know why you went to Kurdistan. Do not play with us, Mr. Roger. Your time is limited."*

I wonder what he means when he says my time is limited.

*"Who sent you here?"* Baldy asks his question without seeming concerned for my answer.

*"Nobody sent me here. I am here to research a book."*

*"Do you know your friend in New York is an agent for the CIA? He's using you. Don't you see that? Do you work for him or for the State Department?"*

They know everything. All my phone calls, all my e-mails.

*"I'm sorry, I know you want me to say something different, but I can't, because there is nothing else to say. I am nothing more than a freelance writer, and I am hiding nothing whatsoever."*

They all shake their heads, even Translator, who I realize is not just a translator after all.

*"You are not helping us to solve your problem. I am sorry."* Baldy is inspecting his fingers and almost mumbling to me from across the room, as if he's lost interest. *"You give us no choice. We are going to have to take you somewhere else for further questioning. Somewhere comfortable. Somewhere you know."*

*"I would like to exercise my right to call the British embassy."*

*Baldy and Translator laugh and shift positions on their chairs. "You are in Iran. You have no rights."*

*Shades doesn't move a muscle. His presence is shadowy, unsettling, even though he does nothing and says nothing, except for an occasional shake of the head. He's like a prop or an extra in a movie scene whose presence sets the whole tone.*

*There is a knock at the door, and a man walks in with my baggage. They must have asked the airline for it before I even sat down in their office. So their questions are no more than a charade. This is all leading to a foregone conclusion, whatever that might be. My answers to their questions are irrelevant.*

*"Please come with us now, Mr. Roger. We will go back to Tehran." Translator is curt now in his directive. I wish they wouldn't call me "Mr. Roger." It reminds me of an affable television personality whose presence in this situation, even in my imagination, is wholly inappropriate.*

*They all stand, and with two behind me and one in front, they walk me out of the airport to their car. I am not afraid. I don't know why, but I feel strangely calm. I feel as if this were a play I landed a part in a long time ago, and now the curtain is finally rising.*

# CHAPTER 1

# writing iran

The inner—what is it?
If not intensified sky, hurled through with birds
And deep with the winds of homecoming.

— RAINER MARIA RILKE

Whenever I think of the color blue, I think first not of the sea or the sky, but of a dome. A dome in Isfahan, Iran. It lodged itself in my mind some thirty-five years ago, one gray afternoon in the British Library, that beautiful building, itself a dome, which at the time housed a few million books and manuscripts on every subject known to man. Oblivious of the scholars shuffling to and fro around me, I gazed for the longest time at a full-color plate of the dome of the Royal Mosque in Isfahan. Its perfection of shape and its blue never left me. It prompted me from that time on to marvel at domes, to appreciate their sensuous precision with a fresh eye, and to love that turquoise blue with a single-mindedness that has dominated my wardrobe and my wall hangings for a lifetime.

It was my Iran phase. Around the same time, I discovered Iranian music and poetry. While my peers were listening to the Stones and Bob Dylan, I would be poring over the Iranian music section of some esoteric record store in London, looking for ethnic folk music or the music of the Sufis, the mystical brotherhoods of Islam. Or I would be in the Middle Eastern Bookshop on Museum Street, looking for translations of the great Iranian Sufi poets, Rumi and Hafez. That music, those poems, had a visceral effect on me. They would bring me down into myself, into my body and the rhythms of my blood: another kind of heart murmur, you might say.

It made for a potent brew, a jumble of feelings and images that somehow conjured the fantasy of a culture that was both sensuous and soulful at one and the same time. For all I knew, my imaginings were mere imaginings. The Shah was in charge then, and his mission to modernize his country made the images of my inner world seem old-fashioned at best, and reactionary at worst. It wasn't cool in Iran then to have an interest in Sufis or anything non-Western. My fascination was probably no more than a young man's longing for a romance and vitality that seemed hard to come by under the somber skies of his native London—a much grayer city then than it is now.

Even so, those images of Iran remained through my lifetime, alive and innocent though never tested by reality. Those colors, that music, that poetry, the beautiful dome, I realize, represented my own personal paradise; a paradise that is neither here nor there, of course, but rather a living sense of presence in which nothing is lacking. A sort of homecoming, you might say.

Those same images linger today in the Persian art on my walls: a large ceramic tableau of overflowing flowers that I bought years ago, and a detailed embroidery, a meter high, of the Tree of Life complete with birds of paradise, that I gave myself from the proceeds of my first book contract. My Iran phase never really went away; neither, it seems, did my nostalgia for the original "home."

We never know until it happens how the images stored in our brains may suddenly leap up out of nowhere to shape our lives.

Thirty-five years later, in the early spring of 2008, I was walking through the redwoods near my home in California with nothing in my mind other than the savor of the forest and the deep trees. I wasn't walking as a writer in search of a subject, even though I had no idea what my next book might be. I was in the positive gap, the one that is empty of content, yet seems to sustain you, like floating in the Dead Sea—as opposed to the kind of gap where you can go into free fall down some endless rabbit hole.

Walking along that path through the woods, my mind was in neutral. Into that empty space, out of nowhere, three words sprang fully formed into my mind: *the other Iran*. I do not know where that phrase came from. I was strolling along with the clouds above and the ground below. My images of Iran had not surfaced for years.

It seems to be one of life's enduring habits to sneak up on us unawares. My next project or enthusiasm (they are usually one and the same) has always arrived unannounced and from left field, rather than through any deliberate attempt to figure it out with pen and paper. Not that I don't try every now and then to dream up subjects and passions I could turn into a piece of work—but they rarely, if ever, materialize that way.

So here I was, embarking on my sixties, out of a second marriage for three years, with a rewarding but precarious occupation that dispenses with the need for a weekly planner, not to mention a yearly one: an occupation that encourages me to follow the lightning wherever it strikes, and in the lightning's time, not mine. I had recently finished writing a long series of books on poetry, and once again, a variant of the perennial question— What do you want to do *now* with your life?—had been flitting about the edge of my mind.

Except it was no longer about doing this or that so much as feeling which qualities and loves really mattered to me, and which I wanted to embody in this world before I left it. None of this was in the shape of an anxiety, or even in the form of words; but as a kind of readiness, or welcoming disposition toward something I could feel was wanting to surface.

Not that I was sitting back waiting for my life to happen. Of course I have wondered at times what on earth I am doing here; of course, as a writer, I have suffered the peculiar sensation, like grasping at air, of not having a subject. In the last couple of years I had flirted with several ideas that seemed promising book subjects. But nothing had had the wings to lift words onto the page.

That's when the rabbit hole can appear out of nowhere: the gap that can open up without warning between the last book, the last painting or start-up project, and what you hope, at least, will be the next one. The kind of gap where you realize that sweating it out means what it says. I went through one of those gaps eighteen months or so before my walk in the woods, and not for the first time. I was having ideas all right; in fact I had ideas aplenty, but my publisher was not impressed. *The Greatest Joy: Having a Purpose Bigger Than You Are.* I don't think so, she said. *On Being Useful.* Uh-uh. No. *Ten Meals to Eat Before You Die: Journey to the Heart of France*—how could anyone say no to that, I thought.

It would save my bacon, so to speak; give me a way forward, let me run round my favorite country for a year. I thought I would use food as the doorway into *La France Profonde,* the culture whose language and literature I loved. I thought it would give my writing career a kick-start into a new future. But no, they were not impressed.

"How can you not be impressed by ten meals to die for? Ten *French* meals?" my brother Mark had asked when I called to tell him. But then he lived in France, was something of a gourmand himself, and ran his own business, the French House, selling the romance of French style to Anglo-Saxons. It was he who had come up with the idea in the first place.

No, they were not impressed. Too regional, too French, too

traditional. The publicity director killed it when she said she couldn't see herself eating *any* of those meals. No *confit de canard*? Really? You don't like the sound, let alone the taste, of bouillabaisse?

A writer's life is about moving on. There's always the hope of the next project, the next great idea. My previous book hadn't turned out to be as great an idea as my publisher and I had hoped it would. Now the *Ten Meals* project had gone the same way before even getting off the ground. My agent tried to cheer me up as I was leaving New York after one of our periodic meetings.

"I have best-selling writers nowadays who have to propose four or five ideas before they get a green light," she said consolingly. (How many more does that mean I have to go?) "It's tough out there," she told me. "People are not buying books the way they used to, so neither are publishers. They're scared." *They're* scared! Don't they know that being a writer with nothing to write about is like being a sailor without a boat, a builder without a hammer, a painter without a brush?

Back home from New York I sprawled on the sofa and gazed unseeingly out of the big window that looks onto one of the most beautiful landscapes I've ever beheld—Marin County, actually, with its big Mount Tam stuck right in the middle distance there before me among contours of pines and madrone trees. As I sat there, I let my eye travel down inward rather than outward for I don't know how long, and let in the true horror of my situation— a writer without a subject, not so long without a wife, fresh from being madly in love with an unavailable woman, and with a most moderate bank account—and I started to smile.

I started to smile, and then I started to laugh. Maybe this was the end of the line for this particular writer, this couch on a Tuesday afternoon in May 2008. Maybe there was simply nothing left for him to say or write. And yet what would be wrong with that? I was still here, and more a lover of life than a survivor of it. I relaxed. Where a moment before I had felt empty, now I felt full.

Not full of myself, in the way that I certainly can be, but full of relief, full of quiet, like after a big outbreath. I had enough money to live on for a year or so, and I would just see what if anything came out of the blue.

It was *the other Iran* that came out of the blue, several months later. I knew instantly that a big fish had surfaced, and that I was going to land it, and soon. When I reflect more deeply on the color blue, deeper still than the image of the dome in Isfahan, I realize that what it really means for me is the sea inside: the deep, uncharted waters of one's own interior life, where unlived desires and loves swim and wheel and turn, calling to us, at times barely audible, at other times with a clarion call, to haul them up into the light before the light goes out.

When I reflect on what is still unlived in me, travel for its own sake, or out of simple curiosity, is not the first thing to come to mind. I have spent a substantial part of my life traveling the world. Nowadays I find the place where I live to be as full of curious customs and enchantments as anywhere. But then, those romanticized images of Iran from my youth had never dissolved, even if they had fallen below the surface; their lingering presence still exerted a magnetic pull that had now emerged in the form of words. Again my response wasn't so much a decision as a realization, a strange elation at the dawning upon me of what was next: Oh! And now *this*! I felt, walking through those redwoods in Marin County, which is so beautiful there is surely no need to go anywhere: *I am going to Iran!* Of course! The power of adventure was upon me again.

As soon as those three words swooped into my mind, I knew the subject was far bigger in scope than my own personal curiosities and subjective story. In recent years Iran has been more at the forefront of people's minds than almost any other country. It is never far from the front pages today, so that phrase, *the other Iran,* arose not only from my personal unconscious, but from the broader context of the current climate. Ever since the hostage crisis of 1979, America's relations with Iran have been strained at best and dangerous at worst. But then it became the crux of the Axis of Evil, as George W. Bush proclaimed to the world. The mullahs, we were told, ran a quasi-fascist state full of terrorists that was on the verge of going nuclear, and that would be the ruin of all of us. With all the help from Ahmadinejad they could have wished for, the White House and the press succeeded in drawing a caricature of Iran that not only demonized an entire culture but dehumanized it.

The image of Iran as a dark and scary place, full of nuke-toting mullahs, remains a difficult one to dislodge from the collective imagination. And, especially in the light of Ahmadine-jad's tirades and intransigence, with good reason. Even more so, since, in June of 2009, the hopes of the Green Revolution were quashed in a stolen election and the violence that followed. And yet, paradoxically, what we also saw at that time on our screens was an Iran that so many Iranians themselves already knew their country to be: a young, vibrant, questioning, highly creative culture with dreams not so very different from our own.

This was the Iran, some six months before those fateful elections, that I wanted to bring to light—to touch and be touched by. I wanted to humanize its culture and its people in my own mind, to resist the temptation to objectify them as "other"—as a people somehow different from and inferior to us and therefore legitimate targets for our aggression; and also to help do something of the same for my readers. I wanted to look beyond the political wrangling altogether, to the truth and beauty of an ancient and sophisticated culture; to know something of life as it is lived there, beyond the slogans and the headlines; to touch the creative spirit of Iran and to be touched by it in turn.

Above all, I wanted to see if the Iran of today could give substance and value to the images I had cherished for decades. Those images—the poetry, the music, the Sufis, the soaring domes—are for me metaphors for wholeness. They have lingered through my lifetime because they represent a culture that embraced both its deepest longings and its delight in the sensuous world—a culture that in my imagination mirrored the possibility of my own synthesis of body and soul, soul and spirit. Finally, they represent a creative genius that has resulted in works of unparalleled beauty.

For my traveling companion I would take along Rumi, guide of souls. Rumi, the thirteenth-century Iranian poet I had been consulting for years—the one whose family had fled Iran before the Mongol hordes, and whose tomb now lay in the city of Konya, in Turkey. Of all poets, Rumi spoke my own heart to me. He knew the primordial sense of home I still hankered for. He knew the loss of it and also the union with it. He called it the "Beloved"; and he sang its praises as no one else has.

So, with Rumi in my pocket, I would set off to discover if the world I imagined was a current reality in Iran today, or merely a chimera of my own making; and if it did exist, whether it might still shine a light on the hidden truths of my own inner world. All this happened and more—more than I ever bargained for.

A couple of months after that walk in the redwoods, I was on a Lufthansa flight to Tehran.

CHAPTER 2

# leaving the known

The function of the imagination is not to make strange
things settled, so much as to make settled things strange.

— G. K. CHESTERTON

There's a cappuccino and some apple cake on my table, a hum
of activity around me in the café at Frankfurt Airport; everything's normal, my flight is on time, and I'm nervous. I've never
been nervous traveling before. But I'm nervous now, sitting here
waiting for my connection to Tehran. I feel like I am about to get
on a plane to nowhere—to nowhere in my known world. The
only other time I have felt anything close to this was when I was
twenty years old and leaving the shores of Europe for the first
time to enter the (then) exotic world of North Africa. Even at
that time, I had felt less trepidation than sheer excitement. Now
the balance has swung marginally the other way.

But why? What about *the other Iran* and the thrill of finally
seeing a land I had dreamed of for years? And then surely I was
used to landing in strange and even remote parts of the world?
I was, but in these last few weeks of preparing to go there, Iran
had already become in my mind a more shifting and complex

world, one with rules and challenges that I had never encountered before. No other country I know of has kept my passport for its visa stamp until the day before my departure. Neither are visas granted automatically, and it was impossible to know beforehand whether or not I would get one. (The same is true for Iranians hoping to visit the United States, I was told later.) Yet I had to book my flights and give them my flight details, leaving it to fate that it would all work out and my tickets would not be wasted. Then they gave me fewer days in the country than there were between my arriving and departing flights; which now meant that I would have to apply for an extension once I got there. At least I am using my British, rather than my American, passport, but I'm not even sure that makes things any easier. Dutch or Irish, perhaps, but British, I don't know. Salman Rushdie is British, and it wasn't much help to him.

"I always wear black," an American professor who had been there a few times confided to me a few days before I was leaving. "I don't stand out that way." Then, "They will always know where you are and what you are doing, so you should know the rules. Sharing a room with any Iranian is not allowed; sharing a room with a woman who is not your wife, not allowed; having sex with an Iranian woman, definitely not allowed; shaking hands with an Iranian woman, not allowed; alcohol, of course not allowed; most things, especially to do with pleasure, not allowed."

I took him seriously. Not that I intended to share a room with anyone, though you never know. But who were *they*? The ones he said would know where I was and what I was doing? I trusted that I would never find out. It remained vaguely titillating, thinking I might be followed or watched. It would be a first, to my knowledge. So whatever it is going to be, and despite any romantic imaginings I might have had, it is not going to be friendly, that is for sure. The Islamic Republic of Iran does not approve of

Western ways, especially American ways. They especially don't like writers. So, American or British, I am probably a marked man anyway.

I'm not feeling much better now on the plane. I am sitting next to a Danish engineer who tells me he is helping to rebuild some antiquated plant. He was there the year before and doesn't relish having to return. He tells me he's worried about his connecting domestic flight, because, he says, none of the signs in the domestic terminal are in English, and they only call the flight gate a few minutes before departure.

He seems as nervous as I am, and he has already been there once. Not a good sign. But then I am embarrassed to acknowledge that I feel a certain relief on looking around the plane and noticing that a large percentage of my fellow travelers are European men. They can't all be as ignorant as I am about where we are going, and they seem perfectly at ease—but then again it is three in the morning, when it's not always easy to distinguish between ease and exhaustion. I also remind myself that one of the two or three women I had seen boarding the plane, a nonchalant Iranian, was dressed in fashionable fitted jeans tucked into high leather boots, with a large silver chain belt draped around her waist. I can see her now, a few rows in front of me, sprawled in her aisle seat. She must know something I don't about landing in Tehran.

I stumbled off that Lufthansa flight somewhere between night and day, half expecting a grim and low-lit airport teeming with humanity, like the ones I had encountered in India. There would be long lines at passport control, glowering men with beards and machine guns, and petulant questions from the customs officer. But I came out, blinking, into a large and spacious structure that could almost have been the international terminal I had left behind in San Francisco. I sailed down an open escalator to the passport queues, which passed along as efficiently as they might in Paris or New York. There were no guns, and no beards that I could see. The woman with the high boots and fitted jeans was just in front of me. As unconcerned as ever, she had now made the small concession of wearing a light silk scarf toward the back of her head. When it was my turn, the officer met me with a smile, looked briefly at my passport, and said, "Welcome to Iran!"

I looked up, surprised, a little taken aback. "Thank you," I said. "You're welcome," he said. My body softened. So did my mind. I laughed at myself for having generated such concern because of some small visa problem. But then it wasn't just that; nor was it only the warnings of the American professor. I don't even have a TV at home; yet in that moment I realized that our collective fear and suspicion surrounding Iran had somehow entered my skin without my ever having been conscious of the fact.

After all, I was a liberal Anglo-American living in the Bay Area, one of the most progressive places in the world. I tended to scoff at the fearmongering of the media and the departing Bush administration; at their clichéd images that neatly divided the rest of the world into good and evil. I liked to think that my European background gave me a more complex and nuanced picture of world affairs. You might call me self-satisfied, smug, and complacent. You would be right. But there we are. These were the assumptions about myself that my anxiety had brought to the surface and challenged all the way from Frankfurt.

And then there were the friends of mine who, on hearing I was going to Iran, said I was either courageous or crazy. Right there, passing through passport control, before even having set foot in this country, I was already feeling sheepish and ignorant for the collective images I'd brought with me despite myself—and on my friends' behalf as well as my own. Here am I, I thought, the intrepid traveler, standing in a perfectly normal airport, waiting for my bags at a perfectly normal baggage carousel, having fallen prey to fears I didn't even know I had—fears, I realized with some relief, that seemed unwarranted by the actual reality that had greeted me.

The lobby of the Laleh Hotel in Tehran is a spectacle of tired and faded opulence: once glitzy chandeliers, red flock chair coverings, banisters with exaggerated scrolls, and polished brass wherever you look. My coffee turns out to be the instant variety. The coffee cup is a white one, thick and slightly chipped, the kind you might find in a canteen or an old-fashioned diner. It is late in the morning the day after my arrival and I am in that purgatorial, faintly jellylike state so familiar to anyone who has recently landed in a country with a twelve-hour time difference from the one they left behind. Before the Revolution the Laleh had been the Intercontinental. Still one of Tehran's foremost hotels, a slab of white some fifteen floors high, it remains in something of a design time warp, layout and design reminiscent of the 1970s, even though it was refurbished some years ago with a distinctly Middle Eastern taste for shiny surfaces.

The lobby is crowded. Like most large hotels, the Laleh is a place for doing deals, having meetings, and holding conventions. Three men in suits (though without neckties, a symbol in the Republic of Western cultural imperialism), briefcases in hand, are standing just by my table. A tall woman wearing jeans under a sort of smock—I learned later that you call it a manteau—and a light green headscarf on her head walks purposefully up to them and shakes each of them by the hand with an authority that seems to confirm her status as a peer rather than an assistant or a secretary. They all stroll off together for their meeting, leaving me to contemplate what the professor had said back in San Francisco.

*You don't shake hands with women.*

For an hour or more I gazed somewhat vacantly at the ebb and flow of people around me. My body had landed. My mind was still between worlds. But then finally, in a burst of energy between one wave of jet lag and another, I hauled myself up to make a brief foray into the city. I stepped out toward the jangle of traffic, blinking for a moment at the unfamiliarity of the street before me, the crowded sidewalks, and the concrete office blocks of the sprawling, dusty, muggy city. The only difference between one building and the next was how tall or small the gray block was. Uniform concrete, everywhere. A hundred years ago the city was no more than a village, chosen as his new capital by the ruler of the time merely because it was near his ancestral lands. The fumes of incessant traffic curled in the yellowing air. Horns honked, motorcyclists rode on the sidewalk, taxis swerved in and out like fairground rides, pedestrians wove their way through the madness with the skill and patience of chess players. Every car had at least one badge of battle—a dent, a missing headlight, a twisted fender. Glowering over everything was a huge portrait of the Supreme Leader, Ayatollah Khamenei, pinned on a wall of one of the larger concrete blocks.

My first impression was of a grim, uninviting scene. Any city in, for example, India, is chaotic, dirty, and filled with exhaust fumes. To my eyes in that moment, this street in central Tehran lacked something that Delhi or Calcutta did not; for all the motion and commotion, there seemed to be an absence of vitality, of exuberant aliveness. Yet perhaps this was merely my perception, filtered through a veil of jet-lag fog.

Whatever its origins, a curtain of gray was beginning to settle over my mind. Perhaps I had made a dreadful mistake. Perhaps I had concocted a whole story that existed nowhere but in the right side of my own brain. One dark thought led to another, and soon there was no stopping them. Who, after all, would want to come of their own free will to a place like this? To this unremitting drabness? And at this particular time, with the Americans and Israelis threatening to bomb the place any minute? In that moment, as I faced the endless gray slabs of the buildings, the madness of the Tehran traffic, the grimness of the general impression before me, the thought raced through my mind that I had indeed been prematurely seduced by my own fuzzy longings, as when you realize you have fallen in love with someone you made up in your own mind, who in reality is a completely different and inappropriate person.

But right then, there in the distance, at the far end of the side street opposite the hotel, my eyes fell upon the herald of an older, saner world: a great mountain, patches of snow still on its sides, raising its bulk against a hazy sky. I stood and gazed for a moment at its sober stillness. I was not in Tehran to appreciate fine buildings and grand avenues, it reminded me. Or inspiring scenery—though this mountain at the end of the street was a welcome surprise. I would go to Shiraz, to Isfahan, to the desert and the mountains for that. I wanted to stay in Tehran for a few days because there were people I wanted to meet here whom I would be unlikely to find anywhere else.

The creative edge of life in most countries is concentrated in the capital city. The capital is an indicator of where the broader culture is heading. It sets the pace of change and exchange in ideas, in art, in fashion, and in cultural and technological innovation. It is the cosmopolitan place of convergence for people of different religions, races, and skill sets. If there is one place in Iran that even begins to match this description, it is Tehran. Only in Tehran, for example, could I expect to meet a figure like Toufan, the woman I was expecting to have dinner with later this evening, if only I could stay awake that long. Toufan—I never heard anyone refer to her other than by her first name—is assistant to Iran's legendary film director Abbas Kiarostami, and known by her friends as the unofficial mayor of Tehran for her pole position in Tehran's social network. I had been told she would open doors for me in Tehran that I never knew were there.

Thirty years ago Tehran was home to four million people. Now its infrastructure is groaning under the pressure of ten million people trying to live and work there. Millions have swarmed in from the provinces in hopes of a livelihood, and life is as difficult and frenetic here as in any megacity in the world. The mountain, the nearest of the Alborz range, which stretches to the Caspian Sea, is Tehran's saving grace. In winter, those who can afford it ski there; in spring and summer, thousands walk in the parks on its lower slopes and while away a Friday afternoon in the teahouses there (Friday being the Muslim equivalent of Sunday).

As I stood now at the edge of this traffic madness, having to launch myself into the fray to reach the other side, the mountain reminds me: stay calm, stay patient, and move like lightning when a space opens up.

A space did open up and I did reach the other side, sidestepping a motorcyclist as he jerked his wheel to miss the taxi in front of him by no more than a centimeter. Coming toward me on the sidewalk was a young woman wearing dark glasses and a nose bandage. A tight-fitting manteau hung down over her jeans and a bright scarf was perched way back on her head. By her side was a tall young man in jeans that he must have been poured into. His black hair was scooped high into an Elvis quiff. Two boys were hawking cell phones and sunglasses. The storefronts were full of electronic goods from Japan and China: flat-screen TVs showing the latest soccer game from Europe, CD players, more cell phones. People pressed around the windows, staring mostly at the soccer. Two young men glanced up from the game to notice my presence. "Manchester United!" one of them said, grinning. I nodded, gave him a thumbs-up, and grinned back.

Such a harmless exchange, but it brought the street to life for me, and my dark mood of just moments before began to lighten. I saw, and not for the first time, how my attention generally overlooks the ordinary, or what I would judge to be the humdrum. I prefer the color and the drama of the graceful line, which were nowhere in evidence in this Tehran street. Until that moment of exchange with the football fan, I had neglected to see the life that was all around me. I was a perfect candidate for the wisdom in those great lines of *Middlemarch:*

> *If we had a keen vision and feeling for all ordinary human life, it would be like hearing the grass grow and the squirrel's heart beat, and we should die of that roar that lies on the other side of silence. As it is, the quickest of us walk about well wadded with stupidity.*

*Well wadded with stupidity.* That would be me, until the soccer fan woke me from my trance. I wandered on through the streams of people in the dusty light of the city, going nowhere in particular, until my attention was caught by a building that announced itself as a *hammam,* or bathhouse. After a long flight there could surely be no better place to soothe my bones. I had once experienced a hammam in Turkey, and remembered well the macho massage I had had there, the effects of which, not altogether pleasant, had lasted for hours. I strolled over to and down the white marble stairs into the Iranian version of a male fraternity club.

The square pool of hot bubbling water had a fountain in the middle, out of which dribbled a sorry thin stream. Every surface was covered in large white tiles, with blue ones bordering the floor and ceiling. A large dome above the pool let in light from the sky. The room was pungent with the fragrance of bay leaves. Several men were chatting in the pool, and others were sitting at tables by a counter where you could get tea and snacks. They all wore towels, white ones. I wondered if Iranian men were genetically more hairy than my own stock. But then, I thought, they *are* my own stock, Indo-Europeans all of us, the word *Iran* derived from *Aryan*. Before 1935 the country had always been known as Persia, but then the Pahlavi Shah, father of the last Shah, changed the name to Iran to impress Western powers with Persia's racial pedigree.

The man at the front desk issued me my own white towel and a pair of Bermuda shorts covered in palm trees, and in minutes I was in the pool along with the others. One man, pensive and on his own, was sipping black tea from a small glass that he held high above the surge of the jet stream. A couple of elderly gentlemen were gossiping in hushed tones, the water up to their necks. I sank down into the swell and let the heave of the water sway me this way and that.

The curtain over my mind lifted away, and I contemplated the fact that I had spent much of my life in the city of Bath in England, and not once in all those years had I immersed myself in its warm waters. Yet the first thing I do on arriving here is to drop into a hammam as if I had been doing so all my life. I made a promise to myself that when I next went to Bath I would go to the baths. Thoroughly soaked and softened in body and mind, I eventually hauled myself out and peered into the massage room that was off to the side. A burly man in his fifties with a mane of white hair and a drooping mustache was just finishing up with a client.

"I will be free in a couple of minutes if you like," he said, in excellent English. With a sudden amnesia obscuring the memory of my Turkish experience, I nodded and sat down to wait. It would be a cultural experience, at least, to know what an Iranian massage was like.

"Where are you from?" This would be the first of countless occasions that the question would be fired my way over the coming weeks.

"I live in America but I am from England," I replied, unsure myself about where I really belonged now after ten years in America.

"I used to live in England," the man said as he began to press the sides of his palms along my spine. "That is where I learned massage, in Leeds, back in the seventies, at the Physiotherapy Institute. I trained there for three years and then came back to Iran. They were the best years of my life. Do you know Leeds?"

I didn't. Leeds is in the north and I am from the south, that distinction being as well defined in the UK as it is in the States.

"I went there in the Shah's time," he went on. "When I came back I had no idea we would vote the ayatollahs into power. We got rid of one tyrant and now we have many."

I remembered the professor's words. There were informers everywhere. Was this man fishing for a response from me? Perhaps he was in the pay of the government, an English-speaking plant who could check out the prejudices of his tourist customers. I was pained to see that, despite the reassurance I had felt on my arrival, my wariness remained just under my skin, even on a massage table. The masseur, a government plant? I mumbled some vague agreement and gave myself over to his work on my back, his confident hands and easy charm ironing my anxieties away in moments. For all I knew, people here could probably speak as freely as they can anywhere.

His image was just what you might imagine of an Iranian masseur in a hammam: the burly, self-confident presence, the big mustache, someone, surely, who had learned the trade from his father, who had learned it from his father before him. But no, he had trained in Leeds. In physiotherapy, which may not quite fit with the aura and smell and venerable tradition of the hammam, but his time in Leeds had served him well and when I eventually rose from that table, innocent of any ill-advised words, I felt like rubber, all flow and bounce.

I returned to the Laleh Hotel to find a swarm of people, nearly all men, filing through its doors. They were delegates for a conference on Rudaki. I had never heard of him, but he was apparently Iran's first great literary genius, and more than three hundred people from all over Iran and Tajikistan were descending on the Laleh for two days to discuss his work. Known as the founder of Persian classical literature, he lived and wrote poetry between 858 and 941 in a region of the Persian Empire now in Tajikistan.

The lobby was humming with excitement over a man who was writing at approximately the same time as *Beowulf* was being composed in Anglo-Saxon England. In the time of Rudaki, Europe was still deep in the Dark Ages. These delegates were as animated at the prospect of discussing this man's work as if he had died only yesterday. But in their minds, he had never died at all. I would come to see that Iranians hold time and history on a far longer wavelength than we do. Their perspective is born from a cultural identity stretching back three thousand years.

Later that evening, I went to visit Toufan. Her husband, a demure older man with brushed-back silver hair, ushered me into their living room. Toufan was leaning back on her sofa, the quintessence of Iranian beauty, grace, and class. She could pass for a Persian Sophia Loren. Dressed in Parisian couture, in middle age and at the same time ageless, with at least one child in his twenties, she had large arched eyes, sculpted cheekbones, midnight-black hair falling to her shoulders, and the easy grace of someone who had learned over a lifetime how to say no without offense.

I followed her husband over to the sofa and shook Toufan's hand. A faint embarrassment fringed the edge of my attraction to her. Three of her friends and her younger sister were sitting around her, and while Toufan made the introductions, her husband wandered back into the kitchen to continue making dinner.

Toufan's world, I was to discover over an informal dinner of spaghetti and eggplant, was the privileged enclave of North Tehran, where everyone seemed to speak fluent English or French, had been educated in Europe, and was wealthy enough to leave the country anytime he or she felt like it. It was a world of affluent families, businessmen, intellectuals, and international artists, a world as passionately Iranian as anywhere else in the country, except that the Iran they inhabited behind their walled gardens might as well have been on Mars for the poor neighborhoods of South Tehran, just as life on the Upper East Side has nothing in common with the reality of the South Bronx.

It was because of a jar of marmalade that I was sitting there in her living room. A few days before I left San Francisco, a woman I had never heard of called me and said she had heard I was going to Iran.

"My name is Judy Stone," she said. "I would like you to take a jar of my homemade marmalade to Toufan, assistant to Kiarostami. I was the film critic for the *San Francisco Chronicle* for thirty years, and she helped me arrange an interview with him. I have never met her, but she has always been so kind to me on the phone. My marmalade is legendary, you know. Would you come over and pick it up?"

Her quirky chutzpah had charmed me. As soon as I had sat down in her kitchen, Judy—a tiny woman with a round face and darting eyes behind large spectacles—produced two jars of marmalade, one very large and one smaller one.

"Which one can you take?" she asked.

I took the smaller one, and that was my calling card for Toufan. Judy had told me that Toufan was not only Abbas Kiarostami's assistant, but his confidante and friend. She had been closely involved in the production of Kiarostami's film *A Taste of Cherry,* which won the Palme d'Or at the Cannes Film Festival in 1997. In 2007 he received the Kurosawa Award for Lifetime Achievement in Filmmaking. He is the most public face of Iran's creative film industry, and he has asked Toufan more than once to play a part in a film. She has always refused.

"I can only be me," she says with just the hint of an imperial air. "I don't want to pretend to be someone else. I couldn't do it."

Toufan was being herself at this very moment, a demure mistress of ceremonies leaning back on her sofa and enjoying the company that she had brought together at a moment's notice. The living room we were sitting in was furnished with fine antiques. She had a good eye; when she wasn't at home she ran her own upscale private antiques store. A selection of Kiarostami's photos—he is a photographer, poet, and sculptor as well as a film director—hung on the walls alongside a few European paintings from the nineteenth century.

Toufan introduced her younger sister by saying she had recently moved back to Iran from L.A. with her two children. I was surprised and puzzled. Why would anyone swap L.A. for Tehran? The reaction was immediate, and I felt exposed for my own cultural prejudices. But her sister assured us she could not have made a better decision. She was divorced, and back in L.A. she had been working day and night to support herself and her children. She would always be exhausted, and could do little more than slump in front of the TV in the few hours left to her before bedtime. Every now and then, only half seriously, she would tell the kids that she thought they should all move to Tehran, where she would have help from her parents.

One night, while she was flipping mindlessly through the channels, her thirteen-year-old daughter said, "Let's do it. Let's go live in Tehran. You're not happy here." It was the permission she had been waiting for without knowing it. Three months later they were in Tehran. She has moved into a complete support system of family and friends. The all-American kids are even starting to like it.

"It's true that we are there for each other in a way that is rare in the West," Toufan said, her enormous eyes on me. "But can you imagine how suffocating that can be?"

I had never thought of it that way. I had never experienced the joys and the pains of a large family. I was seven when my brother was born, sixteen before my sister arrived, and never knew my grandparents. I had always somewhat idealized an Italian stereotype, all ready warmth, touch, caring, and soup. I'd never thought about suffocation, though when she said it, it was obvious. So obvious that I could feel the recoil.

"The family brings with it obligations," Toufan elaborated, "one of which is that you are meant to share everything that's going on in your life with your parents and siblings. Many Iranians actually leave the country just in order to get some privacy! Then, the first thing my brother and I do in the morning is to phone our parents. If I go away for more than a few days, they get sick. They are in their eighties and have been together for fifty-five years. And even now they tell me they wonder if they have chosen the right person!"

Toufan's other three guests were also divorced, all of them looking for their prince. The same story all over, only the scenery different. Toufan changes the subject and tells them what I had written her in an e-mail, that I was hoping to go to Kurdistan in the coming weeks to meet a Sufi sheikh.

"Sufism is all the rage here now," she added, with a glance in my direction. "It's become fashionable with the upper classes, the way Kabbalah has in the West because of Madonna."

*The upper classes*—you wouldn't hear that term often now even in England. Iran, it would seem, was a highly class-conscious society. As for the Sufism she was talking about in fashionable North Tehran, I had heard it was all white robes and candles—New Age Sufism, you might call it—with little relation to the traditional form to be found in the provinces. But at least it was universalist in message and, like its traditional cousins, preached love and tolerance instead of jihad, the holy war of conversion preached by the likes of the Taliban and the conservative wing of the Islamic Republic.

Alienated from the traditional religion of their childhood by their education and their cosmopolitan outlook, the upper classes in Tehran seemed as thirsty as their counterparts in New York or London for genuine spiritual nourishment. Probably none of the people in Toufan's living room would call themselves Muslim. More likely they would describe themselves as "spiritual, but not religious," like many lapsed Christians or Jews in the West.

The evening was far from over when I left. Toufan's guests were starting to discuss their own views on Tehran's current vogue for Sufism; but I could barely keep my eyes open any longer, and seeing my plight, Toufan called for a taxi. On my way out, she suggested I drop by her antiques store the following morning—you never knew who you might bump into there, she said, waving me good-bye.

Two minutes into the ride back to the Laleh Hotel, I was uttering prayers that I might even get to see the next day. The taxi driver, a youth still in his teens, shot off down the street as soon as I had closed the door, just one finger on the wheel, shouting into his cell phone during the whole ride across town. As I would do almost every day, I both marveled and shuddered at the way Iranian drivers regularly reduced traffic lanes to irrelevance. Like everyone else, my driver would straddle two lanes, waiting for the nearest and best opening to move one car ahead in the mass of traffic. The road was one great racetrack with no rules, which accounts for the fact that a day never went by without my witnessing an accident. Iran has one of the highest per capita road casualty figures in the world. Never did a hotel entrance look so welcoming as when I fell out of that battered car and staggered through the revolving door up to my room.

When I turned up at Toufan's store the next day, I discovered it wasn't so much a shop as a house furnished with items for sale, a place that also served as a salon of sorts for Tehran's intellectuals, artists, and filmmakers. People would come in now and again to buy or look at her stock, but mostly they came by to have tea with Toufan and whoever else happened to be there. Toufan's brother, Homayun, was there when I arrived.

Some years before, Homayun had stepped out of one life into another—almost, you could say, into a different identity. During the Revolution he moved to Vancouver, worked as an architect, had two children, and, eventually, grandchildren. But then he divorced, and at a loss and feeling defeated, he returned to Iran ten years ago. He was sitting in the same chair then that he was in now in Toufan's salon-store, feeling then that his life had nothing left to offer him or anyone else—it was over—when Kiarostami walked in, looked at him, and said right there that he thought Homayun would be perfect for the lead role in his film *A Taste of Cherry*.

"You don't have to act," Kiarostami told him. "The film is about a man who wants to commit suicide. He has to feel exactly as you are feeling now."

It probably helped that Homayun has a sort of hangdog expression and large, doleful eyes. Why not, he thought; and he agreed to go for a screen test. He got the role, and when the film won at Cannes, he suddenly had an agent in Hollywood and a new career as an actor. He played the protagonist's father in *The Kite Runner,* and when I met him he had just spent two months in Malta shooting *Agora,* a historical drama set in Roman Egypt, starring Rachel Weisz and Max Minghella. The only limitations imposed on Homayun's career by living in Iran were not to appear in anything offensive to Islam or Iran, which he wouldn't want to do anyway.

"So I don't appear in any kissing scenes, or anything explicit like that," he said, smiling.

He'd had no training at all, he continued, sipping his tea and blowing the smoke from his cigarette over his shoulder, so he would only play parts he could recognize in himself. He and others, too, whom the director had plucked from nowhere owed a great debt to Kiarostami. As a director, Kiarostami rarely used professional actors in his movies. In his most recent film, *Certified Copy,* he cast one hundred women, and Juliette Binoche, the beautiful French star, was the only one with a recognizable face.

"She was here a couple of weeks ago," Toufan said. "Much to the concern of the authorities. The official Mehr News Agency said the appearance of foreign actors in joint productions would result in cultural destruction, since they would turn into role models for Iranian youth."

"As if Iranian youth doesn't already see everything they want on satellite or DVD," said Homayun, laughing. "The DVD is available here almost as soon as a movie is released in the West."

Many of Iran's successful directors, notably Majid Majidi, known in the West for his films *Color of Paradise* and *Children of Heaven,* and Mohsen Makhmalbaf, director of the cult hit *Gabbeh,* have left the country in order to be able to work more freely. None of their films are shown publicly in Iran. Nor are any of Kiarostami's, but he continues to insist on living here, for the same reason that most artists give. His soul is Persian, and his subjects grow from the soil of Iran. He once said, "I feel pain when I see that my country is considered evil. So in all my films, my wish is to give a kinder and warmer image of human beings and my country."

"Art's only mission," he has said elsewhere, "is to make people feel closer."

*To make people feel closer.* Was that humdrum sentimentality, or was he on to something I had never thought of? Those are not likely to be the first words that come to mind when you contemplate the purpose of art. You might be more likely to think of it as a catalyst for a new way of seeing; a call to deeper feeling, to an intimation of beauty; an elevation of the soul to the best that human beings can be.

And yet isn't all this implied in the humble intent *to make people feel closer*? Isn't this a sort of shorthand for why I am in Iran myself, I thought as I climbed into the taxi Toufan had called for me. And I remembered then something I'd once heard the English writer Zadie Smith say: *The true reason I read is to feel less alone, to make a connection with a consciousness other than my own.*

By the time I reached my hotel, I had begun to think that with this understated little phrase Kiarostami had in fact touched the essence of art. When we recognize ourselves in a work—when we feel seen, completed in some way—it is because it includes but also transcends our personal story. It joins the personal with the universal, and so brings us closer to every other living thing. Yes, I thought, art is a transmission of feeling intelligence. It brings us closer to each other because it reveals our shared humanity. Odd that I had to come to Iran to see that.

And yet perhaps not so odd after all. Iran was historically one of the world's great humanist cultures. Hard to believe, perhaps, in its present circumstances, but for centuries it was one of the richest environments anywhere for the pursuit of human knowledge and wisdom. That was in part why it had given birth to so many great poets, scientists, and sages down through the centuries.

Before turning out the light, I leafed through my Rumi book for a few moments. Here was a man who came from Iran some seven hundred years before our time, and yet who was now the most widely read poet in America today. Flicking through the pages, I reflected on what it was in his lines that spoke so deeply to people all over the world. I stopped at a poem I knew and loved:

> Don't be satisfied with stories, how things
> have gone with others. Unfold
> your own myth, without complicated explanation,
> so everyone will understand the passage,
> We have opened you.

> *Start walking toward Shams. Your legs will get heavy*
> *and tired. Then comes a moment*
> *of feeling the wings you've grown,*
> *lifting.*

Rumi's lines evoke a yearning for something that lies buried within us: something greater, nobler than our customary selves, that goes by a thousand names and more. The names change over time, but the yearning remains the same. For all we know, Moses and Jesus and Mohammed may eventually go the way of Osiris, Zeus, and Thor. But the yearning for the transcendent will persist as long as human beings inhabit the earth. It is the heart of every religion and belongs to none. Rumi opens a door to that yearning.

*Start walking toward Shams.* Shams was his teacher, but the word literally means "sun," signifying the true heart of a person's own life. So the walking on this journey went inward as well as outward. Rumi spoke from those inner depths; his passion and desire stemmed from there.

As I turned toward sleep, Rumi's words still floating through my mind, I could feel how easily the journalist in me can be seduced by the stories of others. Yet at the same time I knew my own myth was unfolding here, right here in this hotel room in Tehran, without knowing where it was leading or what the opening Rumi speaks of might look like.

Once, in the early 1970s, a penniless refugee from the Chinese Cultural Revolution came to my door in London. He had my address from some advertisement I had placed in the local newspaper. He didn't know why, he said, but when he saw my name he felt a prompting from his deceased grandfather to make contact. His family had all been killed during the revolution, and the night before his escape to the West he had a dream in which his grandfather was showing him the stepping-stones that lay across the local river.

"At night you can only see one stone at a time," his grandfather's voice had said. "Your life will be like that. Trust it."

Now his grandfather was speaking to me. All I knew was that I was on my way, one step at a time, following the wind, and that was enough to be grateful for.

As I was leaving her place, Toufan had given me the number of a man she thought I should meet.

"The new wave," she had said, enigmatically.

A few days later I was climbing the wide spiral staircase that led up from a foyer to Entr'acte, a café above a cinema. The posters outside were advertising a Bollywood blockbuster. The walls up the stairs were lined with posters of old Hollywood movies from the forties and fifties. Humphrey Bogart and Kirk Douglas gazed down at me with laconic smiles. The stairs spilled me out onto a large open area scattered with a jumble of old sofas and armchairs. At the far end was a counter with an espresso machine and a selection of snacks. Perhaps twenty people, most of them peering into their laptops, were sipping cappuccinos and swapping ideas. Some cool jazz rippled out from the sound system. I could have just stepped into some corner café in SoHo or the West Village, and I felt the balm of the familiar.

I was late for my meeting with Behzad, the person Toufan had wanted me to meet; though in just a few days I had registered that punctuality was not an Iranian priority. A man wearing a cream linen shirt glanced up from a laptop he was sharing with a couple of women, and beckoned me over. Behzad was a tall, clear-eyed man in his forties. He had a calm presence and a direct gaze. He introduced the women: Ladan Nishapour, a video artist, and Mina Nawab, a performance artist.

They had just been looking at Ladan's exhibit in Barcelona on the laptop: photographs of Iranian women's faces, blown up to a meter high, and installed one in each window of an empty high-rise. I bent over to look. Even on the screen it was an unsettling yet moving scene. All those women in close-up gazing down at you with eyes that carried the sadness, the perplexity and complexity, the frustration and the love of their lives in Iran. Each of them covered, some more, some less, in a *hijab*. None of them smiling.

Ladan was a petite, attractive woman in her late thirties. She had wanted to create a situation where passersby would be shocked into standing still for a moment and returning the gaze of the women in the photographs. The faces we passed on the street were usually anonymous to us, and she had wanted to challenge that. She had wanted the people in Barcelona to stop and feel the difference between their lives and the lives of these women—and at the same time to feel their commonality with them.

Even on the small screen I could sense the human connection with these women. One or two faces in a window might easily escape notice. Fifty looking down at you all at once demand at least a few seconds of anyone's attention. I thought of Kiarostami's comment about art making people feel closer.

Behzad was the founder of one of the most popular art and culture websites in Iran, staffed entirely by volunteers and written in English. It was a slightly more intellectual and leftist Slate, and the closest Iran gets to having a community site. MySpace, YouTube, and the other Western interactive sites are banned. Behzad opened the home page and showed me the contents. As well as pages on film, art, theater, and so on, I noticed one with the header *Some Irrelevant Questions*. At my prompting he turned to that page. Among the list of questions were these:

Why do we not have a Ministry of Art?

If Coca-Cola is bad, why is it being bottled in the city of Mashhad?

Why are text messages controlled?

Does Ahmadinejad own a satellite dish at home?

Does the wind also change the direction of his dish?


I didn't know you were free to raise questions like these in Iran, but Behzad said there was a lot of dissent and debate in the press and other public forums about the direction the country should be taking. The only areas that were sacrosanct were the founder of the Revolution, Khomeini himself, and the notion of the Islamic Republic. Everything and everyone else, including and perhaps especially the current president, Ahmadinejad, were fair game.

Behzad earned his living as a translator, and donated his time to the website. Like Toufan's sister, he was someone who had gone against the flow of Iranian migration. He used to live in Colorado, but had been back in Tehran for ten years or so. I could appreciate why Toufan's sister had returned, with all the support she would have for the raising of her family; but I couldn't grasp why someone like Behzad would want to leave the United States and willingly take on all the limitations of personal freedom that I assumed were an everyday part of life here.

He leaned back in his chair and thought for a moment. He could never equate his personal happiness with the American Dream of "making it," he said—whatever *it* might be. He'd never felt at home in a consumer-capitalist culture. What he had always felt the lack of in America, and what he so appreciated here, was the extended sense of community, the way individual identity was always wrapped into the broader culture. He appreciated the more simple life, too: the relative lack of advertising billboards, and the absence of generic, "global" culture and brands. Iran was its own place, he said, with a distinct cultural footprint going back thousands of years. He was nourished by that sense of cultural lineage.

"It gives me a deep sense of belonging. And it's passionate." He grinned. "There's a creative dynamism here that people elsewhere would be astonished by. Look around you. You have record producers, artists, translators, writers, musicians, all bouncing project ideas off of one another. This place is one of the hubs of Tehran's creative world. Most of them are like artists anywhere; they are generally poor, they work different jobs in the evenings and dedicate the day to their artistic vision."

Ladan and Mina came over, and we went out into the day in search of lunch. Walking the few blocks to the restaurant they had in mind, I noticed a couple of young women with nose bandages.

"A nose job is all the rage here," said Mina, a large, jolly woman in her early forties. "Teenage girls, especially, want nothing more than a nose like Angelina Jolie's, or some other star's. I have heard that Tehran has the highest concentration of plastic surgeons in the world outside of L.A. It's not uncommon for men to have it, either. And believe it or not, those bandages are quite commonly only for display. The wearer can get the cachet without the expense or the pain."

A nose bandage as a badge of pride? No woman in L.A. would be seen in the street with a post-op nose bandage, and here it was in Tehran as a fashion statement.

I wondered what could be so wrong with a Persian nose that so many young people felt the need to change it. If Iran was so culturally removed from the rest of the world and Western ideas about beauty, then wouldn't traditional Persian looks, rather than Angelina Jolie, be the height of fashion?

"Look at all the images of Western celebrities," Ladan answered. "These are role models for young people all over the world. Iran is no exception. The young see them here every day through their satellite dishes. Or they call up the local black-market guy and he delivers a DVD to the door in ten minutes."

But a nose job wasn't just about fashion; it was also about increasing your marriage prospects. A woman's best chance of securing a good life in Iran still lay in marrying a rich man. So the more beautiful you were by the current standards of fashion, the more chance you had in the marriage market.

"Did you know you can get anything you like here—movies, alcohol, drugs, sex, anything—delivered like a pizza?" Mina asked, shooting me a sidelong glance. "It just mustn't be done in public. It's impossible for the enforcers to go around and check everyone's private life, so usually we are left alone behind our own front doors. Have you been to a party here yet? All the black disappears and out comes the Hugo Boss, the Armani, the Ralph Lauren, or knock-offs of them from the Gulf. Party drugs and casual sex are as normal here as in Manhattan. I'm not saying it's a good thing. I'm saying it's part of the way of life here just as it is in any Western capital."

Except, of course, everything she was describing was publicly forbidden in Iran—which must make it more attractive than ever. Then it becomes a form of rebellion against the status quo. Nose jobs, Elvis haircuts, masseurs from Leeds, marriage markets: there were more Irans than I thought there were. I could appreciate the influence of the Western media, especially given the Internet; but I couldn't see where the Elvis haircuts fit in. After all, they hadn't been around for forty years.

The Elvis craze had appeared suddenly the year before, Behzad said, and no one knew why. But then Elvis was a powerful antiestablishment figure, and in that sense was timeless. These trends were not merely fashion statements. The energy behind them—creative, antiauthoritarian, a small way of insisting on freedom—was unstoppable. Half the population here was under twenty-five, after all, and there was no way things were going to stay as they were. As for the Elvis haircut, the government had even tried to ban that a few months earlier.

"Would you believe it? A law against a haircut! But as you can see, it hasn't made much difference."

We turned through a door and into a large garden with small trees giving shade to rows of what looked like king-size bed platforms covered with carpets. Along the edges of the pathways roses grew, and water ran in trickling channels. The platforms were occupied by groups of people having lunch. The waiter led us to an empty one and we sat in a circle while he placed water and olives and feta bread in the center. This, I was told, was the Iranian version of a traditional restaurant. Whenever possible the Iranians favored eating in a garden, and always in the presence of running water.

With the waiter laying plates of kebab and raw onions before us, Mina and Ladan told me they were about to go to Athens to take part in an international art conference. Mina, it turned out, was something of a radical performance artist. A few years before, she had distributed drinks to her audience that were laced with a small amount of the poison that the Shah's secret police, Savak, used to finish off their opponents. Everyone, including Mina herself, had a minor stomachache for a week afterward. The point was to identify empathetically with the victims of political abuse and terror, whether of the current regime or the previous one.

*New wave,* Toufan had said, and she would be right. I would never have expected to meet young women artists in Iran who'd had shows in Barcelona and were off to Athens for an arts conference, because in my Western mind Iran was out of the loop, removed from the global community of ideas, stuck in a bubble of its own making. This would be true of much of the conservative political class—the Supreme Leader, Khamenei, hadn't been out of the country for twenty years or more—but not of Iran's young people. The people in Entr'acte represented a small but influential section of the culture that was as engaged in the world as anyone, while Iranian youth in general made full use of the

Web to reach beyond their own borders. Like young people any-where, they were more interested in their personal freedoms than in any political or religious agenda.

I asked Ladan, a single mother, what she appreciated about her life in Iran. She paused for a moment, adjusting her head-scarf, a simple gray one with a blue border.

"It's partly what we were talking about on the way here," she said. "The paradoxes and contradictions of Tehran society are invigorating for me. Especially, of course, the radical differences between public and private life. Then, in the case of the artists I know, the lack of cultural exchange only serves to increase our desire to know, to experiment and to innovate. This is probably why Iranian contemporary art is now such a hot property at the Christie's sales in Dubai."

At the same time it was difficult and challenging to live in Tehran. There was the irritation of knowing that her five-year-old daughter would have to wear the hijab when she started school the following year. Gas was rationed because their re-finery equipment was old, and sanctions prevented them from obtaining new parts. It wasn't easy to earn a living, however qualified you were; most people in Tehran had to hold down two or three jobs to pay the high rents. And yet, for all that, it was an exciting life. The restrictions created an edge, a resistance that could actually serve the artistic process. Constraint forced you to think creatively.

Mina leaned forward. All this was true, she said, yet it was also a fact that too much repression could kill the creative spirit. They lived daily with the uncertainty of never knowing what would be permitted or not. The rules were arbitrary and changed regularly. Two weeks earlier a gallery had been shut down be-cause one of the artists being exhibited knew Salman Rushdie, while another had been on Voice of America.

As we chattered on about life there and my own life in Amer-ica, the waiter brought more dishes of rice laden with currants and saffron, and I could feel how conversation is encouraged to circulate more freely when you are leaning back against bolsters, your legs sprawled before you. Formality is dissolved on those big, rug-covered beds, and lunch lingers on well over the hour. Eating in a garden, perched on a bed platform with friends, the trickle of water nearby, the scent of roses in the air—I wouldn't find this in Europe. I could sense Behzad's meaning, when he spoke of their culture as one in which the individual feels more intrinsically part of a greater whole.

Later, on my way back to the Laleh Hotel in one of Tehran's beat-up Paykan taxis—an Iranian version of the 1960s English Hillman Hunter model—I wondered about my own sense of belonging in the culture I now lived in. I thought back to the previous year, when I had gone to Italy for a couple of months to test out the fantasy that I might want to live in Europe again. . . .

But then, two days before I was going to leave Italy, I lost my green card. It was in my wallet, which mysteriously disappeared on a train. No green card meant I couldn't even board a plane back to the States. I had to go to the embassy in Rome and line up for a few hours for a letter that would satisfy the airline and immigration authorities. I had been given a preview of what it would feel like not to be able to return to the States.

It was then that I realized the obvious: my home was there, in the United States, and specifically in the Bay Area. My whole life was there. Not in Italy, not even in England, though the green valleys around Bath lived on inside me. No, I belonged, for better or for worse, in America now, even as I might consider myself a citizen of the world. My community there was as rich as any you might find: rich in ideas, in creative endeavors, in interests of the heart and the spirit as well as the mind (and it was not insignificant that the climate and topography were as Mediterranean as the Cote d'Azur).

As an immigrant, I had been all too aware of America's underbelly: the blatant individualism that so often trumps the common good; the profit motive and special interests that govern attitudes and public policy on everything from health care to public transport to education. Europeans considered decent health service, good education, and liberal social services to be both civilizing and civilized public policies. The "wild west" attitude of the States was incomprehensible to most people in Europe.

And yet, sitting in that taxi in Tehran, I was aware that I was now an Anglo-American, and there was no going back. I had recently received my American passport to go along with my English one. Losing my green card had brought it home to me: America was my home now, and it needed a commitment from me, an acknowledgment of the fact that I was now American as well as English. And like everyone else—just like my new friends here in Tehran—I would need to take the good with the bad. As soon as I landed back in the States from that trip to Italy, I applied for citizenship.

We were in a gridlock. We had been in it for ten minutes or more, with little sign of change anytime soon.

"Is heavy traffic normal for this time of day?" I asked the driver, who was leaning out of the window smoking a cigarette.

"I am sorry for the traffic," he replied, as if he were to blame. "It is my duty to deliver you to your destination in the shortest time possible. I will do everything I can to carry out my obligation."

I had never heard a taxi driver speak that way before. I was reminded of the first sentence of an exhibition review I had read earlier on Behzad's website:

*That an exhibit should set out to show the relationship between poetry and the visual arts is not such a surprise. What is strange is for it to claim it is something new, especially in this country, where every aspect of life is tied to a lyrical moment.*

I sat back and let the journey take as long as it took. The driver's elegant courtesy was, I supposed, an expression of *taarof,* the Iranian etiquette and formal, high-flown manner of speaking that Iranians often use to initiate a conversation or to greet a stranger. Was it an expression of genuine sentiment, or rather a formulaic response to a difficult situation? Possibly both, and probably the latter, but as an Englishman, I knew the way formal manners could oil the wheels of a sticky situation and could serve a purpose larger than mere accommodation or flattery.

Taarof, I would come to realize, was the perfect metaphor for the layers of truth and falsehood in Iran. It was a formal structure of speech and gesture that aspired in its essence to be a medium for the deepest values of human discourse and respect. And because we do not always, or even often, live at that lofty level, taarof often runs counter to our true intentions, which can be more self-serving than we like to acknowledge. As a result, oil is often mixed with water in taarof, and the foreigner, especially, is never sure where he stands. Nothing is explicit or direct. Everything is shifting innuendo, nothing ever defined or clear. Times are changing, though; I was told that members of the younger generation in Tehran are consigning taarof to history. They are adopting the direct and often brusque vernacular that is the common style of speech in the West.

And yet that is a quality I appreciate in my adopted home, I realized, sitting in the yellowing dust of that late-afternoon traffic. For all the subtleties of this ancient culture, and indeed of my own birthplace, I was grateful for the direct, if at times clumsy, way in which Americans tell the truth as they see it. At the same time, it was not common in America to happen upon a lyrical moment, as the Web writer put it. In Tehran, it can happen even in a taxi in gridlock.

I want to go to Shiraz, and I want to go soon. The whir and excitement of a capital city rarely holds me for more than a few days. But Toufan had told me there was a woman I should be sure to meet before leaving Tehran. She was often away, but Toufan knew she was in town at the moment and said she would arrange a meeting for me. The woman's name was Mania Akbari.

"You will see what I mean," Toufan had said on the phone.

So, following her instructions, I was sitting now in a café by the window waiting for Khosrow. Khosrow was going to drive me to the apartment of his friend Mania Akbari, artist, photographer, filmmaker, lead actress in Kiarostami's film *Ten*. Outside, a couple of North Tehrani women with Dolce and Gabbana sunglasses perched on stylish headscarves were engaged in a heated conversation. There were very few cafés in Tehran like the one I was in now. Illy Italian coffee containers were stacked on the counter, next to a smart espresso machine. But when I took a sip of my cappuccino, I realized it was not cappuccino. "Is this Nescafé?" I asked. "Whipped Nescafé, yes." "Is the espresso machine broken?" "No." "Can I have a cappuccino made with espresso?" "Yes. But it will be extra."

The walls were covered in fine-looking wood, the floor in Italianate tiling. A small roomful of young men and women from wealthy families were whiling away their time here in the middle of the day. The women were wearing large, glitzy rings, their faces were caked with makeup, one of them was impossibly beautiful, and all of them had the requisite large eyes and sensuous mouth thickly applied with lipstick. Every one of them seemed utterly dedicated to being a material girl. Or as Mina and Ladan had suggested, perhaps this was their way—the only way open to them—of expressing a form of revolt against a repressive society. Rebellious material girls.

Khosrow walked in, and though we had never met before, we recognized each other immediately, which wasn't really surprising since we were both thirty years older than any of the other customers. He led me out to his car and I saw that the usual battered Paykan was not Khosrow's style. He opened the door of a shiny Toyota SUV, and soon his English accent was filtering through the fray of the traffic. A suave, handsome man, bristling with energy, he was a graduate of Trinity College Dublin, where his best friend had been the musician Chris de Burgh. They were still close now, some thirty years later, and Khosrow had recently tried to help de Burgh stage a concert in Tehran. His music was enormously popular in Iran, but the Ministry of Guidance was worried about having large crowds of men and women together in the same place, so they wouldn't grant the necessary permits.

Khosrow was in the oil business, and a successful art collector, which is how he knew Mania Akbari. Something of a party man, an international socialite (as distinct to socialist), I fancied. Dubai, French Riviera, that sort of thing. Hardly my world, but I warmed to him immediately. After winding through the narrow streets of North Tehran for half an hour, we were ushered into Akbari's apartment by her assistant. The place itself seemed to have been put together rather like a work of art, all salvaged wood and stone. Two large sofas faced each other across a glass table; a large television screen hung on a wall.

Mania Akbari was thirty-six years old and one of the rising stars in the Tehran art firmament. She came out now from behind a door, a small, vital woman moving quickly in cavalier boots, a pageboy jacket, and a blue scarf around her head. Mania had had breast cancer a year or two earlier, and one of her films, *10+4,* a sequel to Kiarostami's *Ten,* is a searingly honest portrait of her ordeal.

Over the next hour I was to hear some of the most furious, violent, and poignant descriptions I have ever heard of one artist's struggles and joys with her muse. And I heard what it feels like to be Mania Akbari living in Iran. The words and images poured out of her as though someone had switched on a current—except that for Akbari this voltage seemed normal. When I asked her a general question about art, it was like popping a cork out of a bottle.

Art was a huge devil, she said: dark, sexy, alluring. That devil had grabbed hold of her hand as soon as she was born. From that moment on, her fate was sealed. The Ugly Duckling, her father would call her, not because she was ugly, but because she was so different from the other children. And still now, when she was alone, this being called Art, this man-devil, would always be there with her. She and Art were like Jonah and the whale. It was so all-consuming it had swallowed up the whole of her life. Its presence was so vast she couldn't allow anything else into her world, and that was painful. Art would attack her, seize her, rape her. Art was her violent lover who took her by storm. They would make love, she would get pregnant, and give birth. When she finally cut the cord, she would feel relaxed. Like a baby. And when she had given birth to it, she would feel grateful and happy. She would bathe for hours in exhausted bliss.

Often as she talked, the great devil Art would shift shape and become the great devil Iran. She belonged to Iran, she said; Iran was her husband. That was why she couldn't imagine living anywhere else. Iran was her abusive husband and she had twenty-two children by him—all her art—and she could not leave her husband because of them. Every time she got off a plane in Tehran from abroad she would shout, "You ugly brute of a husband! Husband that I love!"

"When you are in Tehran and you belong here," she said, looking across at me with her strong gaze, "it gives you everything. At the same time it takes things away from you, too. It's an ongoing exchange. It takes away comforts. It compromises your security. But then that energizes you again, because it prompts you to find your own security in your creations. In art. Both Iran and cancer challenge my ideas of who I think I am. Cancer has given me more courage to survive, like a soldier in battle. I get injured in the battle with cancer, and I get injured by living in Iran."

I asked how she was injured by living in Iran. Because she belonged here, she said, whether she wanted to belong or not; and living here was a struggle. Iran was her husband, she repeated, her abusive husband, and she had to stay with him. She couldn't be an artist without living in Tehran. She couldn't even be a true individual. She didn't choose to be born Iranian, but she was, and she had to embrace the difficult conditions that this brought with it. Anyway, she added, the idea of living in a foreign culture had always scared her.

That surprised me. I couldn't imagine Mania Akbari being frightened anywhere. Her work was well known in Europe, and I assumed she would have a ready community if she ever chose to live there. Maybe she was more vulnerable than she appeared.

"I like to think my work is appreciated abroad because when art comes from deep within, it is universal and is appreciated everywhere," she said. "But that doesn't mean I am universal in my personal life, that I can live anywhere. No, I need Iran."

Then she added something extraordinary. What she meant by universal, she said, had something to do with holes in the head. She talked about people literally having holes in their minds, and creativity coming from there. It was an amazing image, one I had never thought of before. And it made sense somehow: a personal microcosm of the great black holes from which pours the whole of creation, creativity coming from a source beyond our conscious control or awareness. Yet the conscious mind plays a role in any creative process, too, I thought. Creativity doesn't just pour out of a black hole straight onto a canvas. Technique, too, plays a role. I asked if she had any notion of what she was saying in a work of art as she was saying it.

She replied that if she knew too much, she wouldn't say it. She had to both know and not know. She never knew how it was going to turn out. Art was like life, she said. It seemed to come out of nowhere, and then she just couldn't help herself. It was like a rage. But however it came, Art was completely alive for her, a beautiful being, just like a gorgeous man who could jump and fly with wings and swim. A gorgeous man who could overwhelm her.

I could almost feel her *daemon* in the room by her side. Some being with wings of light and a dark streak in his heart. For some reason I thought of death then, and asked her if it had ever been a spur in her work.

"Always. I have been near to death and spoken to him a lot. I love death, but I love life, too, and I have no time for death right now. This is why I chose to take the chemotherapy instead of choosing death."

She has no time because she is working on several projects at once. An exhibition of her photographs, titled *The Many Faces of Eve,* had just ended in London. Now she was writing a new movie script and she has another ongoing photographic project. And yet she has no particular love of either film or photography, she says. They are tools that she needs to say what she has to say. Which led me to ask her about painting, but no, she had no love for that, either. Painting was not her tool. She realized at an early age that her paintings did not give her the answers she wanted from her work. For her, painting was like drinking wine out of a cup instead of a glass.

I thought of Andre Agassi, the tennis star who always hated the game, and yet could only keep playing, driven on by the specter of his father's ambitions for him. I couldn't help wondering if some similar drive, perhaps unknown to her, was fueling Mania's ferocious tussle with art.

I asked her if she was aware of anything missing in her life. She didn't miss a beat.

"The thing I really miss in my life is any understanding of motherhood and of being a wife. I'm sad about that. By the age of thirty-four I had separated from three men and produced a seventeen-year-old son who doesn't live with me. This is part of what I meant when I said that Art has swallowed me and my life."

She was so raw, so immediate, this woman; and for all the force, the visceral power she carried, I realized now that she wore her vulnerability like an open wound. Mania's passion was urgent and tangible and didn't let up. It was the big wave that as a listener you just had to ride; I took the ride and it took me. It moved me to think; but more than that, it moved me to feel. It touched me. Her living, raging, tender humanity touched me; so much pain and joy in *her one wild and precious life.* Like all of us—except that she was giving voice to it with a wild exuberance that few others could bear the passage of.

I got up from our encounter filled with thoughts and feelings about intensity; the different kinds of intensity, and which kind I was aware of in my own life and work. These lines in a poem by Jane Hirshfield came to mind:

> *I want to give myself*
> *Utterly*
> *As this maple*
> *That burned and burned*
> *For three days without stinting*
> *And then in two more*
> *Dropped off every leaf . . .*

I have always loved this poem, "Lake and Maple." I love the ease with which the maple gives itself over to burning—to its leaves reddening deeper and deeper—and the simplicity with which it lets those same leaves fall. Surely most of us have longed to feel so engaged, so entirely given over to life, that every last drop of us is fully used up. Yet the maple points to a different— not better or worse, but certainly different—kind of intensity from the one Mania knows in her life.

Mania, it seemed to me, was in a long tradition of larger-than-life artists whose gargantuan energy and creative forces cut a swath through time. Van Gogh, Jackson Pollock, Dylan Thomas, Ezra Pound, Anne Sexton, Jimi Hendrix—the list is endless. Their gifts to us all are priceless. Yet because of people like these, creativity is often considered synonymous with an obsessive energy that as often as not seems to end in either burnout or an early death.

I left Mania's apartment wondering whether it was really necessary to burn like a fuse in order to be given utterly to life. Was I missing something, or did you have to be on fire in that urgent way in order to live fully? In her poem, Hirshfield wants to give herself in the way the maple does, which is to say effortlessly, without struggle or torment. The intensity of her desire is for union, not specifically with this or that project or work of art, though it may include that, but with all life. It is the abandon of open arms, itself a form of intensity, though one with a different frequency from the fury of the passionate artist.

Hirshfield's is a long, passionate, poem-length cry of life to Life. And I knew how much of the time my own life had fallen short of that quiet intensity. I had spent many of my allotted days just bumbling along. (I don't imagine Mania Akbari has ever bumbled in her life.) There had been frequent periods when I had had no idea what I was meant to be doing or why I was here. I had spent an embarrassing number of hours wondering if I was living in the right place, with the right person, or feeling the emptiness that no food can fill.

But surely this—the ambivalence, the emptiness, the uncertainty—was all part of it. Part of life, that is. My life. Along with all the delight and the love of this or that person or beautiful creation of either man or nature, along with all the joys of the senses, all the curiosity about the world and what it meant to be human, I longed for this kind of intensity, so gracefully depicted in Hirshfield's maple; the willingness to *feel* it all, to say *Yes!* to all of it, in whatever shape or form it came.

This was how I wanted to live the life I had left: with my feeling intelligence, my arms wide open. Iran was certain to offer me experiences I had not encountered before; experiences not just in terms of what happens, but of what is felt in the marrow as a consequence. Iran would surprise me, I always knew that. It had already done so in just a few days in Tehran. There would be times when I would forget what I was feeling now. But as I went on my way to Shiraz the next day, I wanted to take this quiet kind of passion with me. After all, Shiraz was the city of Hafez, who lived all his life drunk on a wine of this vintage.

# paradise and poetry

Your thousand limbs rend my body.
This is the way to die:
Beauty keeps laying
Its sharp knife
Against
Me.

— HAFEZ (TRANSLATED BY DANIEL LADINSKY)

In Mehrabad, Tehran's domestic airport, the scent of rosewater
hung in the air. Incongruously, a Mr. Bean movie was playing
on the flight to Shiraz. Every time a woman walked across the
screen revealing more than she should, which was always, her
image was scrambled. I wondered how the distinctly English
tone of Mr. Bean's gaffes and jokes might sound in Farsi. But
then nobody in the plane but me was paying any attention.

I was leaving the smog and the clamor of Tehran for this, an
ancient city in the south of the country: the city of roses, nightingales, and wine. (The wine connection lives on today in the name
of a famous red wine, Shiraz, made from the Syrah grape.) Today
there is no wine in Shiraz itself, of course, except in the poetry of
Hafez, the poet who brought renown to the city in the fourteenth
century. Even now his tomb is the main attraction, and a constant

flow of Iranians comes from all over the country as on a pilgrimage. He was the main reason I was on my way there, too.

Somayeh was at the airport to meet me and take me to my hotel. She was a local guide, a young woman in her twenties and a government employee, dressed from head to foot in black. She withheld her hand when I reached out to shake it. "Not allowed," she said. A small, somewhat distracted woman, she led me to a taxi and we headed off down a wide, tree-lined avenue to the center of town.

The hotel was on the city's main boulevard, called Zand after the short-lived dynasty that ruled Iran before the decadent era of the Qajar shahs. A large citadel with four circular towers looms still today over the top end of the avenue, a reminder of the power once levied here across the whole country by Karim Khan, the Zand dynasty's first and most enlightened ruler. He made Shiraz his capital in 1750, and aspired to make it the equal of Isfahan, the capital of the Safavid dynasty before him.

Isfahan would be a tough act to follow for any city in the world, and even Karim's Shiraz didn't come close. But then he didn't have a lot of time on his hands; his dynasty lasted only some forty years, at which point the first Qajar shah destroyed the city's fortifications and moved the capital to Tehran. Before doing so he blinded the entire male population of Kerman, a neighboring city, for having had the insolence to defy him.

I dropped off my bags and went out to join in the street life, telling Somayeh I would meet up with her later that day. Both sides of Zand Boulevard are lined with stores selling jeans and watches and cell phones. Street traders sell knock-offs of Ray-Ban sunglasses and pirated CDs. Zand is worn at the edges, a little tawdry yet lively, an Iranian equivalent of Canal Street in Manhattan's Chinatown. Curls of smoke filtered out from kebab joints in little holes-in-the-wall. There were more women in black here, though many younger ones were dressed as they were in Tehran.

A couple of cinemas were showing the Bollywood fare I had seen advertised in Tehran, but there was no sign or mention of the Iranian filmmakers who have become international figures in the last decade or so. Kiarostami's global success focused the attention of the world on Iranian cinema. Younger directors have made and continue to make strikingly innovative films set in Iran, often with an almost fairytale-like simplicity, always with a deeply poetic, humanist sensibility, and frequently with children in the lead roles. Majid Majidi's *Children of Heaven* and *Color of Paradise*, Mohsen Makhmalbaf's *Gabbeh,* and many others have become art-house favorites across the West.

But rarely is the work of these directors ever screened in their home country. Even though the work is not overtly political in theme, it's firmly in the liberal and humanist tradition of Persian literature that runs all the way back to Hafez and even further. It stands against the restriction of civil and individual liberties and repressive authority in general.

I walked up the avenue toward Karim Khan's citadel, and on to the great bazaar. This was the old part of Shiraz, and in the neighborhood of the bazaar, the cheap little shops and street vendors of Zand Boulevard give way to premises from a more dignified era, many of which today sell carpets and curios. Karim Khan hoped his bazaar would make Shiraz the trade mecca for the entire region, and for a while it did. Bazaars are always a hub of life and scents and savors and bustle, and the one in Shiraz was no exception.

It also happens to be rather beautiful. Vakil Bazaar, as it is known, after the adjoining Vakil Mosque, is built on a cruciform plan, its wide avenues protected by vaulted roofs of light-colored brick, with endless little side alleys to draw you into mysterious nooks tumbling with local goods and foodstuffs. For all the jostle and banter and the hundreds of traders selling everything from carpets to cashew nuts, the place is all light and air, a tribute to Karim's aesthetic as well as his architectural sensibilities.

I wandered without thought for direction, letting myself be carried along by the waves of smells—cardamom, saffron, rose petals—the sounds of artisans hammering metal, of women scolding their children, men crying out to sell their wares; and the sights of piled nuts and fruits, of carpets unfurled, of a barrow stacked with pomegranates, all delicate shades of yellow and red. By the barrow, a man with a press was squeezing the juice out of the pomegranates and selling glassfuls of red liquid to passersby.

I had never seen a barrowful of pomegranates before. The only pomegranates I was familiar with came in the form of elixir at the health-food store. The fruit grows everywhere in the Mediterranean and the Middle East, and every culture there pays tribute to it in its own way through its cuisine as well as its folk stories. In Iran the pomegranate has been fused with the national identity for thousands of years. It is nothing less than a symbol for Persia. Later, among the ruins of the ancient capital of Persepolis, I would see in the murals that the sword handles of Xerxes' guard carried a representation of the "Pomegranate Brigade," an elite unit that fought in the battle with the Greeks at Marathon in 490 B.C. Pomegranates symbolized fertility (all those seeds) at the rites of Mithras, god of light and truth in eastern Iran. It says in the Koran that he who eats the pomegranate will free himself of envy and spite.

Apple trees were not known in the Middle East in biblical times, and in the early versions of the story it was almost certainly a pomegranate with which Eve tempted Adam in the Garden of Eden. It is valued still today both as a fruit and for its medicinal properties, and has served as an image of beauty since King Solomon's time: "Like a broken pomegranate are the cheeks of my beloved," Solomon says in his *Song of Songs*.

Happily losing myself in the maze of alleys, I emerged at last in a small open square with a long rectangular pool in the middle. A second story had an open terrace that looked down onto the square below. It was quieter here, and warmer, too, because there was no roof but the clear open sky. A couple of trees grew by the side of the pool. Under one of them an elderly man, tall and stooped, was selling glasses of hot tea from an urn. I took one, and sat on the ledge that rimmed the pool. All the traders here sold antiques and curios: tiles, samovars, jewelry, paintings on wood, turquoise and lapis lazuli. No one was pushing to sell; most were sitting down in the sun, a glass of tea close to hand, gossiping idly with their neighbors. I began to dream I was in old Persia, in a time before the mullahs, even in a time before the shahs. A time out of an illustrated book; a time out of time.

I stood up eventually and strolled over to a corner shop that had an array of old tiles in the window. They were beautiful, nineteenth-century Qajar period mostly, all those pinks and yellows, images of animals, a deer, a lion, a songbird; of men on horseback, and dazzling arabesque designs. The vendor, sitting on a high wooden stool, offered me another tea and asked me the inevitable question in English. When I said America, he smiled. His son was over there, he said, in Texas, studying engineering. He told me that the square was in fact an old caravanserai that had been restored and incorporated into the bazaar, which accounted for its shape and its two floors, as well as the central pool.

For centuries, traders coming to the bazaar from other cities and farther afield would have unloaded their camels right here in this spot where I was now. Countless stories from across the whole region, personal and tribal dramas from Turkmenistan and Afghanistan to Baghdad and the Persian Gulf, must have been exchanged here in this little enclosure. People would have propped themselves up on a blanket under the stars and eaten, gossiped, argued, and traded together through all the twists and turns of the city's political fortunes. They would have recounted tales of their fathers' times, when life was more honest and simple; bemoaned the sorry conditions their rulers obliged them to live under now; and they would have dreamed of happier days ahead. Life would have gone on, as it always does.

How far have we come since then? We live in a powerful narrative of progress, the idea of an upward linear march of consciousness of which we who live now are the finest achievement to date. Yet can we be so sure that the world of those who peopled a caravanserai like this, perhaps a hundred, two hundred, five hundred years ago, was defined by sensibilities any less civilized than those we pride ourselves on now? Far from being less enlightened, they surely rather defined their time by different values and skill sets. They wouldn't have had a GPS, but they would have known by the wind and the stars and the curve of the dunes exactly where they were in the desert and how many more days it would have taken them to reach Shiraz.

Their clan, their community of people, was their protection and the source of their belonging; they would not have comprehended the loneliness of the modern city dweller. Their community was itself under the protection of the Divine, and whatever happened was God's grace. If love, and the wisdom that grows from the enduring values of the heart—friendship, community, generosity, trust—are ultimately what matter in a life that ends in death, then theirs wouldn't have been a bad way to live; no more perfect than ours, perhaps, but no more imperfect either.

I bought a couple of tiles from the man at the corner shop, one portraying a deer and the other a lion, and continued on my way, leaving the bazaar through a different entrance from the one through which I had come in, and found myself at the gates of the Vakil Mosque. I stepped through a small opening in the huge wooden door into a large courtyard. A few men were scattered around the great open space, sitting reading the Koran or kneeling in prayer. They were here, as was I, owing to the generosity and vision of Karim Khan, on whose orders the mosque was built.

At the far end of the courtyard stood the *iwan*, the vaulted hall rarely seen in mosques outside of Iran. A sort of extension of the courtyard, the iwan is a space enclosed on three sides. Like so much else in Islamic culture and architecture, its origins lie in pre-

Islamic Persian civilization. It is a legacy of the Sassanid Empire, which ruled for four hundred years before the Arab Caliphate finally overthrew it in 651 and installed an Islamic state in Iran.

For the Sassanian kings and their Zoroastrian priests, the iwan represented an opening in the world of material form onto the realm of spiritual realities. What more appropriate place, then, for the Muslims who adopted the iwan to place the *mihrab,* the niche in a mosque that points toward Mecca—the direction to which each Muslim turns as he falls down below his daily cares to commune with God. How many Muslims today, I wondered as they knelt there in the iwan, knew that they were also paying homage to the genius of the world of Persia that existed for centuries before the arrival of Mohammed?

The iwans in Vakil Mosque—there are two, at opposite ends of the courtyard—are beautiful; tiled in the style not of Karim Khan's time, but with the floral and arabesque designs that I had seen in the trader's shop in the old caravanserai. They were added by the first Qajar rulers who immediately followed the Zand dynasty, and their pastel swirls and colors contribute a lively gentleness, if not quite a decadent touch, to the sober square and geometrical rigor of the mosque's overall structure.

I had barely given myself enough time to get back to the hotel for my appointment with Somayeh, the guide. She was going to take me to the tomb of Hafez. I left the mosque to those who were using it for its proper purpose, and walked down a short street past a stack of carpets piled up by the sidewalk. Men were heaving them into a courtyard and from there into a store. Around the corner was the Pars Museum, a small, delightful octagon of a building where Karim Khan used to greet foreign dignitaries, and which now houses his sword and his grave. But I hurried on, still as yet in the grip of wanting to be on time.

Somayeh was sitting in the hotel lobby when I arrived, speaking into her cell phone—which she did, I would come to see, with predictable regularity. She continued speaking to the person on the other end of the line as she hailed a taxi and we sped toward the tomb of Hafez.

Waiting at the entrance to the garden that encircled the tomb were a few men with caged songbirds. If you paid a little sum, the man would offer a pack of small cards to the bird, which would dutifully take one. The man would then take the card chosen by the bird and read the couplet by Hafez that was written on it. Hafez's couplets, Somayeh said, were often used in this way by Iranians as a fortune-telling device. It remains a custom in every household to pick a Hafez couplet from a bowl of cards on the shortest day of the year, the festival known as Yalda. We walked through a rose garden by a long rectangular pool toward a dome tiled in robin's-egg blue and supported by four slender pillars. Beneath the dome lay a simple tomb.

A fine tenor voice was singing Hafez poems over a sound system, water fountains trickled away, a general ease hovered over the poet's resting place. I walked up the seven steps to the tomb and sat down by the long, narrow slab of alabaster that marked his grave. I had come all this way to sit in this spot. Rumi is as beloved of Iranians as is Hafez, but his tomb is in Turkey. Without any physical evidence of his presence here, Rumi lives on for Iranians through his verses, and I have had to be content with bringing a book of them with me. But the physical presence of Hafez's tomb, and the story of his life in Shiraz, makes his name in Iran a tangible reality.

The tomb draws thousands of pilgrims every month. And now I, too, a wanderer from another world, have come to pay homage here. Strange, really, how something you have imagined for so long can seem so natural in its ordinariness and simplicity when you are finally in its presence. All the images fall away and you are left with the tangible reality of—in this case—a slab of alabaster with some lines of the poet swirling down its length in the beautiful Farsi script.

Huddles of Iranians were filtering by to pay their respects. It is rare to see an Iranian alone, and most of the groups seemed to be families. They would touch the tomb briefly while muttering a prayer beneath their breath; others knelt down, dipping their forehead to the cool stone. I, too, was touched, to see the honor and reverence they so naturally bestowed on a poet. I laid my own hand on the stone, tracing with my finger the sinuous aesthetic of the Farsi script, feeling the flow of the line to be the course of my life and the love of poetry that had brought me here. The letters were like vines, twirling along in a leisurely, winding movement from right to left. Farsi is an Indo-European language, as is Sanskrit, and in both spoken and written form it flows like water, fluid and sibilant.

I don't read or speak Farsi, though anyone could appreciate the easy grace of the way those letters rolled down the alabaster slab. But even Hafez in English (his multiple meanings are notoriously difficult to translate) had been enough to draw me here. Hafez has become popular in the West today because of recent translations that capture the wild and free spirit of his lines, if not the letter of them, but when I first read him I had to make do with far more literal and sometimes clumsy renderings. He was first translated into English in 1771, and Goethe and Emerson, among many others, were greatly influenced by his ability to praise this world and the next in one and the same breath. Hafez's two main themes are love (both of woman and of God) and wine—both the kind you find in the tavern and also the wine of God communion.

He and Rumi appeared together in my life—how often you hear people say this about a book, a poem, a person—at the perfect moment. I was in my twenties and tussling with two themes that I was finding difficult to reconcile. One was my budding career as a freelance writer in London, and the other was the pull

I felt toward a contemplative life of reflection somewhere in the woods. (This was the sixties, after all.) The world of the spirit and the big wide world—to my mind at the time they seemed to point in different directions and require different priorities. Should I pour myself into my career or should I direct my attention inward and be content to live a simple life? The question was not uncommon at the time among my generation. Then there was another matter, not insignificant: I had just fallen hopelessly in love for the very first time. All in all, I was ripe for an intervention.

I was walking past the Middle East Bookstore in London— across the street from the British Museum—when not one but two books in the window caught my eye. One had a red cover with decorative scrolls on it. It was the poetry of Hafez. I had never heard of him, but I had had some contact with Sufi groups in the city, and my curiosity was aroused by the words *The Great Sufi Master* under his name. The other had a green cover, and announced *The Masnavi,* by Rumi, whom I had heard of but never read.

I went in and opened the Hafez book at random. The words were few enough to remain aglow in the memory even now:

> *Life's a riddle—give it up.*
> *There's no answer to it but this cup...*

Whoever he was, I liked this man's sense of humor. And then which cup was he talking about? His lines themselves contained a riddle. I flicked through the introduction and read that the cup of Hafez gladly accepted both kinds of wine, the earthly and the divine. In his world there was no contradiction between the life of the spirit and the life of the tavern. This was exactly what I needed to hear, and of course I felt he was speaking to me alone—which in that moment, in that bookshop, he was. Your mind, he said to me, will never see into the heart of your deepest questions. So relax! Everything is out of control, as it always is.

I turned to Rumi's *Masnavi*. On the first page I opened to, it said something about love that almost made me weep. An erotic energy poured through the lines. My heart was already full, and his words and his passion tipped me over. What I remember was that he, like Hafez, allowed no contradiction between divine love and its earthly reflection. He fell in love with God through another human being, the mysterious wandering dervish whose name was Shams, which means "sun."

Rumi was already a revered preacher and scholar when they met, but Shams's initial greeting to him, it is said, was to throw his books down a well with the line that the only true knowledge was in the heart. In that very instant, Rumi the scholar became Rumi the mystic. Shams soon disappeared, however, realizing that Rumi's students would become jealous of the intensity of their association. The separation broke Rumi's heart, and his love and longing poured out in poetry—a longing not only for Shams, but for the Beloved for which Shams was the doorway.

I, too, like countless others before and after me, felt I was falling in love with something I had no name for (I resisted calling it God) through the agency of another human being. Waves of feeling—of joy, delight, wonder, anxiety—would wash over me and have me wide awake before dawn, even then a rare occurrence for me. I would feel I was being touched by the stars, and all by the grace of a young woman from Davis, California, who was living in London then.

I forgot about the British Museum that day, and spent much of the morning in the bookshop. When I finally left, it was in the company of Hafez and Rumi. My relationship with their verses has matured over the years, but both of them have moved me, inspired me, instructed me, and given me solace down through my lifetime.

"We Shirazis spend our leisure time in the Garden of Hafez more than anywhere else in the city," Somayeh said. "Especially when we are in love."

My eye wandered over the people strolling between the rose-bushes and sitting on the steps by the tomb. There was a pervasive sense of ease among people here, in their simple way of being together, in their natural way of reclining on the steps by the tomb. The word *suave* came to mind. Smooth, like Esau. A culture can be sophisticated even in simplicity, especially one as old as this. It was in the way people held themselves, loose and easy; innocent in a way, as in a time before the global markets made everyone anxious to get ahead, bend their head into the wind, and "make it." There was not a lot of "making it" in Iran, and people seemed happy enough for that, even if they could do with more than they are earning now.

Hafez's real name was Shemsuddin Mahommed, and he was given the title *Hafez,* which means "one who knows the Koran by heart," because he is said to have learned the holy verses from an early age. He was the son of a coal merchant in fourteenth-century Shiraz, and when he was still very young, Hafez himself worked in a bakery, which was to lead indirectly to heartbreak and his life as a poet. It's that timeless story: one day while delivering bread, he saw this beautiful young woman whose name was Shakh-e-Nabat, and his heart was pierced forever.

Even though he later married someone else and had a son of his own, he continued to love Shakh-e-Nabat from afar just as Dante was loving Beatrice in fourteenth-century Florence. Like Dante, his love and heartbreak were the source of some of his greatest verses, and also like Dante, his human love transmuted into a love of the divine. The same was true for Rumi, who fell in love through Shams to a greater love.

Hafez is known as a Sufi, but he was not the kind to enter a monastery or to wander the streets as a beggar, the common practices of Sufis at that time. In fact he often rails in his verses against the hypocrisy of those Sufis who set themselves apart from society and wore distinctive clothing as a badge of purity. Their hearts, he would say with his incomparable irony, harbored the same sins as everyone else. His own spiritual teacher, Sheikh Mahmud Attar (not to be confused with the poet Attar from Nishapur), was a fruit-and-vegetable seller in Shiraz and something of a renegade who was never recognized by the established Sufi schools of the time.

> *Now that I look back at my wasted life*
> *It is better to have fallen down drunk in the tavern corner*
> *Prudence and proper thoughts lie far from the dervish way*
> *Better to fill your breast with fire and your eye with tears.*

When Hafez was barely out of his teens, the poetry he was already writing caught the attention of the local ruler, who made him court poet, and for some years the young man enjoyed a certain celebrity in his hometown for his spiritually romantic ghazals. The ghazal is a Persian poetic form based on rhyming couplets and a refrain. But then with the following ruler, who was highly orthodox and instituted prohibition laws, Hafez and his wine-soaked verses fell out of favor. He fled to Isfahan for a few years, and wrote reams of ghazals on his longing for Shiraz; for his beloved, Shakh-e-Nabat; and for his teacher, Attar.

The fourteenth century was like today: you never knew what was going to happen next. Another ruler, Shah Shuja, a liberal by inclination, seized control of Shiraz. Hafez was invited back to teach Koranic studies at the madrasah. As he grew older and more prolific, his verses became ever more spiritually subtle and abstract. He wrote more than half of his ghazals in his sixties. On turning sixty he undertook a *halvet,* a forty-day retreat, during which he kept within a circle that he drew on the ground. It is said that on the last day he went to Attar, who gave him a cup of wine, and when he took a sip of it he experienced cosmic or God consciousness. He refers to his realization in a verse in which he encourages his reader to attain the "clarity of wine" by "letting it sit for forty days."

The halvet, which usually takes place in a darkened room, is still practiced on occasion in Sufi circles. The idea is that a period of solitude in the dark removes the fascinations of the exterior world and gives an opportunity for sustained spiritual practice, known as *zikr,* usually the repetition of God's name. Depending on your inner development and the workings of grace, you might receive profound spiritual insights or even, as in the case of Hafez, a realization of union with the Divine.

Some decades ago I read a book titled *Halvet,* by a German woman who wrote on her experience of forty days in a darkened room under the supervision of a Sufi sheikh in Turkey. Ever since then I had wanted to experience a solitary period of darkness for myself—out of curiosity, but also out of a wish to dive deeper down into silence than my ordinary life normally allowed. The opportunity to do my own little dark retreat finally came some years later: seven days in a darkened room with food being pushed through a slot every evening.

My mini-halvet took place somewhere in the Black Forest in Germany. I had been put in touch with a man there who had turned the top floor of his house into a permanent dark retreat that he managed for individuals who had peculiar desires similar to my own. Apparently there were quite a few of us.

Without the stimulus of light, the inner world becomes the only real world. Thoughts slow down and the space between them grows large. Sometimes I would see lights that could only have come from inside my own mind. I discovered that there was something deeply restful about the dark once the mind had settled down and you became accustomed to not knowing whether it was day or night. At one moment the presence of my father filled the room. He had died a few years before, and there in the dark I felt closer to him than I ever had in my lifetime. It was a communion of sorts—one that had been a long time coming—and something was put to rest in me because of it.

When I crawled out on the morning of the seventh day, the sky was turning pink with the first hint of dawn. I walked up the hill through the forest to a little chapel that stood in a clearing all on its own. Every sliver of light on the walls, on the trees, on the grass danced and glittered as it surely does every fine morning—except I was seeing it for the first time, my own first dawn. I may not have known Hafez's clarity of wine, but I felt a deep gratitude for the beauty of this world and the restful silence that stayed with me for days after.

When Hafez died at the age of sixty-nine, the orthodox clergy refused him a Muslim burial, but the whole of Shiraz rose up in protest. It was finally agreed that an oracle should be consulted, and that the oracle should be Hafez's own words. His verses were put in a pot and a young boy was chosen to pick one out. He drew verse 7 of ghazal 79:

> *Neither Hafez's corpse nor his life negate*
> *With all of his misdeeds, heavens for him await.*

No wonder he unsettled the clergy. More than a Sufi or a Muslim, Hafez was a universal mystic who saw into the heart of humanity and shared his vision and wisdom with others through poetry. Why poetry? Because poetry can dive down below beliefs and theories, philosophies and religion, to capture a deeper truth; which is why it has spoken to me for so long. In one of his later ghazals, Hafez put it this way:

> *I have learned so much from God*
> *That I can no longer call myself*
> *A Christian, a Hindu, a Moslem, a Buddhist or a Jew.*
> *The truth has shared so much of itself with me*
> *That I can no longer call myself*
> *A man, a woman, an angel, or even a pure soul.*

> *Love has befriended Hafez so completely*
> *It has turned to ash and freed me*
> *Of every concept and image my mind has ever known.*
> (translated by Shahriar Shariari)

This is the kind of poem in which I feel the poet is speaking directly to me. It is why Hafez has stayed with me for so long. In my twenties, I used to fret that I could never seem to feel at home in any spiritual tradition. It stirred me deeply to take part in Sufi movements in London, but it didn't mean I was a Muslim. I appreciated sitting in silence with the Zen people, but was equally reluctant to call myself a Buddhist. Yet I always felt I must be missing something, that I was a spiritual window-shopper who was reluctant to get more than his toes wet.

As I have grown older and come to trust more the promptings of my own inner world, those concerns have fallen away. What is free of *concept and image,* as Hafez would say, is sheer alive presence—the love that ultimately burns us away. My faith is in that and in the aspirations of secular humanism; together they make for a secular spirituality. The equality of men and women, human rights, education and the democratic process, environmental action, medical research—achievements like these surely embody some of the best of what it means to be human. They are exercises in practical compassion, a greater leap forward for the daily welfare of humanity than anything achieved by the medieval hierarchies and rituals of religion. Secular spirituality works for the betterment of this world while acknowledging the immanent mystery inherent in everything.

After all, it was from God—the nameless wisdom and compassion beyond reason—that Hafez learned to go beyond religion, not from a good humanistic argument. In his eyes, secular ideals without the acknowledgment of the Divine would have been nothing more than a mark of human pride.

Like all other versions and translations today, this poem of his is drawn from the *Diwan of Hafez,* a collection of five hundred ghazals that were compiled into a single volume some twenty years after his death.

It stirred me, to be sitting by the tomb of a man who knew my own thoughts before I even knew them myself. And at the same time I realized I was longing for tea. Tea or Hafez: there it was, the competing interests of heaven and earth right there in the mind of man.

But the teahouse in the Hafez garden was closed. "It was the best in all of Shiraz," Somayeh said, somewhat reproachfully. "And they served coffee, too, and sherbet and ice cream. Maybe it's different in Tehran, but the cafés here are still closed because of a government edict from last year."

Why would a government close the cafés? Well, she said, the government was concerned for the health of young people, who were increasingly becoming addicted to tobacco through the use of the water pipes that were often available in cafés. I didn't believe her. I had been warned before I had even set foot in Iran that anything to do with the pursuit of pleasure was suspect there. Perhaps even beginning with the apple in Eden, pleasure stands forever against puritan orthodoxies of every kind.

We strolled away from the tomb toward a long, low building off to the side. In one of the rooms a woman shrouded in black was holding forth at the front of a packed class of men and women. "A class on Hafez," Somayeh said. "They are yearlong courses and are always oversubscribed. Everyone in Iran, from the taxi drivers to the intellectuals in Tehran, can recite a verse of Hafez. He is in our blood and in our soul. He is a Persian hero."

Later that evening, on meeting Mahsa Vahdat, I would come to appreciate how true this was. Mahsa Vahdat, the woman with the golden voice.

I knocked on the door of the address I had been given, and a woman, perhaps in her late thirties, with large, warm eyes and a gentle presence, appeared and ushered me into a spacious, light-filled apartment in central Shiraz. Her name was Mahsa Vahdat. Her husband, Atabak, got up from the sofa to greet me. Bowls of nuts, fruit, and small chocolates were spread out on a low table. Another woman and a man were adjusting a film camera at the far end of the room. Mahsa and Atabak lived in Tehran, but they were in Shiraz to develop a film on Iranian women artists.

Traditional Iranian music had been part of my record collection since those early days in London, and it had survived technology's progressive advances to migrate finally in recent years to my iPod. I wanted to know if it was still alive and well in its country of origin. I knew it was not a happy time for music and musicians in Iran, and I wondered how artists were able to negotiate their way around the rules of the Islamic Republic and still make their music. A friend in Tehran had told me about Mahsa and Atabak. Not only were they exceptional musicians, he had said, but much of their repertoire consisted of the poems of Hafez and Rumi. "Mahsa, she of the golden voice," he had said.

Atabak was several years older than his wife—a calm, dignified presence, with hair beginning to show hints of silver. He composed much of the music that Mahsa sings; he also accompanied her on the setar, a four-stringed instrument in the lute family. However, if you are a female singer in Iran, you face a formidable obstacle: a woman is not allowed to sing in public. A woman's voice can incite desires in the men in the audience, the authorities say. A man, on the other hand, can give public performances, even though music in general is frowned upon by the authorities. You are not even allowed to show traditional musical instruments on television. You can still hear the music, but the view of the instruments is blocked by flowers. A grand piano or other Western instrument is perfectly legitimate and needs no camouflage because it does not, in the government's estimation, stir the passions the way Persian music can. Mahsa, who sings mostly traditional music along with her sister, performs in Europe, and occasionally in the United States.

"Of course, it's not easy being an artist in Iran," she said, as Atabak and I made ourselves comfortable on a long red sofa. Mahsa sat opposite us in an armchair patterned with faded roses. "But no matter how difficult life here may be, I could never think of leaving my native land. I draw my inspiration from the country's soul. The culture's longings, its poets, its beauty, the centuries of tradition—all of it nourishes me in a way that nowhere else could."

She was echoing the same sentiments that Mania Akbari had voiced in Tehran. Through the window behind her, the yellow leaves of a large tree fluttered down now and then, as if into her hair.

"Coming here to Shiraz, being able to sit by the grave of Hafez himself—how could anywhere else give me that?" she went on, leaning back in the sofa and needing no response from me. "Living in Iran is essential for me if I am to continue to make music.

"As for the restrictions and obstacles, you just have to find your way around them. You create your own world—a parallel world of art and artists and thinkers which has connections with the world outside and finds its way around the political class and their regulations."

There were only two music schools in the whole of Iran for a population of seventy million. The Taliban imposed the same restrictions on music in Pakistan and Afghanistan. It is a distraction from prayer and from God, they say—even though nothing in the Koran forbids music.

For Mahsa, on the other hand, music was the highest form of prayer. It was a prayer said not by the lips or the mind alone, but with every fiber of her being. It was a means of transport, a doorway to communion—which was exactly what the authorities must fear. And not just the authorities in Iran; music and dance, followed closely by representational art of any kind, have always been viewed with suspicion by the conservative wing of every religion. I will never forget a woman I met in Tennessee telling me that in the town where she grew up, dancing was against the law, owing to the local influence of the Church of Christ. (Maybe it was no accident that she later spent some years as a Playboy bunny.)

Whether in religion or in politics, the more conservative a faction is, the more patriarchal it is. The patriarchy acts like a collective superego that wants to make sure you don't step out of line. If you have people singing and dancing, things might spin out of control.

Ecstatic experience of any kind has always been the province of the feminine. That is why women are controlled as they are in Islam and in the traditional sects of other religions, especially their sexual power. Here was Mahsa, sitting in this simple but elegant Shirazi apartment, all white walls and a large tribal rug on the parquet wooden floor; an urbane woman who travels the world, having to wear the hijab in public. It didn't add up in my foreign mind, but she told me she never gave the hijab a second thought. She had even grown used to the rule that required her to sit in a different part of the bus from male passengers.

The reasoning in this is that if a man were to sit in the place a woman has just moved from, he would be aroused by the heat trace her body has left on the seat. It's the usual complaint: women are responsible for men's arousal, so even in cases of rape, the victimized woman in Iran is more likely to be blamed than her male attacker.

The law only makes life more difficult for women. Right now a nine-year-old girl can be punished as an adult. There is even inequality when it comes to capital punishment in Iran. When a woman is murdered, her family has to pay the murderer's family before there can be an execution. If the victim is a man, no money changes hands. The only logic in this is that a woman is a lesser being. In a divorce the children go automatically to the husband. And while it is easy for a man to get a divorce, it is extremely difficult for a woman unless she has it written in her marriage agreement to begin with.

Iranians laugh at these rules and restrictions just as anyone would, except their laughter is more rueful than ours, tinged with the irony and cynicism that grows from having to confront them on a regular basis.

Yet for all the restrictions on their liberty, Atabak said, pouring more black tea into my glass as he spoke, there were ways in which women's self-expression had grown more vocal since the Revolution. He asked if I had heard of the One Million Signatures Campaign that lobbies for gender equality. I had. It was a popular grassroots movement, and an example of how women had become the most visibly active voice of dissent in the country. Not just educated women, but ordinary women, too, were finding their voices. They were becoming active in grassroots campaigns to address social and political issues, which was why women were considered by the authorities to be more dangerous than ever, and they were paying the price for their courage. Women who were peacefully demonstrating for equal rights were now being arrested and charged with threatening national security. The government was depicting their movement as a vehicle for sexual anarchy and "moral corruption," a persuasive argument among many traditionally minded Iranians.

For all the humane literary and artistic culture of Iran that Mahsa and Atabak themselves represent, and that I had already seen something of in Tehran, it is a fact that a second culture exists in Iran, an ugly dimension that people have to deal with on a daily basis. Public hangings of murderers and drug dealers take place routinely; torture is common in the jail system. Suppressed violence spills into road rage and makes driving a daily hazard.

So how can one live a moral and compassionate existence in the midst of such cruelty and violence? How can you live in an Iran of the imagination that is so at odds with the reality all around you? This is the irony and the paradox that people like Mahsa and Atabak live with: the challenge of living up to their own principles and yet also taking responsibility for their own complicity in the world about them. After all, they and others like them have chosen to be part of this society along with everyone else.

So many contradictions in being human, and we have to negotiate them wherever we are. I, too, live in a society with millions in jail, with rape and murder a daily occurrence on city streets, with hopelessness and despair cutting swaths through what is nevertheless a magnificent country of dreams. The dark always follows the light wherever it goes, and none of our transcendent ideals will ever eradicate human cruelty, injustice, and greed. In Iran, though, the stakes are higher than in many parts of the world. A wrong move at the wrong time, Atabak said, and your life as you knew it could disappear. I hadn't expected our meeting to have this sober edge. I had thought we were going to talk about music. But then, for all the fine music they made, this was the world they had to survive in.

Mahsa was quiet for a moment, gazing at the glass of tea in her hand. Despite all the darkness, she said eventually, Iran was an exotic place. It was so mysterious, it defied easy categories. Sometimes she had to go abroad to see and feel this other Iran. In Paris or Rome she would sit in a café and realize she had brought Iran with her. She would feel Iran as a living thing inside. She would feel part of an ancient culture that still survived through its poets, its music, its love and respect for human life in and of itself, independent of any particular creed or political ideology. For thousands of years there has existed this tradition of upholding human rights and dignity. Iranian poets have always sung of the joys of this life, and how this world and the next are one and the same. Not just Omar Khayyam, whom most people have heard of in the West, but many others; and perhaps no one more than Hafez. This was the Iran she inhabited.

But what was it about Hafez in particular that made these two want to sing his poems around the world? For Mahsa and Atabak, it was personal. They identified with him in a more immediate way than I did. People like me in the West appreciated Hafez for his universal spiritual themes, but for Iranians—and for these Iranians in particular—he lived on in their blood and soul, as my guide Somayeh had said. And yet I would have thought his life and circumstances in the fourteenth century could have had little bearing on the Iran of today.

Quite the opposite, I learned. The political climate of his time apparently had uncanny echoes in the present. The governor of Shiraz, where Hafez lived all his life, banned music and wine. Hafez complains often in his poetry about the closing of the taverns. He had to buy his wine from the Zoroastrians, just as people today go to the Armenian Christians for their wine. He lived in a very conservative society that did not understand him. He even challenged Sufis when he felt they were not genuine. He was a free spirit who could not speak openly in a repressive time of theocracy and religious dogmatism. The struggle between those forces had colored Iran's history for centuries.

But then Hafez would say that we could never expect happiness from the material world alone, because everything was always changing. No social or political ideal could ever satisfy the longing in a human heart, he would say. Human beings were unique among all created beings in their capacity to love. Hafez said that even the angels, who were full of goodness, did not know love, because you could not have love without sorrow. Love was the treasure of sorrow, Mahsa said then, and I savored the beauty of the phrase as it dissolved in the air.

So Hafez, too, lived in another Iran in his own time, an Iran of the imagination that stretched back to pre-Islamic times and forward to include Mahsa, Atabak, and others like them. They were kindred spirits of the same lineage; a spiritual and artistic, but also cultural, lineage that was part of the Iranian story—the same story that had brought me here. That was why it was so important for them to continue to sing his poetry today.

Hafez was such an intrinsic part of the culture, Atabak said finally, that for all his veiled criticisms of orthodoxy, no government would risk being critical of him. Even many of the mullahs knew some of his lines by heart. It was different with Rumi, however, because after his life-changing meeting with Shams of Tabriz he threw away his books and moved from being a traditional preacher himself to a full-blown ecstatic mystic. A few years earlier, many of the mullahs would not even touch a book of Rumi's. His work was unclean, they said. But now that the whole world had come to know him in translation, they could no longer deny his worth.

Just then the doorbell rang and a tall young man with an instrument case came in. He had recently arrived from Germany, where he had been on tour. His instrument was the ney, the traditional wooden flute that is well known in Turkey as well as Iran. They were getting ready to film a music session for the documentary they were working on. They had invited me that afternoon because it would be a rare chance for me to see them in action.

See them in action I did. I heard their own expression of traditional music forms, with the words of Hafez as they were written in the *Diwan of Hafez*. For the next hour or so I was lifted on the wings of Mahsa's extraordinary voice, so clear and so strong, and at the same time with a purity and depth of feeling that brought me to the verge of tears. I wondered why all Persian music seemed to be so plaintive, so steeped in the language of longing. Perhaps it was melancholy for its own fate, having been forbidden so frequently through Iranian history. But listening to the rise and fall of Mahsa's voice, and to the wistful moan of the ney, I felt the melancholy to be far older than that.

"The still, sad music of humanity," Wordsworth had called it. Surely it was an echo of the oldest longing of all, the ancient sadness of Adam as he was told to leave the Garden. For wasn't it here in old Persia that the Garden of Paradise was first brought to earth? "Love is the treasure of sorrow," Mahsa had said. Listening to her, feeling my own life sailing by, the joys and the loves and the disappointments and sorrows, it was easy to gather her meaning. I am here in old Persia, I said to myself as her minor chords washed me clean. Here in old Persia, where a Garden of Paradise was first made by man. And tomorrow, in Shiraz, I would be able to enter the gates of a paradise garden to see for myself the fruits of man's labors. Just as I had done so often before, all those years ago, in England.

Our English word *paradise* derives from the old Persian word for "garden," *pardis*. So important was the garden in old Persia that when a new city was planned, the gardens would be planted before any building foundations were laid. Cyrus the Great, father of the Persian nation and founder of its first great empire, planted acres of gardens on the site of his new capital city, Pasargadae, as long ago as 550 B.C. Gardens spread across the world from Persia to become one of the earliest civilizing influences on the minds of mankind.

They were not intended to be mere decoration. Nor were they planted as a food source. They were a mirror of the glory and beauty those early Persians saw in the created world about them, and a witness to the creative role of human stewardship. They were an act of imagination through which the first gardeners consciously sought to create a heaven in a little corner of earth.

I discovered my own little heaven on earth when I was ten years old, not knowing then that it was a far echo of the original version in Persia. My family had come to live in St. Catherine's

Valley, that steep cleft in a Cotswold ridge on the edge of Bath. Along the valley lay St. Catherine's Court with its tiny church. Originally it had been a retreat house for the monks of the abbey in medieval Bath. Mrs. Strutt, the old lady who lived there when I was a child, used to let me wander in the garden and play on the crumbling steps that led to the ancient fishponds made by the monks a thousand years before. Golden carp swam there still, under the leaves of the water lilies. Grasses and forget-me-nots sprouted around every flaking stone, a fountain trickled in a recess in the garden wall.

In the springtime, beds of daffodils and bluebells would trace a path of yellow and blue around the edges of the garden. Wildflowers—snowdrops and cowslips—would scatter themselves across the lawn. Beyond the ponds, through an arch cut into the high privet hedge, I would sit by the ancient swimming pool, all made of flagstones, with its changing rooms of privet, one with the name *Adam,* the other with *Eve* carved in formal lettering into its stone step. The pool was always dappled with crimson leaves, tongues of flame, whenever I saw it. I would while away the afternoon there, nourished in a way beyond my knowing, until the sun was low, and long shadows would streak the pool and tell me it was time to make my way home.

In Shiraz there were several paradise gardens, some of them centuries old, but Somayeh wanted to take me to the garden of Naranjastan, the garden of roses and orange blossoms. (The Persian *naranjan* gives us the word *orange,* via the Spanish *naranja.*) The very garden, Somayeh told me, where she would often stroll with Ali, her soon-to-be fiancé, and with whom she was headily in love. She dreamed of studying abroad, in Paris perhaps, and having a son when she was older. "Life is too difficult here for a girl," she confided, looking up with a cursory glance between sending texts and checking her messages. Wanting to connect, but Ali didn't call. Except for the black chador, she could be from anywhere.

We stopped in a dusty street by a stretching wall that gave no clue to what lay behind it. When you pass through the narrow entrance, you see a long, rectangular water basin with fountains sweeping away toward a shimmering building at the far end, all slender marble columns, and glittering mirror work covering the large portico. With its multiple reflections dancing in every direction, the mirror work—a common device in Iran—is intended to suggest the infinite work of creation. The roof is punctuated along its length by three equidistant and tiled semicircles. On the central crescent directly facing the water pool, two lions in yellow and blue face each other. Each of them holds a scimitar in a raised paw, and a golden sun is rising over each of their backs. This, Somayeh said, was the Qajar dynasty's symbol for Persia when they were in power in the nineteenth century, though the rising sun was a Zoroastrian symbol that had survived through the centuries of Persia's Islamization.

Naranjastan is the smallest and newest of the gardens in Shiraz—only 130 years old and a confection of the Qajar era, built by the leading Shirazi figure of the day. The building was his summer pavilion, and he would allow the garden to be open to the public for much of the year. A narrow path runs along each side of the long pool, lined the whole way with a row of orange trees, then rows of red and white roses, then more orange trees; both formal and natural, somehow, at the same time. As we gazed at this inspired work of the mind of man, a young couple strolled in, hand in hand. Which of course is forbidden, but then, this is the garden of roses and orange blossoms...

We sat by the pool for a while, the summer pavilion casting a hint of its reflection in the far end, the rose blossoms wafting their scent in our direction. The design of the whole was all straight rows and neat circles; and yet somehow, as in the garden in St. Catherine's Valley, the illusion of naturalness remained. A garden is always a taming of the wild, yet the success of the result depends on the balance between the two. If you tame nature too much, the result is a dry formalism; too little, and the garden will seem to have returned to nature. The designer of the Naranjastan garden had held the line in a delicate tension.

Sitting in that oasis of harmony and tranquillity, the dusty street outside and the bare mountains not far away, one would find it tempting to think that the notion of the garden first arose as a refuge from the harsh land all around. Iran's bright light and vast sky can make the world seem so infinite that it would be only natural to want to fashion some more intimate corner.

But the evidence suggests that the first gardeners had a grander vision in mind. They wanted to do nothing less than imitate the work of God, to create a dynamic harmony of the four elements available to the original Creator—earth, air, fire, and water. With these elements they wanted to generate life, as the Creator had done; to pay homage to the fertility of this blossoming world. The fire is the light of the mirror work and of the reflected sun in the water pools. Without its spark, no seed would germinate. The air carries the scents of the flowers, which are an expression of the presence of invisible realms. The water reflects the sky, and when earth and sky (woman and man) are united in waters, life is born. Water, love, woman, fertility—all are the one source of life. Finally, the tree, sacred in every religion, joins heaven with earth in another symbol and gesture of love and union.

The garden, then, was a form of devotion, an offering in honor of the original creative, fertile force. It was a sacred space, literally an earthly paradise set apart from the mundane concerns of the world—a place where man could return to his original nature, in harmony with the rest of life. Then, if it was too cold to sit outside, you could always sit on the garden inside your own home, since the garden carpet has always been one of the most famous of all Persian designs.

Later, in the courtyard of my hotel, I sat in another kind of garden for which, over the ensuing couple of days, I developed a certain wry fondness. There, surrounded by five floors of wall

and windows, was a fake cherry tree with plentiful white blossoms, a little fountain, and carpet-covered beds with bolsters
where guests could sip their tea. For Iranians, even a fake garden
was better than no garden at all.

I sat back on one of the daybeds, and took out Rumi to read
with my tea. The kind of garden he spoke of was beyond the
reach of the senses and mind, yet was as real as the garden of
Naranjastan. Rumi's garden was inside him, unknown and hidden from the rest of the world, though the perfection of the outer
garden served as its mirror. In the hotel courtyard, my own inner
garden had only this fake cherry tree for its reflection, but even
that had its uses, raising the question as it did of how contrived
or genuine my own garden really was.

Or whether it even existed at all. Maybe I just liked to get
drunk on another man's words, whipping up a sentimental
storm to mask my own poverty of feeling. Rumi could console
and awaken, I knew that well enough. But I also knew I was as
capable of self-deception as anyone. How easy it can be to imagine we share exalted feelings that in truth we have no knowledge of. I opened up the book even so. The first lines I saw were
these:

> Remember the proverb, Eat the grapes.
> Do not keep talking about the garden.
> Eat the grapes.

Rumi always came through. I thanked him out loud. And
then I read this:

> We tremble like leaves about to let go,
> There is no avoiding pain,
> Or feeling exiled, or the taste of dust.
> But also we have a green-winged longing
> For the sweetness of the friend.

I gazed around me. Two families were huddled on their day-beds, while a young man was sprawled back on another, working on his computer. Looking up from those lines of Rumi, I felt myself to be a part not only of this little community of tea drinkers, but of the unceasing swell of human affairs that had somehow washed me up against this particular shore; brothers and sisters, all of us, both in our trembling, *like leaves about to let go,* and in our *green-winged longing* for something without a name.

The garden, I thought as I got up to leave—even this garden—was yet another expression of the same humanist sensibility that, despite the ongoing tyranny and repressive policies of successive rulers, had fed Persian art and literature for centuries. The next day I would be paying my respects to the father of all humanists, who lay at rest not far from Shiraz.

Cyrus the Great, the man Iranians still speak of today in tones of reverence and respect, as if he were some recently deceased family relative, was the first known humanist anywhere. Somayeh was keen to take me to his lonely resting place out in the desert beyond the city, and to Persepolis, the city his descendents made, the marvel of the ancient world. Her fiancé, Ali, she said, would often cry when he went to Persepolis, and she herself was always grateful to go there. For Iranians it was like visiting a shrine—one sacred to the memory of a great culture whose qualities and values were still alive today, in spite of everything. I was as interested in the idea of their place in the Iranian soul as I was in the ruins themselves, and we had agreed to go the following day, our last one together.

# talking stones

"My name is Ozymandias, King of Kings:
Look on my works, ye Mighty, and despair!"
Nothing beside remains. Round the decay
Of that colossal wreck, boundless and bare,
The lone and level sands stretch far away.
— PERCY BYSSHE SHELLEY, "OZYMANDIAS"

There's a piece of clay shaped like a corncob, known as the Cyrus Cylinder, that was found in the late nineteenth century, when the British were everywhere they shouldn't have been. The cylinder is now in the British Museum, along with half of Egypt and most of Mesopotamia, it might seem at first glance. I saw it the last time I was in London, sitting on its own in a glass case in one of those cavernous corridors. You would walk right by it, this unassuming lump of clay, unless you knew how pregnant it was with significance for one of the burning issues of our own time.

It is inscribed with a decree known as the first charter of human rights, and with a little license it can be read as a call for religious and ethnic freedom. It abolished forced labor among the Jews in Babylon, restored the temple in Jerusalem, banned the seizing of property by force, and gave member states the right to subject themselves to the rule of Cyrus or not. "I will impose my monarchy on no nation. Each is free to accept it, and if any of them rejects it, I never resolve on war to reign."

Cyrus was the world's first enlightened despot; perhaps the first in all of history to recognize that ordinary human beings, as distinct from the rich and powerful, had rights—simply by virtue of being human. This was the Persia that Iranians like Somayeh were nostalgic for still today, however far it may be from their present reality: a benevolent, humane, and fair-minded superpower.

Cyrus, the Abraham of the Persians, father of the nation, progenitor of its first glories, was only twenty-one when he defeated his own grandfather, King Astyages of the Medes, on the Pasargadae plain. That was in 550 B.C., when few had yet heard of a city called Rome, and the Jews were languishing in Babylon. For the Iranians, it could have been yesterday. The remains of their great king lie there still in a rectangular burial chamber supported by six stone tiers.

You drive over a flat brown desert to get there from Shiraz; not a desert of sand but of endless horizons of dust and rubble, a desert without relief that yawns on for hundreds of miles. Pasargadae is a lonely place, a wide plain empty now except for the tomb and a few small remnants of what was once the king's capital city and its beautiful gardens. Just two cars were in the parking lot. A white sky spread over us, so shroudlike, so overarching that any human being could not fail here to acknowledge his or her small and humble place in this vast world. We walked over to the monument and gazed up at its somber stones. You could almost smell the poignancy, a savor in the air; the king of the greatest empire of the ancient world lying right here, with nothing to show for his magnificent achievements but a small pile of stones in a desolate emptiness.

And yet Pasargadae is potent with meaning still. For all its desolation, it is a crucial symbol of Persian identity even today—

especially today, when the reigning authorities are so keen to stamp an Islamic, as distinct from Persian, identity on a people who stubbornly identify with their glorious, pre-Islamic past. The government has deliberately allowed Cyrus's tomb to fall into disrepair, and a few days before we arrived there had been a spontaneous demonstration at Pasargadae to clamor for the tomb's restoration. People had text-messaged each other on their cell phones, and a few thousand had shown up out of nowhere. There were no speeches, no ceremony, just an honoring of Cyrus and their own ancient origins.

Just one man had done more than anyone else to revive the identification of the Persian people with their past glories. His name was Ferdowsi, and he lived a thousand years ago in a town called Tus, in the east of the country, some three hundred years after the Arabs invaded Persia and embedded Islam into the culture. He wrote Iran's greatest epic, the *Shahnameh*—Book of Kings—and in so doing he became the father of the modern Persian language. His book reinstated Farsi as the language of preference over Arabic. Still today, it is the most widely read text in Persian. It no doubt played a part in drawing the recent crowd to Pasargadae.

It is hard to imagine spending thirty years writing a single work of no fewer than sixty thousand rhyming couplets. Ferdowsi did just that, and ended up producing one of the great classics of world literature. The *Shahnameh* begins the story of the Persian kings and heroes some seven thousand years ago and ends with the defeat of the last Sassanian king by the Arabs in the seventh century A.D. Along the way it provides an entire system of laws, of court etiquette, and details of the teachings of Zoroaster, founder of Iran's native religion. It was the inspiration, and possibly the source itself, for the chivalric code of European courts in the Middle Ages, with all its clanking armor, jousting, and the dedication of one's honor to some fair lady.

For a thousand years the *Shahnameh* was the definitive text underlying the structure of the legal system and court protocol in Persia and all over Central Asia as well as in Mughal India. And yet, as so often happens with a towering genius, Ferdowsi died in poverty at the age of eighty-five and went unrecognized by the royalty of his time until after his death. Of all the great poets of Persia, Ferdowsi was perhaps the only one who was not a Sufi. Nor did he show any great interest in Islam, since his subject was pre-Islamic Iran, and he portrayed the final defeat of the last Persian king by the Arabs as a tragedy.

One may wonder how a book could have such resonance over a thousand years, but then we do not have the pedigree of a culture like Iran. Neither have we had to submit to a foreign power and religion when our own was already more than a thousand years old. A thousand years of cultural memory do not disappear easily. So when a great chronicle emerges that mythologizes its glories, it is given wings by the longings and also the pride of an entire people. That wistful pride continues still.

If you stood by the Colosseum in Rome, you might imagine you could hear the cheers and jeers of that antique world echoing still. But on the empty Pasargadae plain, the echoes of an even greater empire than Rome's have long since fallen silent, unless you have the ears of a Persian. Hard though it was to believe, the forlorn spot where I was standing now was once the heart of the largest empire of the ancient world. The Achaemenid Empire, founded by Cyrus the Great, spanned three continents and is thought to have been the wealthiest and most magnificent in all of history. It was Cyrus, not God, who delivered the Jews from the bondage of Babylon; it was he who introduced the first postal service and created a network of paved roads stretching from one end of the empire to the other.

But then Cyrus crossed a woman, a perilous move even for an emperor. Despite his promise not to impose his rule on those who did not want it, he subdued a powerful tribe in the northeast by getting their army reeling drunk before engaging them in battle. The head of the tribe was a Queen Tomyris, whose own son had been killed by Cyrus's forces. In revenge, the queen marshaled her forces and destroyed most of the Persian army. Then she heaped scorn and insult upon the vanquished by ordering the slain Cyrus's head to be cut off and dunked into an animal skin filled with human blood.

It's a sober and salutary tale, not just for Cyrus but for all of us, I thought, as we turned to go back to the car. Cyrus swept to power on a wave of altruism whose memory is preserved by the cylinder on display in the British Museum. His belief in the value and freedom of the human individual was carved in stone. Once in power and with the whole world at his feet, he forgot his own high principles and committed an act of treachery. That's when fate and a woman took power into their own hands and he was dispatched to his unseemly end.

During the Achaemenid dynasty that Cyrus founded, his tomb was surrounded by gardens and was revered for generations. Eventually, when it was the turn of Alexander the Great to dominate the world stage, the old tomb was plundered by his own troops, to the genuine sorrow of Alexander himself. The Greek saw himself in the image of Cyrus, and held Cyrus the Great in the highest esteem as the creator of the largest empire to exist before his own. Pasargadae fell into disrepair, and was eventually overshadowed by Persepolis.

We left Cyrus to his stately silence and continued on under the same white sky across a dun desert. Persepolis lies half an hour out of Shiraz and an hour from Pasargadae. I'm glad it wasn't more, because there seemed to be as many traffic regulations in Shiraz as in Tehran, which is to say none. We even met one or two cars driving down the wrong side of the freeway. My driver simply weaved around them without comment.

His works aren't invariably beautiful, but they all bespeak beauty as an operating principle: the catch in consciousness when mind and body merge in a state of praise for existence, just as it is.

— PETER SCHELDAHL, ON THE WORK OF THE ARTIST GABRIEL OROZCO, *NEW YORKER*, DECEMBER 21, 2009

Persepolis, the greatest surviving masterpiece of all ancient Near Eastern civilizations, the city that Alexander the Great destroyed, spreads itself before you across a dry and empty plain like some ghostly specter, half in this world and half in some other that the millennia have retired from view. Two great winged creatures, bull-like, in stone, loom over me at the threshold, reminding me of my relative stature in the scheme of things. Beyond, two monumental staircases with shallow steps lead you up toward wide ceremonial avenues and scattered pillars that once supported the magnificent wooden roofs of the king's palace and reception rooms.

The whole vast complex begun by Darius the Great in 522 B.C. was developed and extended for generations before it was burned to the ground by Alexander the Great in a fit of pique in 330 B.C.—in revenge, some say, for the burning of the Acropolis in Athens by the Persians some time before.

Once I was past the winged bulls, the first thing to catch my eye was not the lonely columns soaring to the sky or the great causeway at the heart of the city, but a graffito. Two graffiti, in fact. Scrawled in an untidy script on blocks of stone that had stood there undisturbed for more than two thousand years were the words

*Stanley. New York Herald. 1870.*

Above that, in precise upright lettering and straight lines, was a second message for posterity:

1911–12
39TH KGO.
CENTRAL INDIA HORSE
CAP. JOHN MALCOLM. ENVOY

Two individuals asserting the significance of their own story over and above that of the old stones. One of them was a servant of the imperial power of the time, and I felt vaguely complicit in the stone's defacement, owing to my own racial connection with that faded empire. Captain John Malcolm's signature carried the hubris of a nation along with it. The English were everywhere then, and especially in this area because of their need for clear supply lines to India, the prize of their empire. As for Henry Stanley, the year after he left his mark on Persepolis, he ensured his place in history by finding the long-lost Scottish explorer Dr. Livingstone, who had discovered the source of the Nile.

I followed Somayeh in the mounting heat, gazing at the walls with their yards of fine reliefs, mostly of princes and ambassadors from around the ancient world laden with tribute for the king of kings. I imagined the stunning red of the original floors, and the elegant black columns of the Hundred Column Hall.

For nearly two hundred years before it was burned to the ground, Persepolis was the multicultural heart of a great Persian empire that stretched over dozens of different lands and cultures. It was the ceremonial capital, where princes would come from far and wide at the time of the New Year festival to pay tribute to the emperor. In its time it was a glorious display of architectural styles and design skills drawn from all over the Middle East and as far away as the Bosphorus and India.

And now it lies in ruins. Alexander did such a thorough work of destruction that most has to be left to the imagination. Yet ruins of any kind are food for the imagination, especially the romantic imagination, which—among other things—feeds on nostalgia, memory, and the wearing effects of the passing of time. Poets and artists relish a dialogue between their private imagination and a faded reality whose gaps they can fill in with their own dreams and longings.

It's a small step from there to ruminating on the vulnerability of empire, the fragility of art, and our own ephemeral lives. How eternal these things seem at the time; how fleeting they are with hindsight, the stones of a ruin say. Shelley, Byron, Keats, the painter Constable, Edgar Allan Poe, and other reflective spirits of the nineteenth century all drew inspiration for their art from ruins.

Yet in truth, confessed romantic though I am, just a whisper of the old glory of Persepolis reached my ears. I was impressed—how could you not be?—but not really touched by such a distant world. Distant not only in time but also in space; Persepolis lay beyond the habitual geographic borders of my imagination. I could not summon more than vague outlines: the pomp and ceremony of the king of kings, the lines of ambassadors with tribute in hand, the guards at the gates, the warriors in their skirtlike tunics, the women of the court in diaphanous trails of white, the whinnying of horses and snorting of mules—nothing cast more than a faint shadow in my mind.

But then I am not Iranian. Somayeh walked through the remnants of her stately past with a discernible reverence that touched me more than did the ruins themselves. Her cell phone in her pocket for once, she was building her own Persepolis, her own Persia, from the old stones through which we passed. The few other Iranian tourists were likewise deeply absorbed and quiet.

After a few hours among the faded glory of Persepolis, I finally turned to Arthur Upham Pope to summon some deeper feeling for the place. Here was a man who, like Somayeh, had built his own Persepolis from the raw materials he had found, not only on the site but in his library. Passing between the winged bulls on our way out, I read again what the American scholar of Persian architecture had written about the ancient city:

> *Humane sentiments found expression in the nobility and sheer beauty of the building: more rational and gracious than the work of the Assyrians or Hittites, more lucid and humane than that of the Egyptians. The beauty of Persepolis is not the accidental counterpart of mere size and costly display; it is the result of beauty being specifically recognized as sovereign value.*

*Beauty... recognized as sovereign value.* What an extraordinary claim to make on behalf of a culture! It made me wonder what the sovereign value of our own culture might be. The word *freedom* sprang to mind; so did the word *dollar*. What, then, of my own sovereign value? Could I say *love*? Was that what my own life was honestly given to? If I said *truth* or *authenticity,* if I said *goodness*, would I be doing anything more than mouthing mere platitudes?

No, it was Upham Pope's *beauty* that struck a chord in me—not as a concrete object, nor even in the form of a beautiful thing or scene, but as a visceral sense of the moment. Beauty as a moment of harmonious proportion, everything in its place. In those moments I felt my self-awareness fall away. The only thing missing in moments like those was myself. Such moments entailed a self-forgetting, as when I would while away hours in the garden at St. Catherine's Court.

The usually ever-present and separate observer falls away when you pay attention so utterly and completely that there is only the leaf floating on the pool, the brush painting the painting, the pen writing the line. When we disappear like that, a presence arises that encompasses everything. Nothing is separate, nothing is left out, everything glows in its unique distinctness, an irrevocable part of the whole.

I had found a name for moments like these in my teens, a name borrowed from Stendhal, my favorite author at the time. I saw myself in the young heroes of *The Scarlet and Black*, the *Charterhouse of Parma*, in the tension they lived between their worldly ambitions and their greatest happiness, which lay in their simple delight in timeless moments. Stendhal called these *moments de beauté*, and when I first moved to London to work for Thomson Newspapers, I would spend my lunch hours sitting in Trafalgar Square or by the Thames, collecting my own "moments of beauty." Impossibly, shamelessly romantic, the phrase sounds today, forty years later, so very nineteenth century, yet it still captures the spirit of a moment like that. The power of Now, you might say today; or just being. Whatever you call it, being in the moment is life's simplest, most available treasure.

Stendhal's heroes would stand transfixed with some detail that had caught their eye: this bowl, that face, this carpet, this cup of tea. But it wasn't the object of appreciation itself that mattered so much as the growing intimacy with it; a gathering of love, one might almost say, that ushered the character into a deeper revelation of the light buried in all matter, and ultimately in the character himself.

Persian culture, too, has always been big on particulars, which is why it, too, is a doorway to beauty still today. It knows that the world teems with vernacular loveliness. Traditionally it was why the aesthetics of a house mattered: the way you sat down at meals, the food itself, its presentation, the bowls you ate from—why everything mattered to the Iranian. With the right attention, the physical world was known to be a portal into our own deeper nature.

We all have one foot in this world of time and another in eternity—here and there at one and the same time. Like the singer Mahsa Vahdat, like Hafez himself, whose lives testify to the challenge of marrying our inner reality with the outer reality of our time and place. The call to bridge that gap comes with the package of life itself.

This was what I was doing in Iran, I realized then. This was what Rumi was pointing to in "Unfold Your Own Myth," the poem I had read in my hotel room back in Tehran. I hadn't thought of it that way before, but it dawned on me that I was on a pilgrimage of sorts. A pilgrimage serves to stitch time and eternity back into one piece again, one step at a time. And so it was that, there in Persepolis, I could feel the thread of my life weaving in and out, in and out—for even now, in the afternoon of my life, I am still making my coat as I go.

CHAPTER 5

# *return to the source*

For make no mistake: Evil does exist in the world. A
nonviolent movement could not have halted Hitler's
armies. Negotiations cannot convince al-Qaeda's leaders
to lay down their arms. To say that force may sometimes
be necessary is not a call to cynicism—it is a recognition of
history; the imperfections of man and the limits of reason.

— PRESIDENT OBAMA, IN HIS ACCEPTANCE SPEECH

FOR THE NOBEL PEACE PRIZE

The white Paykan in which I had bounced along through the
desert for five hours lumbered finally to a halt outside a small
wooden door in a long, low wall. Outside the door was a square
of rough ground that resembled a cross between a building site
and a dumping ground. I felt dazed from the journey, and not in
the best of sorts.

I staggered with my bags through the doorway and then down
a dark corridor to find myself in an open courtyard with a pool in
the middle and daybeds scattered around. Narrow double doors
flashed with stained glass—red and yellow mostly—signaling
the entrances to the dozen or so bedrooms in this, a traditional
hotel in the city of Yazd.

We were in the Jewish quarter, next to the Jameh (Friday)

Mosque. I never knew Jewish quarters existed in Iran. A young man in tight jeans with slicked-back hair introduced himself as Ali, the hotel manager, and offered me tea in a small glass. There were still a hundred or so Jews living in Yazd, he told me, with one rabbi and a functioning synagogue. There were many more before, but most had retired to Israel. Some had moved to other cities because of the difficulty of finding kosher meat in Yazd. Some 25,000 Jews live in Iran still, more than in any other Muslim state in the Middle East. Even so, life in the Islamic Republic can hardly be an advertisement for the good life; their population is a quarter of what it was in 1979.

My dazed head clearing now with the tea, I left my bags with Ali and set off to explore the old Jewish quarter around the hotel. It was built entirely of adobe, and the soft contours of the buildings and its narrow lanes gave the area an intimate feeling of a village within a town. A donkey rounded the corner as I did, pulling an empty flatbed cart with a boy perched in the front. Nothing else stirred. I was the only person in the lane. Soaring above me in every direction were tall chimneys designed to catch the wind and direct it down into the rooms below. Known as a *badgir,* such a chimney was an ingenious and ancient form of air conditioning, with flaps down its sides to redirect the wind. Yazd is a desert city, and its people need all the air they can get in the stifling summer season.

A cascade of blue bowls in a window caught my eye. I stepped into the tiny shop to find an elderly man scrutinizing the workings of an old watch with a jeweler's loupe. *"Salaam aleikhum,"* he said, with barely a glance in my direction. I returned his greeting, glanced at a collection of old pistols he had under the glass counter, and then turned to look at more blue bowls that were stacked on some shelves.

"Qajar time," the man said, still peering into his watch. "Date is on bottom of bowl. All hand painted."

I picked one from the shelf. It was as delicate as porcelain, with the figure of a bird surrounded by branches in the bottom and trees in niches around the sides. What is it about a simple blue bowl that can arrest the mind and fill it with wonder? The hesitant shape, almost but not quite round, as if the potter had included a slight but intentional fault line? The vibrant strength of the blue, synonymous in my mind with Persia itself? Whatever it was, I wanted that bowl. The man pointed to some Arab numerals on the base.

"Eighty-five years old," he said.

He wanted next to nothing for it, and there was no need to go through the usual bargaining ritual. I asked him if he was Jewish, and he replied that he was Iranian first, and Jewish second.

"We are part of this land," he said. "We have been part of it since our ancestors came here from Babylon. So we are Iranians and also Jewish."

For all I knew, this was a stock sentence to be rolled out to every inquiring tourist who might wonder about the condition of the Jews in Iran. But I pressed him no further. Only a few Iranian Jews spoke Hebrew, he said in stilted English, although their community had become far more religious in the last thirty years.

The Jews in Iran had always been merchants and scholars, and more secular than devout, but perhaps the political Muslim environment they were surrounded by now had prompted this turn toward their own faith. More likely, however, it was the need for a tangible and solid cultural identity in the face of diminishing numbers. It was true that the Islamic government did not look kindly on any minority faith or culture within its borders. I thanked him and wandered back out into the empty lanes, getting lost for a while before finding my way back to the hotel.

If I hadn't expected to meet any Jews in Yazd, I did think I might encounter some Zoroastrians. Ali told me his bookkeeper was a Zoroastrian, but he wouldn't be in until the next day. Ali himself was more typical of a younger generation less interested in religion of any sort and more preoccupied with what most young people everywhere are busy with—the opposite sex, and personal ambitions. I spent the afternoon lounging on a daybed under a warm winter sun until, in the early evening, with the sky still light, I walked out of the Jewish quarter onto a wide boulevard that took me into the downtown area of the bazaar.

Yazd, one of the oldest cities on earth, has been in existence for at least five thousand years. It was for centuries a major layover on the Silk Road. "The noble city of Yazd," Marco Polo called it. Its position in the middle of a forbidding desert a long way from anywhere has allowed it to keep much of its traditional culture and architectural heritage safe from marauding armies. In the twelfth century it was a haven for artists, scientists, and intellectuals fleeing from all over Persia before the invasion of Genghis Khan. As a young man, Rumi must have passed this way with his family, as they fled along the Silk Road toward the haven of Turkey.

This evening the boulevard was filled with the sound of Iranian pop music tumbling out of a tiny Internet café. Pop music, yet with the same notes of longing in minor key as any music played here in the last thousand years. The lover calling to his beloved down through the centuries. I went in to ask who the artist was, and the man at the counter responded by saying he would make a copy for me. Moments later I had a CD in my hand, and left in sheepish gratitude after he had waved away all offers of payment.

Down an obscure tunnel of an alley somewhere in the main bazaar, I came across an open door that, after a couple of turns, led me to a central courtyard. I found myself standing in one of the finer examples of domestic architecture I have ever seen. Though not adobe like the buildings in the Jewish quarter, it, too, was a nineteenth-century Jewish merchant's house, carefully converted to its present use as a hotel in a way that allowed for original imperfections and the occasional hole in the stained-glass windows. The usual pool occupied the center of the courtyard, and wooden daybeds were arranged around the walls. The light of the day's end was violet, and the small pieces of stained glass that ran around the high windows glowed softly in the last embers of light.

I had never seen windows like this before. But then I had never stood looking at windows before, unless they were in a Gothic cathedral. A wooden lattice, in a crosshatch pattern with tiny pieces of stained glass, soared two stories high and occupied all the wall space between columns interspersed every twenty feet around the courtyard. The oak frames had a rough and bulky charm, and the whole made for the spectacular impression of a work of sculpture.

Through a door by one of the windows was a formal dining room with an ornate ceiling painted in gold. In the elegant fireplace, the fire damper was shaped in the delicate figure of a peacock. From the inside, the glass in the windows shone rainbows all over the walls and blazed with a radiance that was barely noticeable outside. For a hundred years or more, successive families would have dined night after night in this gracious room. I imagined them here around a long oak table, candles flickering all down its length, the sound of water or wine being poured, the smell of saffron and grilled meat filling the room, the windows flashing their colors over animated faces, the conversation humming along, all beneath the protecting arch of a golden ceiling.

Whoever this Jewish merchant had been, and whatever his trade was, he had acquired an aesthetic sensibility you might normally associate with nobility. But then beauty such as this was never solely the work of one man's imagination. The merchant, as Upham Pope made clear, was living in a culture that made beauty a *sovereign value*. It was a religious as well as an aesthetic sentiment: a form of praise. Far from being a mere display of wealth or culture, a house like this seems designed to induce a state of mind, to conjure a feeling that takes one below appearances to the primal experience of Beauty. Both Judaism and Islam extol Beauty's virtues and value. In Islam, Beauty is one of the names for God. This merchant's house had the name of God written all over it.

Out in the courtyard a woman was sitting alone on one of the daybeds. Although she was draped in a full black hijab that fell over her shoulders as well as her head, I could see that she was European. She introduced herself as Barbara, a lawyer from Zurich, and invited me to eat with her there in the courtyard. Over a plate of shared kebabs, she told me she took full advantage of the long European summer vacation and went away every summer for several weeks, usually on her own.

The previous year she had gone to Uzbekistan and Turkmenistan. She had been astonished to see how widespread Sufism still was, especially in Turkmenistan. She had even been shown the tomb of a Sufi wrestling saint. Wrestling, an ancient art in Iran and all over Central Asia, has for centuries been a spiritual as well as a physical practice in this region, rather like some of the Chinese martial arts.

"I have heard there is a wrestling club here in Yazd," Barbara said. "A *zurkaneh*, they call it in Iran."

Yes, the zurkanehs; I had heard of them, and thought I might come across one somewhere. I remembered seeing a group of wrestlers working out by the Ganges in Benares, India. All these old martial arts with a presence from India across to Iran must have originally come from the same source. Long ago the Persians and the Indian Aryans were one people who later split into two camps. One group settled along the banks of the Oxus River; the other, along the Indus. That's why Old Persian and Sanskrit are so close, and why Zoroastrianism and Vedic Hinduism, both of which emerged around three and a half thousand years ago, share many of the same terms.

It was the Zoroastrians who were still uppermost in my mind; so when Barbara invited me to join her in a taxi she had booked to go to the Towers of Silence the next day, I ditched my usual habit of traveling alone and took up her offer.

It was she who told me that Zoroastrianism was far from merely a quaint relic of the past. If you believe in any of the following, she said, then Zarathustra lives on in you: good and evil, angels, the devil, heaven and hell, the coming of a Messiah, the Day of Judgment at the end of the world, and resurrection. It was a humbling thought, that some of our deepest cultural beliefs led back down through the millennia to a single man—a true revolutionary, the very first prophet living somewhere out on the Iranian plateau, who was inspired to write down in songs the wisdom of a voice he called God.

Though none of them say so, all three religions of the Book—Judaism, Christianity, and Islam—inherited their foundational beliefs from this, the first prophet of them all, the one who none of them recognizes directly: Zarathustra. He received the teachings known as Zoroastrianism as a direct transmission from Zend Avesta, the One God, some 1,200 to 1,500 years before Christ. The teachings of Zarathustra were passed to the Jews via the exiled Judeans in Babylon at the time of Cyrus the Great. Through them they were passed down to the Christians and Muslims, becoming in the process as foundational to Western civilization as Hellenism or Judaism.

Long before Moses or Christ or Mohammed, Zarathustra was the first person in the world to proclaim that there was only one God, Ahura Mazda, and that God had spoken to him directly. He addressed the problem of evil by claiming it to be the work of a force completely outside of God, known as "the Lie," or *Ahriman*. During the history of the world, these forces of light and dark are locked in a struggle that will end in the destruction of evil and the ultimate triumph of good. The same struggle plays out in the heart of every human being. Every individual, he said, has the freedom to choose between good and evil. This is a core belief of Western civilization today. Zarathustra's way was rational, pragmatic, and anti-ritual: choose truth over lies; strive for good works, good thoughts, and good deeds.

Two low but steep hills stood out against the desert plain a few minutes beyond the city. Each had a trail spiraling to a flat, tabletop summit encircled by a low wall. Between the hills lies the ruin of an old caravanserai in a cruciform shape. Two brick domes finished in a pattern of herringbone still bend the air, while the remains of two other domes lie in a heap of rubble on the ground. We sat for a few moments among the broken bricks and listened to the curl of the wind before heading for the nearest mountain.

They are known as Towers of Silence. When you climb one, you see why. This is a lonely, isolated place, with nothing for miles around but the barren brown earth and a range of hills in the far distance. It would have been even more isolated a century ago, when these towers were last used for their traditional purpose. Since then the city of Yazd has crept ever closer toward them.

The Zoroastrians believe that a dead body is unclean, and that the corpse demon rushes into it and contaminates everything that happens to come in contact with it. So they would place their dead on the tabletop surface of the mountain and leave it there for vultures to pick the bones dry. Then the bones would be collected and placed in a burial pit. The practice was outlawed in Iran in the 1970s, and today the Zoroastrians either bury or cremate their dead; though in Mumbai, in India, the ancient ritual still continues.

The stones are black and sharp on the way up the Mountain of Silence. The path fades at times to become almost indistinguishable from the surrounding scree. It is cool still at this time in the morning, though in summer, with temperatures over 100 degrees Fahrenheit, it would be stiff exercise to reach the top. The last few meters are spent scrambling over large boulders; then a gap appears in a parapet wall and you find yourself on a circular dusty plateau, with nothing to see but a big sky and the endless plain. All trace of what used to take place here has disappeared; no circling birds of prey, nothing to show the passage of generations of Persians from this world to the next. Yet it provokes an unusual sensation even so, to stand on the place where countless bodies of the faithful were torn to shreds and recycled into the food chain. I felt my own impermanence for a fleeting few moments, my own body and mind heading the way of all things, there in that lofty departure lounge.

On the other side of the plateau the city sprawled below. The Jameh Mosque hurled its spindly minarets far into the air, a few others emulated it on a lesser scale; but all in all, old Yazd seemed fragile and also temporary, hovering there in the morning shimmer against the great backdrop of silence and space.

It struck me again up there on the hill how current the ideas of Zarathustra still are today, when we are as taken as ever with notions of the end of the world and the ongoing struggle between good and evil. If you are not a religious conservative and scoff at the notion of a returning Messiah, chances are you will still think we are on our way to catastrophe through climate change or general environmental devastation. And despite Nietzsche's attempt in his great classic *Thus Spake Zarathustra* to overthrow Zarathustra's stand for a moral choice and to declare that there was no such thing as good and evil, history since then has seemed to suggest otherwise.

The twentieth century gave us plenty of cause to think that evil was not just a result of excessive egoism and pride, that, as the old prophet said, it was a force beyond the human will that could enslave human beings for its own purposes. President Obama could have been quoting Zarathustra when, in his acceptance speech for the Nobel Peace Prize, he said that the doctrine of nonviolence would never be enough to counteract the force of evil.

Before Zarathustra, only priests and aristocrats were thought to have eternal souls. The prophet threw out that idea along with all the other lesser gods. Everyone had a soul, he said, and anyone could develop a personal relationship with God. This was radical stuff in a time when every culture propitiated hundreds of gods and was presided over by an elite priesthood with exceptional privileges.

To believe, with Walt Whitman, that *every man shall be his own priest,* is radical even today. It's West Coast self-empowerment taken to the ultimate level; and of course it brings with it the dangers of grandiosity and self-delusion. The priests hounded Zarathustra out of the community and he had to flee for his life. He ended up in what is now Afghanistan, where he found service in the court of the local king and rose to prominence. It was there that he composed his *gathas,* or songs, just a few of which survive today.

We sat on the crown of the hill in silence for a while, a desert wind whipping lightly over our shoulders. Rumi would have seen this same barren landscape in his own time, and probably this very hill we had just climbed. Little had changed in the intervening centuries. Because Yazd was a major city on the Silk Road in Rumi's time, his family must have lodged somewhere nearby on their flight west, perhaps with the local Zoroastrians. Yet he and his father would have had very different beliefs from those of their hosts. They would have subscribed to the Muslim teaching that evil was a creation of God, which He permitted to exist in this world so that man could know the good by contrast. While evil was intrinsic to the world itself, it could be purified in the individual by spiritual practice.

Which is not to say that Rumi was an ascetic or a monastic. No, he was an ecstatic who was borne away on the wings of love. His practices were not really practices, but spontaneous outbursts of praise accompanied by dance and music. Rumi never wrote down a word of his poems. He would spin around a pillar in the mosque, absorbed in the depths of his loving, and words would fly out of his mouth like honeybees. A scribe would catch them on the wing with his quill. Out of his spinning the Whirling Dervishes arose, those Sufis whose principal form of devotion still today is to whirl on their axis deep in prayer.

If any purifying were to take place in me, it would likely have to happen through the school of life or the good offices of grace—or both. Looking out over the great plain below us, I recalled a few lines of Rumi that I knew by heart:

> Be helpless, dumbfounded,
> Unable to say yes or no.
> Then a stretcher will come from grace
> to gather us up.
>
> We are too dull-eyed to see that beauty.
> If we say we can, we're lying.
> If we say No, we don't see it,
> That No will behead us
> And shut tight our window onto spirit.
>
> So let us rather not be sure of anything,
> Beside ourselves, and only that, so
> Miraculous beings come running to help.

I always loved how this poem cuts to the quick, how it urges us to drop all pretense at being the master of our own lives. I was glad for Rumi's imperative, pressing us to stand where we are with our jaw dropped open, dumbfounded before the immensity, the impossibility of it all. I could feel the rigorous truth of it, looking out over the plain from the crest of that Tower of Silence.

I turned to ask Barbara if she knew of Rumi. She looked at me in surprise. Of course, she said. She carried a small volume with her everywhere on her journey through Iran. She pulled a tattered German paperback out of her backpack. I asked her to read me something and to translate what she could.

> *You must be set on fire by the inner sun.*
> *You have to live your Love or else*
> *You'll only end in words.*

If there is a universal religion, this must be it, I thought, Barbara's voice drifting away on the wind. That is why, on Rumi's death, not only Muslims but Christians, Jews, and even Buddhists and Hindus flocked to pay their respects at his funeral in the city of Konya, in Turkey. Rumi's religion is the heart of hearts, and no one is turned away.

> *Come, come, whoever you are.*
> *Wonderer, worshipper, lover of leaving.*
> *It doesn't matter.*
> *Ours is not a caravan of despair.*
> *Come, even if you have broken your vow*
> *a thousand times*
> *Come, yet again, come, come.*

We climbed back down the way we had come, leaving the mountain to the ghosts of the past, and asked our driver to take us to the Atashkadeh, the Zoroastrian Fire Temple, which was back in the town. The driver stopped at an unassuming gate in a wall, and pointed the way in. We walked through a small garden and came to a circular pool in front of a modest brick building the color of honey. A wide flight of steps led up to a portico supported by four columns, above which hovered the large figure of a winged man with a long beard and a fantail, all blue and gold—the Zoroastrian symbol for Ahura Mazda, the one God. Around his waist was a large circle of gold.

Inside, framed paintings of Zoroaster hung on the walls, along with the three principles of his religion: think good thoughts, use good speech, do good deeds. Principles like that know no boundaries.

In a chamber set apart was the sacred fire, brought to Yazd in 1474. The fire is said to have been burning continuously since A.D. 470, having been carried from place to place throughout Iran before ending up here. It put me in mind of the old joke about grandfather's ax, the handle and blade of which had been changed so many times, it was a stretch to think of it as grandfather's anymore. The fire itself was a symbol of the divine, life-giving light; the force of God that eternally opposes the darkness of Ahriman.

Two or three Zartusht (the name Zoroastrians give to themselves) women stood by the fire in colorful headscarves and clothes, while the men beside them were wearing white skullcaps. They all seemed to be murmuring a prayer, their palms outstretched to the sky. At one point the men pulled out a thread from around their waists—a humility belt—and chanted yet another prayer, probably one of Zoroaster's hymns, in a long, low, plaintive chant.

When they had finished I asked one of them, a banker from Isfahan in an open white shirt, who thankfully spoke some English, how many Zartusht were left in Iran. He seemed uncertain, but he thought about thirty thousand.

"There were many more before the Revolution," he added, reminding me that the same was true for the Jewish population. "It's difficult for us here. We can perform our religious ceremonies, but like other minorities in Iran we are viewed as second-class citizens, especially when it comes to employment. Most young people now try to emigrate to America. As Zoroastrians they can easily get a visa."

The Zartusht spoke their own language, he said, distinct from Farsi; and they had their own schools where their children learned their traditions and rituals. He went on to tell me about angels: that they believed angels to be the army of light in the service of Ahura Mazda; that every species on earth had its guardian angel. It appeared that one of the more common beliefs in Marin County, where I lived, had its origins right here. This was where angels came from. To this day, the man continued, the Persian months still bore the names of Zoroastrian angels.

"Were you here for Nowruz," he asked, "our New Year festival at the start of spring?"

I wasn't, which was a pity—it was the greatest occasion for joy, dancing, and laughter in a Persian calendar dominated by Shia festivals of mourning and martyrdom. The festival, originally in honor of Ahura Mazda, begins on the last Wednesday of the old year with people jumping over public bonfires.

On New Year's Day and the following twelve days, everything shuts down and people celebrate with feasting, dancing, and the reciting of poetry. Incredible to think that after nearly fifteen hundred years of Islam, everyday life in Iran today was still infused with the influence of Persia's ancient religion.

Later that afternoon, Barbara and I discovered that the zurkaneh was yet another pre-Islamic tradition with a lot of life left in it still. When we went in search of the one in Yazd, people were only too keen to point down this alley and that, except for one man who walked quickly away when we started to ask him for directions. With people generally so eager to help, the place wasn't difficult to find, even among the tangle of lanes around the bazaar.

We bent our heads to pass through a low, narrow door that took us down a flight of steps into a basement. All zurkanehs—it means "house of power"—are belowground because they were originally centers of resistance to the successive invasions the country has suffered ever since the Mongols in the twelfth century. We emerged from the dark, narrow passage into a room with a domed roof, below which was an octagonal pit with a wooden floor. On a ledge around the pit were rows of clubs of various sizes, and surrounding the pit were a few rows of chairs. All around the walls were framed photographs of past champions of the zurkaneh. We sat down opposite a sort of booth in which a man was fiddling with a microphone and a large drum. Hanging in front of him were two or three bells. Several men were doing stretching exercises in an open space to one side.

We sat there for a few minutes feeling faintly conspicuous, though nobody paid us any attention. The man in the booth arranged himself in front of the microphone and began to beat his drum and to sing, or rather chant, in a rhythmic baritone voice. We were told later that he was singing stories of heroes past from Ferdowsi's great classic, the *Shahnameh,* singing with a pride and vigor worthy of the venerable book itself.

The men, all wearing culottes, strode into the pit one after the other, bending to touch the ground as they entered in recognition of where they had come from and where they would return to. They reminded me somehow of the Morris men—traditional folk dancers with swords and ribbons who still today dance around the maypole on village greens all over England, except these Persian warriors would not think of having bells around their ankles, which the Morris men continue to wear as they have for centuries.

The men in the zurkaneh were mostly in their fifties, though there were two in their teens and one who looked as if he could be in his seventies. They spread themselves around the perimeter of the pit as one man leaped into the middle and began to spin fast on his axis, his arms stretched out horizontally. After a few minutes he was replaced by someone else, and then another, and as each man took up the central position, the singing drummer would strike his bell and change the rhythm.

Then someone took a pair of clubs from the ledge and began to twirl them around and above him. Others began to do the same, and soon the pit was a mass of swirling clubs. Sometimes someone would throw his in the air, spinning around and catching them as they fell. Then a man appeared with a pair of heavy wooden shields and performed what looked like a weightlifting drill with them. Someone else took a thick metal bow with a row of heavy metal discs for its string and threw it around from hand to hand as if it were a feather.

We were watching a dedicated team workout, whatever other layers of meaning it may have had. Finally the clubs were put away, the shields and the bows put aside, and two men faced off in the center. The bell rang, the rhythm changed again, and they lunged forward to grapple with each other. But this was not wrestling as we might know it from American TV. These men were engaged in a time-honored ritual, as much a display of chivalry as a show of strength. The noble virtues—generosity, forgiveness, forbearance—are intrinsic to how participants comport themselves in the zurkaneh, which is why it is a moral as well as a physical discipline. The two men ended by kissing each other on the cheek, and then bowed before they gave the center over to another pair.

The practices had evolved from hand-to-hand combat perhaps two thousand years ago. The clubs were ritualized maces, the wooden shields were an imitation of the metal ones soldiers used to protect themselves in trenches as well as in sword fights; and the bows were the shape of those to be seen on the walls of Persepolis. On our way out I picked up one of the clubs that the men had been throwing about like juggling sticks. I could barely raise it above my waist.

Barbara and I had been witness to a stirring performance. No, it was more than stirring, I thought later that evening, lying on my bed with the light of evening filtering over the walls of my little room. It was a privilege. It was a privilege to have been able to witness local men—a blacksmith perhaps, a fruit seller, a cabdriver—give a time-honored display of chivalric skills and qualities, long forgotten in the West, as we, two aliens from Europe, whose own culture was more used to happy hour at that time of day than anything else, sat with our jaws open somewhere down in the bowels of the earth under the city of Yazd.

As I drifted into sleep, the name of another city floated through my mind. I saw the image of the blue dome again, the one I had brought with me down through the years. The following day I would be going to Isfahan, the city of all cities in Iran, the realization in this world of the dream of a king.

CHAPTER *6*

# the blue dome

Mankind will be saved by beauty.

— DOSTOEVSKY

The journey to Isfahan did not begin well. Waiting for me the next morning outside my hotel in Yazd was Mohsen, who, when he saw me, unfolded himself from his taxi in one languorous movement and shook my hand limply with a simpering smile. I had hardly closed the door when he backed out of the yard in a cloud of dust and headed off into town. For a couple of minutes I said nothing, but then I could restrain myself no longer.

"Why are we going back into town?" I asked. "I thought the road to Isfahan was the other way."

He nodded vigorously, and made a gesture with his hands that had no meaning for me. He spoke almost no English, though he had clearly anticipated my question.

My temperature continued rising as we drove deeper into the city, until finally he turned down a side street and stopped at a battered wooden door. Turning around to me in the backseat, he gestured as if to say everything was going according to plan. But whose plan?

He disappeared through the door and returned in a couple of minutes accompanied by a woman with several bags and a toddler.

"My wife," he said, pointing to the woman. "My boy." He smiled proudly.

I gesticulated uncomprehendingly, my mouth open but no words spilling out.

"Tomorrow Friday, holiday," he explained. "She not know Isfahan."

The woman, meanwhile, was stuffing herself and the child in the front seat, along with a bag.

"They are coming with us?" I was torn between righteous indignation and feeling a spoilsport for even thinking of objecting to the family outing they were taking at my expense. "How can she sit in the front with a child and no seatbelt? Let them sit in the back and I will sit up front."

His child screamed and cried and wriggled for the whole six hours that it took to cross the desert monotony. I thought I had paid for a taxi to avoid the crowded buses. When he wasn't trying to distract his child, Mohsen fiddled with his cell phone and kept turning to banter with his wife in the backseat. Buses would sweep by us a centimeter away and blow us close to the ditch at the side of the road. Mohsen would drive to within a centimeter of the car in front of us, and then, with his hand on the horn, sweep past with an imperious swing of the wheel, like the King of the Road. Even on the open highway, driving here is a sport whose principal skills are intimidation and brinkmanship.

I spent no small part of the journey reflecting on my need for private space—on whether it was a neurosis or simply my cultural conditioning (they may be the same thing) and how foreign such a concept as privacy was to the average Iranian, and to Mohsen in particular. It was evident he had no idea that his family holiday might pose a conflict of interests. When we finally reached the outskirts of Isfahan, we took a tour of the ring road for nearly an hour, despite my pleading with Mohsen to follow the city-center signs that even I could read. It wasn't only his wife who had never been to Isfahan.

When I finally staggered into my hotel, I thought my troubles were over. But as I stepped through the narrow entrance into the central courtyard, I failed to notice that the ceiling suddenly lowered. I hit my head and nearly knocked myself out. Over the course of the next week I would hit my head several times, reminded each time a little too late that you were advised by the lowered ceiling to bow before the company already present in the courtyard.

My hotel in Isfahan, as in Yazd, was the restored traditional house of a merchant, with the rooms all opening onto the central courtyard, in the middle of which was the statutory pool with a fountain. Conversions like this are beginning to catch on, as Iranians respond to the fact that the kind of travelers coming to Iran are people who tend to avoid the usual tourist destinations and their cookie-cutter facilities. You don't go to Iran for more of the same. All the Western chain hotels were nationalized at the time of the Revolution, and in this respect as in many others, Iran was, for good and also for ill, almost entirely free of global corporate influence.

When I had recovered from my lack of humility, and my bump on the head had been dressed by the receptionist, I sat on one of the beds and took in the scene. As in Yazd, each guest room had an old double wooden door lit with a panel of stained glass. Whenever a door opened, shards of red and blue would flash briefly across the yard. Large, sensuous pots, narrow at the base and top and wide at the belly, stood at each corner of the courtyard. Small trees lined the sides of the pool. The low roof was reached by a broad stairway that had its own plants on each step.

Again, a house designed to induce a state of mind. Of course you should bow your head on entering such a scene. I was beginning to have a whole new respect for the notion of intelligent design.

The hotel was in the bazaar—appropriately enough, since it had been a merchant's house. So when I emerged from the long corridor that served as its entrance (a common feature, serving as an intermediate state between the inner and outer, private and public, worlds) I found myself smack in the middle of all the daily business and trade—another reason for the calm oasis that you find deep within those private walls.

Like all the best bazaars, the one in Isfahan was large, covered, and labyrinthine, with each lane given to a specific trade or type of goods. I wandered down the metalworkers' lane, where men hammered pots into shape and chiseled designs into brass and silver; down the artists' lane, where men sat on stools and painted scenes on trays and dishes in meticulous detail; and down the carpet lane, which kept me busy for an hour or more.

I eventually emerged into the daylight and onto the great central square. Unlike Shiraz, Isfahan has a square. I was so glad—no, relieved—to see a square. For a European, the square is central to civilized life, both in the village and in the town. I have so missed the square in my American years. A square is a public stage: it blends theater with commerce, intrigue with leisure, flirtation with serious proposals, seeing with being seen, dressing up with dressing down. In Iran, by contrast, much of all this happens in private rather than in public space. Families gather with their friends in the courtyards of their houses, like the one in my hotel. Aside from the public garden, the other most popular public venue is the bazaar, which could be a perfect metaphor for the Iranian psyche—all secret corners and serpentine alleys.

But here indeed was a square, and like no other I had ever seen. It was early evening, and hundreds of families were sitting on carpets, camp stoves flaring and food of all kinds being pre-

pared. Children ran and skipped and played with balloons. A
few Rollerbladers coasted by. It was Thursday evening, which
for Muslims was the start of the Friday holiday. With a general
lack of public entertainment—film, theater, music are all hard
to come by, and of course there are no bars or clubs—the single
most popular pastime in Iran is the picnic, and the whole extended family takes part. There is no grassy meadow to picnic in,
so the natural place is the public garden or square.

It seemed to me that the entire population of Isfahan was
sitting in that square. As I ventured somewhat tentatively out
among the families, I was beckoned from all sides to come and
share in their meal. With a cursory glance at the overall scene—
the mosques I had heard so much of at the far end and to the side,
including the one with the blue dome that I had seen so long ago
in the British Museum—the summer palace, the fountains playing, the horse-drawn carriages clip-clopping along, I sat down
with one of the first families I passed. I did not want to rush
straight to the mosque whose image had captivated me so long
ago. I preferred to inhale it all in small gasps.

The young woman of the family was the only one who spoke
English, and then only a few sentences. She was a teacher, she
told me, and these were her father, her aunt, her cousin, her
uncle, and her two sisters. Their mother was coming soon with
more food. Where did I come from? America—broad smiles all
around. Did I like Iran? Yes, very much. More broad smiles. Can
we take your picture? Of course. Giggles. All so innocent, well-
meaning, so immediately at ease with a stranger.

I accepted some tea and a slice of melon and cucumber, and
lingered for a while. "How old are you?" the girl asked. "I can
see you are young at heart." I agreed, and slipped over her question. "You are alone? You have no wife?" They looked at me for
a moment, uncomprehendingly. "This is my older sister," the girl
said out of nowhere, pointing to a tall girl with glasses. "I love
her, I love her!" I tried imagining a Western girl introducing her

sister that way, half wondering if she was offering her sister as a solution to my single state. (Marriage with a foreigner is one of the few avenues offering an Iranian woman more possibilities in life, and most foreign men have at least one proposal from a stranger during their time there.)

I finally made as gracious an exit as I could, and began to take in the sheer scale of the place I was in. The whole remarkable complex at the heart of Isfahan was designed on the orders of Shah Abbas in the seventeenth century. The shah had made Isfahan the capital of his Safavid dynasty, and was intent on making it the jewel of the entire Muslim world. He succeeded beyond all measure. What is now called Imam Square is the second largest square in the world after Tiananmen Square. You could fit four Red Squares in this Isfahan square, which is in fact a long rectangle. Its original, and more appropriate-sounding name, was Naqsh-e-Jahan, meaning "Pattern of the World."

Shah Abbas came to power at the age of seventeen. It was he who finally established a homogeneous state of Persia with— under pain of death—the one Shia faith and the one language of Farsi. He also instituted a single currency. Like his contemporary in England, Queen Elizabeth I, he had inherited a fractured nation with multiple foreign enemies, and his immediate priority was to establish a new sense of national identity.

In 1598, when he was just twenty-seven years old, Shah Abbas moved his capital to Isfahan, and began one of the greatest and grandest endeavors in city planning the world had seen since the construction of Baghdad in the eighth century.

The shah built his new city center on the southern edge of the old Seljuk town. He designed its main artery as a grand avenue of gardens. The Chahar Bagh, meaning "the Fourfold Garden," was to reflect the heavenly paradise. In the seventeenth century it was a mile long with a central canal made of onyx interspersed with pools, fountains, and cascades and lined with rows of cypress, juniper, and plane trees. Rose hedges and jasmine scented the thoroughfare from end to end.

Alongside it were the mansions of the court officials, royal ministers, diplomats, and the shah's favorites. Even the court jester and astrologer had their own miniature kingdoms there, complete with personal wine cellars and harems. To the east of the Chahar Bagh lay the vast imperial complex with the royal palaces, the harem, and all the workshops serving the shah's household. And there, too, lay the great square, Naqsh-e-Jahan, where I was standing now with my mouth open.

At its south end is the Royal Mosque, known now as the Imam Mosque, with its dome to one side and at an angle to the entrance. My feet were leading me there, as to a magnet. Winding my way through the picnicking families, I took in the many-arched arcades, echoed by a second tier of smaller arches above, that lace their way around every side of this "half the world," as awed foreign travelers called it. In the days of Shah Abbas, the lower arcades were for the trading of handicrafts, as they are still today. The upper floor served to lodge the travelers who came not just from the region but from as far afield as India, Istanbul, and Europe. There was a Dutch and an English presence, too, because the East India Company, with an eye for new markets, had established a warehouse in Isfahan.

The shah knew what he was doing. He not only built caravan-serai and bridges across the river to develop trade, not only developed a capital of political power, but also expected his city to awe and amaze people from around the world with its beauty, its royal pomp and extravagant display. Isfahan was the showcase for his vision of the new Persia and its emerging influence. And the great square was to be both the epicenter of its religious, political, and economic power and also a supreme work of art and beauty designed to impress the growing stream of visiting dignitaries. It was a deliberate and carefully conceived strategy to colonize the mind of any foreigner who set foot there—an "empire of mind," as the historian Michael Axworthy has described it.

The Royal Mosque looms over the south end of Naqsh-e-Jahan, its entrance portal in the middle of the flow of arches. As I stand before it finally, my mind is already conquered. Blue dominates everywhere. The richness of this blue before me now is what springs to most people's minds when they think of old Persia. Brilliant, radiant turquoise blue, alternating with the deep dark glow of lapis lazuli. Swirling and twirling tendrils and foliage, fired into the tile, wind their way among black-and-white geometric designs, while Arabic calligraphy streams along and separates one panel of tiles from the next. I look up to see a ceiling of improbably intricate stalactite moldings in a honeycomb pattern, each hexagonal panel with its own exquisite design, the whole defying my mind to absorb it all in one gaze. Surely a swarm of bees had suspended a vast, multifaceted, delicate hive from the roof, and someone had come along afterward and spent months painting the most subtle and beautiful patterns over the whole of its surface.

I step through the door into a passageway that directs me to the right and around a slight turn. There before me is the great inner courtyard, with its ablution pool in the middle and a recessed sanctuary at either end. The blue and yellow flower patterns weave around me on every side. Not a square inch is left unattended to. Wherever I look, shifting colors and patterns hold my eyes. It's like sitting inside a child's kaleidoscope. The whole effect is to stun the mind; to take me out of myself into some deeper, quieter place.

I walk slowly over to the main sanctuary, the south one, with the dome that can be seen from the city square. I go to the far corner, sit down, and look up at the vast and perfectly proportioned upturned bowl floating weightlessly, it seems, in space. A great sunburst of yellow, made of a myriad of tiny flowers, fills the highest point, and streams of interweaving tendrils cascade from this central sun down to the base. The whole creation, an overflowing flower basket, seems to move and dance and proceed from the center like some great symphony.

When my gaze lowers at last, I notice the two turquoise minarets that soar over the entrance portal across the courtyard. Each one is capped by an elegant little dome, with a projecting balcony for the muezzin to give the call to prayer. In brilliant white calligraphy, the names of Mohammed and Ali wind around the slender, delicate needles.

Isfahan is the Florence of the Orient, without the tourists. I sat under the great dome for half an hour, and during that time just a trickle of visitors came by, all of them Iranian except for a French couple. Mostly young, they would stand for a moment under the center of the dome and clap their hands or whistle to hear the legendary echoes—twelve are audible to the human ear—just one more testimony to the mastery of the architect and builders. One young man with a neatly trimmed beard stood at the black spot marking the center and sang the call to prayer in perfect pitch. He set the whole building ringing, a resonating chamber, and my body shivered with a rare form of pleasure.

The Royal Mosque was begun in 1612 and took nearly twenty years to complete, including several years during which all construction stopped because of the mysterious disappearance of the architect. When he eventually returned, he explained that the delay had been necessary to allow the foundations to settle. Presumably he had not dared to tell the shah beforehand. The shah ordered an inspection, and when it was confirmed that, indeed, to have placed the great dome on the walls any earlier would have caused a disaster, the architect was duly rewarded for his foresight instead of being hanged, drawn, and quartered for his insolence.

This place is Heaven's Gate if ever there was one—the Crowning Glory, Wonder of Wonders. Sheer, sinuous, spiraling Beauty. And since every shape and every form—the flowers, the leaves, the tendrils, the sunburst—is drawn from the organic living world of Nature, the building is a soaring tribute not only to God but to the beauty of Creation and the genius of the human spirit. Leaving only by necessity, as the door was closing, I was sure I had just seen the most beautiful and perfect structure that could issue from the mind and hand of man.

Out in the gathering dusk I sat down on the entrance steps for a few moments and gazed over the great square before me. I had just fulfilled a dream that had lingered in my mind for forty years. It was as if my life had come full circle. What had begun as a gasp of wonderment in the British Museum had been fulfilled with a greater astonishment, a reverence even, at the sight of the blue dome itself.

And I knew now why the image had meant so much to me. The perfection of the dome, its exquisite proportions, its glowing color, was in some way an image of the possible that lay deep down inside my own person. It was a symbol, you might say, of the truth and beauty inherent in any human journey. The dome itself was an epiphany, a showing forth of our better nature.

While I was sitting there a tall, genial young man strolled over from the bookshop he ran near the mosque. His name was Omid, he told me. We chatted for a while about his earlier life in Yazd, and his love of Isfahan. He pointed me to a tea shop that overlooked the whole square, and when I mentioned my friend Jason Elliot, the Englishman who wrote a fine book on Iran in 2006, he said I should meet Zizou, whom Jason refers to in his book as someone who showed him things about the works of Shah Abbas that he would never have known otherwise. When I mentioned that I needed to call Tehran, Omid immediately offered me his cell phone.

I realized over the course of our conversation that here was a shopkeeper who was not trying to engage me for the obvious reason of making a sale. He had a genuine interest in foreigners and in life as it was lived elsewhere, and in the simple pleasures of casual human exchange. It dawned on me then that, unlike in India, say, or elsewhere in the Middle East, I had not for one moment been hassled or pestered by hangers-on anywhere in Iran. People everywhere in this country were curious about a foreigner, especially one traveling alone. But it was genuine curiosity, and always expressed with friendliness and courtesy. Young women, especially, surprised me with their spontaneous greetings and welcomes. I rarely passed a gaggle of students who didn't stop to ask me where I was from and how I liked Iran. Such openness and simplicity were a far cry from the common stereotype of women who were trained to withhold their natural femininity and always to look at the ground rather than at a man.

Thanking him for the call to Tehran, I left Omid to wander on through the arcades to the carpet shop where he had said Zizou could be found. There on a stack of carpets an intense, wiry young man sat watching his friends playing backgammon. When I told him I was a friend of Jason's, he leaped to his feet with a shout and shook my hand vigorously. "Tell Jason I want him to write a book on my homeland," he beamed. "Lorestan. I am from a tribe of nomads in the Zagros Mountains near Shush [Susa]. That is the real Iran, untouched by modernity, all wild nature and traditional ways. You should come, you would love it. What do you do? You are a writer, too? If Jason won't write the book, then you can. I have made a DVD of the region, I will give it to you, and you can come there with me and see for yourself."

I fielded Zizou's urgencies with as much grace as I could muster, and mentioned that I had never seen anyone playing backgammon in Iran. Was it an import from a neighboring country? "It is forbidden," said one of the young players, whose name was Faisal. "That is why we are playing here, at the back of the shop. Everything is forbidden here. Do you think I could get a visa for Australia? My father is Turkish, so do you think I would have a chance?" "Probably a better chance with a Turkish passport than an Iranian one," I replied, feeling the poignancy of the young man's question.

Zizou led me out into the square and pointed to two posts, both around five feet tall, at the southern end, in front of the Imam Mosque. "Polo goal posts put there by Shah Abbas," he said. "The whole square was used as a polo field in the seventeenth century. Do you notice anything about them?" I didn't. "One is a little shorter than the other," Zizou declared. "Take a closer look." He was right. "It's a deliberate fault, to remind us that God alone is perfect. You will see the same thing everywhere in the mosques. One pillar will be covered with intricate designs, and its twin on the other side of a portal will be plainer. Or a tile in a pattern will stand out as an odd one. If you haven't been to the Lotfollah Mosque yet, the one on the other side of the square, opposite the palace, then I will go with you, if you like, tomorrow."

I agreed, and left him to stroll through the picnickers (they stay out until midnight or later) to the north end of the square, where Omid had told me the tea shop was. It was a strange feeling, everyone in a family or walking in couples, except, it seemed, for me. For all the beauty around me, for all the gentleness of the scene, I realized how alone I was, and, in that moment, lonely. How rich it would be to share this with someone, a special someone. As much as I had appreciated my last couple of years of single living, the romantic dream had continued to linger. Perhaps it always does, if we avoid the pitfalls of cynicism and despair, until the final moment of aloneness, the one we can never share, sets us free. Part mammalian instinct, the wish for closeness of body and breath, part longing of the soul for its outer reflection, the romantic impulse seems lodged in our DNA.

Strolling through the gracious beauty of Naqsh-e-Jahan, the light fading, you can't help puzzling over the extraordinary contradictions of the person who had dreamed it all. Here was a man, Shah Abbas, who in today's terms might have been called a liberal. His priorities were religious tolerance, capitalism, state Shiism, Sufi reverence for saintly teachers, and a genuine concern for the welfare of the masses. Across the Zayandeh River he created the suburbs of his new city, reached by a glorious new bridge at the south end of the Chahar Bagh. Armenian Christians lived there alongside Muslims, while the area also had room for a Zoroastrian cemetery and Hindu places of worship.

The Italian traveler Pietro della Valle was astonished at the shah's knowledge of Christian history and theology, which did not, however, prevent the shah in 1615 from suppressing a rebellion by the Christian Georgians by killing 70,000 of them and deporting over 100,000 to Iran. He later had the Georgian queen Ketevan tortured to death when she refused to renounce Christianity.

His own faith was fervent and devout. In 1601 the shah made the pilgrimage barefoot from Isfahan to Mashhad, a distance of several hundred kilometers. The shah had a special reverence for Imam Reza, whose shrine is in Mashhad. Imam Reza was the only one of Shiism's twelve holy imams (the rightful successors to the Prophet Mohammed) to be buried in the country, for which reason Mashhad is still today the most holy city in Iran.

Yet this was the same devout man who began to suspect his eldest son of plotting to murder him during a hunting trip, when the son broke protocol and killed a boar without deferring to his father's privilege of first kill. Abbas had his son put to death, and almost immediately regretted it. He made the executioner kill his own son, too, so that he would understand the anguished remorse of his king. Abbas later had his two surviving sons blinded and imprisoned, also because of fears of a plot. Ironically, on his death in 1629, Shah Abbas was finally succeeded by his grandson, whose father the shah had killed in 1615. Shah Safi, as he became known, loathed his grandfather for obvious reasons, and murdered the surviving son of Abbas, who was still alive in prison.

I found the tea shop up a winding flight of narrow stairs in the entrance to the bazaar. The stairs lead you up to an open terrace on the second row of arcades lining the square. The entire square lies before you up there, the Royal Mosque at the far end just visible in the twilight, the outline of mountains beyond, the fountains lit with colored lights, the arcades still busy with their business at this late hour. In the tea shop, a few Iranians were smoking hookahs. The rules on cafés and hookahs were evidently more relaxed here than in Shiraz.

When I first noticed Paolo and Gabriela, I thought they were Iranian. They were in their early thirties, and sharing a hookah. Gabriela wore a thigh-length coat over jeans, and a dark blue headscarf over jet-black hair. Paolo, too, had dark hair, and both of them had fine, aquiline features. They turned out to be Italians from Perugia.

It was not the first time I had confused the two. The Iranians and Italians have more than high cheekbones in common. They are the foremost exponents, East and West respectively, of the cult of beauty, art, and an impossible but all-consuming spiritualized love. Think Dante, Petrarch, Rumi. Their politics are Byzantine and Machiavellian. They are temperamental by nature, they have similar driving habits, and they both have world-class cuisines. In Tehran I had heard more than one person refer to Iran as the Italy of the East.

When we started talking, the couple from Perugia told me they had always wanted to visit Isfahan, that it had for a long time been a sort of dream city for them, made even more mysterious by the apparent difficulties of getting there. So I wasn't alone in my private romance, which was both gratifying and at the same time the tiniest bit disappointing. It was as if someone else had dreamed themselves into a world that I thought was mine alone. There were doubtless people all over the world who shared the same dream, without ever having looked at that picture in the British Museum; and I never knew it.

Paolo was a marketing manager for Kimberly-Clark, the paper company, and Gabriela was a school counselor. We joked that Iran would be a huge potential market for his company, because paper tissues were used everywhere there—in cars, on tables, in the bathroom, and in restaurants in place of napkins. Their friends thought they were crazy to come to Iran, but they had traveled the world and never met a more welcoming people. They told me they were photographing the graffiti on the old American embassy in Tehran—Death to America, etc.—and people kept coming up to them and saying, "This is only government propaganda. We love America. We love it."

The next morning I awoke in gladness, I don't know why. I made my way down to the square and over toward the Sheikh Lotfollah Mosque, named after the shah's father-in-law, a revered preacher at the time. While I appreciated Zizou and his scraps of information, I wanted to go there on my own. It was the first of the great buildings in the square to be completed. The portal is again a dazzle of blue with flowing floral designs and arabesques. Hovering over it and slightly to the right is a pale dome of the most perfect proportions, its cream-colored tiles unusual for a mosque, the blue and turquoise only appearing around its crown. I walked up the steps to the door, and immediately realized that this was a mosque like no other.

It has no minaret and no central courtyard. Beyond the door a narrow tunnel, entirely covered in magnificent tilework that glowed in the half-light, led me off at a forty-five-degree angle and then abruptly turned ninety degrees to usher me into the sanctuary below the dome—an intimate enclosure after the great spaces of the Imam Mosque.

It was empty except for a guard half asleep on his chair. Doves were cooing and flitting between the circle of latticed arches, alternately blind and open to the sky, that form the base of the dome. The dome itself rests on the square of the building, the miraculous squaring of the circle, symbol for the union of heaven and earth. Every wall is a bewildering complexity of beauty in blue and yellow and green. The entire floor is laid with turquoise tiles.

I gazed about me. I was caught between wanting to spend the rest of the afternoon there and spending some more time with Zizou, remembering he had said he was leaving town for a few days. Taking a few moments more to let the colors pour through me, I decided to leave the Lotfollah Mosque until I could give it my full attention, and went out into the day and over to Zizou's carpet shop. He was just leaving as I arrived—in search of me, he said. I explained I had come from Sheikh Lotfollah Mosque, and he took my arm and led me out into the square.

"Did you notice that the pattern on the interior of the dome is an open peacock tail? All those lozenges streaming down from the center are the eyes."

It was obvious now that he had said it, but the peacock had not come to mind for me at the time.

"Now look at either end of the square. Do you see how the Imam Mosque in the south is set exactly opposite the main entrance to the bazaar in the north?" he asked. "Shah Abbas was a wise man. He did that so we remember that when we enter the mosque we turn our back on the commerce of ordinary life."

He began leading me over to the Ali Qapu Palace, opposite the Lotfollah Mosque. I asked him how he got the name Zizou. He grinned cheekily.

"There are not many tourists who come to Iran," he said. "They think we are all terrorists. Even in Isfahan we don't have many. It's difficult to earn a living here. So I started thinking about how I could attract foreigners into the carpet shop. More French people come here than most other nationalities, so I thought, 'What do French people like?' They love, love their foot-baller, Zidane Zidane, whom they call Zizou. So I had 'Zizou' printed on a white T-shirt and immediately I had a talking point.

"It worked well for quite some time. But you know, I am not really a *bazaari*, a merchant. I don't really care for it. I'm a phi-losopher at heart, a student of buildings like these and the sacred geometry that Jason speaks of so much in his book—the way the whole construction of the square and the mosques and the Ali Qapu Palace is based on the Golden Mean, the mathematical ratio that is repeated over and over in nature, as in the way roses wind 'round their stem."

I didn't quite share Jason's and Zizou's enthusiasm for sacred geometry, though I was glad to share in the results of their explo-rations. I had never been adept at grasping the beauty of math-ematics; I was content enough to bask in the ensuing harmony of color and proportion. But certainly the odd angles and position-ing of both the Lotfollah Mosque and the Royal Mosque made sense when considered in the light of an overall mathematical plan that Shah Abbas wanted to bring into form.

The Ali Qapu Palace was not quite a palace. Built at the very end of the sixteenth century, the six-story building was intended primarily as a monumental gateway (Ali Qapu means "Gate of Ali") from the great square to the royal palaces that lay in the parklands beyond. But it is also believed to have served as a pal-ace for the great shah, or at least as a vantage point from which to watch over his wives as they came and went from the Lotfol-lah Mosque opposite.

For that, Zizou informed me, was the purpose of the Lotfol-lah Mosque. It was for the shah's harem only, which is why it had no need of a minaret. The shah didn't want another man, the muezzin who normally sings the call to prayer, among his women. There was no need of a courtyard, either, since it was not for public use.

At the entrance of Ali Qapu, Zizou ran over to one corner and told me to go to the opposite one and face the wall. He whispered something from the other side, and it resonated like a transmitter down to the corner I was standing in.

We went upstairs to the elevated terrace with its eighteen slender columns, all cedars from Lebanon. In the center was a dry pool with a fountain. The ceiling was supported by elegant exposed beams and was covered in ornate inlay work. Persian miniatures adorned the walls, women in languorous poses, feeding a bird or picking a rose. There was a painting of a woman with child, clearly influenced by the Italian Madonna with Jesus. On the opposite wall was a painting with Chinese influences. Both were advertisements for Isfahan's pivotal position along the world's trade routes, as well as its cosmopolitan court culture.

All this sophistication needed paying for, and trade, as well as the spoils of conquest, was the way to do it. When Shah Abbas force-marched tens of thousands of Armenians from Armenia all the way to Isfahan, it was partly to make use of their skills as craftsmen in the construction of his projects, but it was also because he was aware of their knowledge of the silk trade, and their contacts stretching from China to Europe. During his reign he diverted the Silk Road to pass through Isfahan. He rewarded the Christian Armenians with the freedom to practice their religion and to build Vank Cathedral, which is still the heart of the Armenian quarter today.

As impressive as the palace itself was the view from the upper terrace, with the harem's mosque opposite, the Imam Mosque to the south with bare, rugged mountains beyond, the vast square gathering all the various sights into a unity.

Gazing over the parapet, I learned that Zizou's father had been damaged in the 1980s by chemical weapons in the war with Saddam's Iraq, and was now mentally unstable. Zizou's brother had died in a car accident just the year before, and a few months later, his sister had died in a fire. "My mother, too, she is a little crazy because of all this," he said. "So much bad luck in one family. I think there must be a good reason that God has kept me alive. This is why I am not so worried about selling carpets. I know there is more to life than this.

"First of all," he said, clutching my arm and leading me down the stairs, "I want to get this book written on Lorestan. Will you e-mail Jason? Or you can do it. I know you can!"

I could appreciate how Jason had taken to Zizou. He had an authentic, passionate spirit. He was an intellectual without a university degree or a library of books. He cared; he cared about his homeland, he cared about the creations of Shah Abbas, he cared for the mystery of what living is. When I told him that I had no plans to go to Lorestan, at least on this trip, he took it as the workings of fate, and said that he trusted it would happen in good time and with the right person. I had to agree with him. We parted, and he strode quickly away to his carpet shop.

# drink the wine

Wayfarer, indulge me in a sober moment.
Please set down your glass.
I can help you write a letter of resignation
To all your fears and sadness.

— HAFEZ

Isfahan is a difficult place to leave. It's the kind of place that nurtures dreams, where you may even imagine living a part of the year in one of those fine old Safavid houses near Imam Square. Who wouldn't want to wake up in the morning to a shower of red and blue light, wander through the bustle of the bazaar, and spend the first hour of the day up in the teahouse overlooking the spread of Imam Square? The traders unfurling their carpets, the gaggles of children on their way to school, the flashing silverware and brass trays, Persian miniatures set out in rows, the fragrance of orange and roses from freshly lit hookahs, the new shoal of tourists brought in overnight. And embracing it all, the palace, the floating blue domes, the fountains, the far mountains. Iran does not have a great Internet service, there is no Starbucks, no *New York Times,* no kissing in public, no public forum to speak your mind freely. But there are things we don't have, either.

I have a friend who grew up in Isfahan and only left it two

years ago to marry a man in San Francisco. She dreams of Isfahan every day, and not just because it was her home, where her mother still lives. She thinks of the women leaning their heads in to share confidences in the street, she says. What simple and intimate friendship they share with one another; they know they can call on each other any time of the day or night. She thinks of how close to the earth the living is there; how the senses are fed with the smell of roasting pistachios and spices, the billowing call to prayer, the bustle of bodies in the narrow lanes of the bazaar. She thinks of the simple warmth and courtesy of daily life. It's just not the same, she says, in her life by the Bay.

But for all its charms, I had to leave Isfahan. A traveler is always leaving. On my last afternoon a great wind began to blow in clouds from the mountains and sand from the desert beyond. The sky turned a muddy polenta, veiling the domes and the mountains with a haze of dust that swirled in the air. I spent my last evening in the courtyard of the Abbasi Hotel, a magnificent old caravanserai of the Safavid era that was turned into a hotel in the 1960s. Its size bears witness to the streams of visitors and merchants who came here in the days of Shah Abbas. Now there was just a small group checking in from Dubai.

The great courtyard is a miniature Imam Square, with a water channel and fountains down the middle and a double story of arches flowing all the way around it. Couples and families were sitting at tables by the water, drinking the Iranian version of Diet Coke. Looming over one end was the blue dome of a madrasah, a theological school founded by the great shah. I ate my thick soup of green noodles and sat back as the stars began to peek out again, the wind dying down. There is an old Persian saying: *When it is dark enough, you can see the stars.*

The stars that watch us always from long ago, I thought, returning their gaze. And as the thought passed on its way, I felt myself to be an intimate part of the great wide world and at the same time strangely alone, a speck in a vast and timeless universe.

There I was with my soup of green noodles, alone yet not alone, wheeling along on some fateful trajectory not of my conscious making, under the wheeling stars.

I finished my soup, paid my bill, and rummaged in my backpack for Rumi. I knew what I was looking for. I turned to the poem "Buoyancy." I wanted to eat these words:

> *So the sea journey goes on,*
> *and who knows where!*
> *Just to be held by the ocean*
> *is the best luck we could have . . .*
>
> *Why should we grieve that we've been sleeping?*
> *It doesn't matter how long we've been unconscious.*
> *We're groggy, but let the guilt go.*
> *Feel the motions of tenderness*
> *Around you, the buoyancy.*

The next morning I rolled up at the bus station and was glad to discover there was no confusion, no chaos, no scramble. The bus to Tehran was about to leave, on time. More modern, more spacious and comfortable than any bus to JFK, it had only two things to contend with: the video turned up loud and the driver counting his bills at the wheel while driving at seventy miles per hour all the way to Tehran. But at least you are up high and larger than anything else on the road.

The following morning I left the sanctuary of the Laleh Hotel and made my way along the street and into a park. I would be in Tehran just long enough to meet up with an old friend from San Francisco who happened to be in the country at the same time I was. A few moments on the exercise machines that are common in most Iranian parks—bright yellow bars that you push and pull against your own weight, even a rudimentary running machine—and I strolled over to watch the chess players. Several older men were sitting, intent, over their game. They reminded me of Cezanne's painting of the card players—the tall, erect figures, the gaunt, unsmiling faces—although playing cards is considered un-Islamic, so chess had to suffice in a public park. I had arranged to meet my friend here, and Faisal turned up a few moments later. He and I would often meet in our local coffee shop back home, and it was by sheer coincidence that we happened to be in Tehran at the same time.

Like most Iranian Americans, he had left his native country at the time of the Islamic Revolution. His family had been part of the ruling elite, and he was back here for only the second time in thirty years. Like thousands of others in the same predicament, he was hoping to reclaim some of his family property, which had been confiscated and redistributed during the early years of the Revolution. The recovery process entailed an extraordinarily Byzantine legal process with no guarantee of any success. He had come to realize that the only way he might ever succeed was if he went at regular intervals to Tehran himself, to oversee and assist in the process. His family property was worth many millions, and if he only clawed back a small percentage of its value, he reckoned the effort would be justified.

Faisal had just come from a visit with his lawyer, and the news wasn't good. He gazed absentmindedly and somewhat gloomily at the chess players for a few moments, until I asked him if he would like to join me for a few days as translator on a trip to Kurdistan.

"I'm only offering you one unlikely venture in exchange for another," I said. "I'm going in the wild and remote hope of meeting a Sufi sheikh whom I heard about from another friend back in San Francisco."

His face lit up. Faisal had never been to Kurdistan before—it was almost another country for someone who, as a young man, had only known a privileged life in Tehran, with summers by the Caspian Sea. Faisal had a few days to kill while his lawyer filed yet more papers on his behalf, and he was more than glad to come along.

I had heard about the Sufi sheikh from a friend who had been traveling in the area a few years earlier when he was robbed and beaten in his hotel room—a rare occurrence in Iran. All his money, his passport, his credit cards, and his driver's license were stolen. Later he suspected it to be the work of the Iranian Intelligence Services. It was a warning, he thought, not to continue with his cultural research in the area.

He had been given the number of this Sufi sheikh by a friend in Tehran, and he called him, the only person he had any connection with in Kurdistan, to see if he could help. The sheikh responded by saying he would send someone to fetch him in an hour. On the hour, a young man appeared in the lobby of his hotel and drove him to another town, a few hours away. He stopped outside an enclosed building in a residential part of the city, and motioned my friend to follow him inside.

A couple of hundred people were crammed in the building. The sheikh had assembled them in the space of an afternoon for the benefit of the American. When my friend walked in, they all began singing and swaying, and holding their arms out toward him. It was a gigantic celebration designed solely to fill him with the compassion and loving attention of the community. It continued for an hour, by the end of which my acquaintance felt fortunate for having been robbed. The sheikh had also phoned the authorities to rearrange his visa and deal with his passport troubles.

"I've never heard a story like that," Faisal said, looking faintly cynical. "But why don't we go to Jamshidiyeh—the gardens up on the mountain slopes on the edge of Tehran. The air is so much better up there on the mountain, and there are some wonderful restaurants where we can have lunch. Then you can tell me about this sheikh. And you can tell me something about Sufism. I was never interested in it when I lived in Iran. It always felt like a relic of the past."

On the way to Jamshidiyeh, Faisal told me there were several hundred parks in Tehran, and that without them the entire population would have been asphyxiated long ago by smog and exhaust fumes. The trees and the greenery at least help to keep the air breathable some days, if not all, though scores of people still died every day from the appalling pollution. I had already taken to wearing a traffic mask, along with most other people— a first for me. Even the receptionist in the Laleh Hotel wore one, and when I first walked into the hotel I thought in my ignorance that she must have had some face injury. The problem was not only the overwhelming traffic, none of it ecologically minded, but the geographical location of the city. The mountains nearby, while they offered respite for those who could go there, served to trap the pollution in a wide circle over the city.

Jamshidiyeh was like no other park in Tehran, or anywhere else for that matter. Nothing stands between it and the Alborz mountain range, which stretches empty and large all the way to the Caspian Sea in the north. You crawl in your taxi up to the northern outskirts of the city, and the road ends in an area that, while clearly man-made, already appears half wild. Graceful paths lace their way this way and that, varieties of trees and shrubs shaping their course. Soon the trees give way to the first open slopes of the mountain, and in the near and middle distance, restaurants and tearooms perch on crags and rocky outcrops. The park itself begins seamlessly to merge with the mountain.

Faisal and I hiked up a trail that soon left the last buildings of the city behind, stopping eventually at a restaurant that rose up like a Swiss chalet from a rocky outcrop. We sat outside on a wide balcony overlooking Kolakchal Mountain, the nearest of the Alborz range, squatting on carpet-covered cushions at a low wooden table. The mountain peak gleamed white against a brilliant blue.

Over *faisanjan*—a delicious stew of chicken, pomegranate juice, and walnuts—and *korme sabje*, the same thick green soup I had first tasted in Isfahan, I told Faisal why I wanted to meet this sheikh. I told him how the romantic image of the dervish had lingered in my mind for decades; how the image had been burnished through the years, not only by my familiarity with the poetry of Rumi and Hafez, but also by meetings I had had with such men in Turkey and in northern India.

The Sufis, as they are known, represent the mystical dimension of Islam, and exist as brotherhoods still today all over the Muslim world. Rather than contenting themselves with the dogma and observances of orthodox Islam, they follow a path of personal experience of the divine through silence, prayer, communal chanting, and ecstatic dance, known as the *sema*.

They follow the spiritual guidance of a sheikh, the leader of a brotherhood. And the brotherhood may, like the Naqshbandi Order or the Bektashis, extend all over the Muslim world, and have different sheikhs in different countries. The Sufis are not monks, and have no monasteries. They are householders, and their practices take place largely within the community and context of their everyday lives. In many parts of Central Asia they remain the primary binding force of the community.

Not long before arriving in Iran, I had read an article in the *Guardian* by William Dalrymple, in which he had suggested that the Sufis were the only viable counterweight to the fanaticism of the Taliban that was sweeping Pakistan. Their shrines of the saints were still centers of pilgrimage across the country, and remained powerful symbols of another, more interior and apolitical form of Islam that we heard little of in the West.

"But surely this kind of thing is only for simple, uneducated people," Faisal interjected. "I've always thought a pilgrimage to a shrine was about nothing much more than blind belief. People go there hoping for a miracle of some sort—a cure for their ills, help for their impoverished families, or to ask for a child."

I wasn't so sure. It was my own experience that there were values and qualities that could emerge on a pilgrimage that might soften the shell that keeps us absorbed in our own self-concerns. It could also blur the boundary between our usual rational perspectives and other dimensions that were normally opaque to us.

I told Faisal how I had once joined a pilgrimage to the shrines of saints all around Turkey, led by the Sufi sheikh Uruch Gevenc, a master musician from Istanbul. Within a few days I had begun mixing up one tomb and saint with another; but as important as the shrines, I learned, was the wandering, circuitous journey itself. Before long the journey had lulled me into a kind of porous dreamtime, helped in large measure by hours of doing nothing in a clattering van that frequently broke down, by sleep deprivation, and by my ongoing ignorance as to where we were going next.

It was like life really, the one great pilgrimage all of us make, round and round, often not knowing where we are going until we get there, with a few watering stations along the way. It followed the wind, rather than a schedule, this Turkish caravan of dreams, this pilgrimage in honor of the saintly dead. And in doing so it unsettled the usual solidity of my frames of reference.

Once, in the city of Bursa, we sat through the small hours of the night with a local sheikh and his disciples. Everything they touched they kissed. They kissed the table we ate on, the sheikh kissed the book he read to us from, and when the time came to take photographs, he even kissed his camera. Everything deserved gratitude and respect in the eyes of those sufis.

The climax of the journey was to arrive in Konya for the day of Rumi's Wedding Feast, as the day of his death is called. Sufis of the Mevlevi Order, founded by Rumi, were there from all over the world, and when we opened the door of the hotel lobby we were hit by a wave of sound. Sixty or seventy people were chanting at the top of their lungs. A row of men, arms linked, were bending their knees and rising up and down with the breath, their bellies rising and falling like bellows. At one end was a group of musicians next to the sheikh, who was looking around the room, slowly nodding his head.

The sheikh greeted Uruch with a kiss on both cheeks, Uruch took his oud from its case and began playing, and our group joined in along with everyone else. The bellows breathing started up again, everyone joining hands, circling the lobby, the hotel staff oblivious, our luggage still in the van. For hours, first one sheikh then another led the music, until sometime after three the night finally ended with a speech from each sheikh paying his respects to the others.

The following day we took our seats in the sports hall for the *sema,* the ceremony of the Mevlevis, or Whirling Dervishes. The sema had been officially banned in Turkey since the 1920s, when Ataturk secularized the country and outlawed the Sufi orders. The sports-hall event was organized not by the Mevlevis themselves, but by the Ministry of Culture, and was as much a tourist event as anything else. We and the other Sufi groups in the audience were there for the symbolism of an event that had been held almost every year for centuries.

I was surprised, even so, to see the Coca-Cola advertisements all along the sports-hall windows and to hear the drone of political speeches opening the event. The musicians who preceded the sema played with the grandiose gestures of television light opera. The sema was better served in London, I thought, where I had once seen the Dervishes from Konya perform at the Royal Albert Hall. At least the surroundings were more fitting, sort of austerely gracious, and the audience, unfamiliar with the reality back in Turkey and thinking they were attending a spiritual ceremony, brought a respect to the gathering that did something to imbue it with dignity.

In the Konya sports hall the dancers, in high felt hats and long white skirts, lined up in front of the sheikh, heads bowed, arms folded over their chests. The hats were their ego's tombstone, the skirt its shroud. The ney struck up its bittersweet tone. Each of the dancers peeled away from the line, bowed before the sheikh, began to turn on his axis around the hall, turning, turning around the heart, like the stars, the atoms, the blood in his veins, arms spread wide, right hand open to the sky to receive God's grace, left hand turned to the earth to pass on the gift of grace.

Perhaps fifteen of them finally, one or two of them boys still, some elderly men, turning for love, dissolving away before our eyes under the Coca-Cola signs. For half an hour or more they whirled along, absorbed in their private bliss—or at least I imagined so, for in truth I had no way of knowing what was going on behind their closed eyes.

Faisal was looking at me somewhat quizzically, and I felt I had gone on too long. I stopped to take in the view while he ordered a water pipe with rose-scented tobacco. Our acquaintance in the local coffee shop did not extend to these kinds of stories, and I imagined he was wondering how he had agreed to team up with this character who had spent weeks running around the tombs of old saints from a tradition that was not even his own.

"Well, what I do know is that the ayatollahs don't approve of Sufism," Faisal said, drawing on his water pipe. "Just as they frown on Zoroastrianism, and positively detest the Baha'i faith—with 300,000 adherents, the largest minority religion in Iran. The authorities have torn down the principal Baha'i place of worship in Tehran, have imprisoned and tortured many Baha'is, and do not even deign to grant it the status of a religion."

While that was true, Sufism, like any form of mysticism, had always been at odds with the prevailing political and religious powers of the day. There had been exceptions, certainly, like Sheikh Safavi, the founder of the Safavid dynasty. But the exceptions tended to prove the rule. After all, if you wanted people to follow a party line, whether you were a pope or an ayatollah, you didn't want them giving priority to their own inner experience. You wanted to do their thinking for them, and to decree what was right and wrong. When people start listening to their own authentic experience, even if it contradicts external authority, there's no knowing where it might end.

The Islamic Republic had effectively purged Sufism from public life in most of Iran, though it was a growing undercurrent behind closed doors, especially among the younger generation. The house of worship of the Gonabadi Sufis—the largest Sufi order in Iran—had been demolished in Isfahan by the authorities in 2008, and the following day, dozens of Sufis were arrested and injured when they gathered in protest next to the tomb of the Dervish poet Naser Ali. Similar scenes had taken place in Mashhad, Qom, and elsewhere since Ahmadinejad became president in 2005. Soon after his election, a Sharia scholar in the holy city of Qom, Ayatollah Hossein Nouri-Hamedani, declared that Sufis were a danger to Islam.

Kurdistan, however, was different. It was a troubling area for the authorities in many ways. First, the Kurds were a different people, spread over the border areas between Iran, Iraq, and Turkey. They were essentially a tribal culture with their own customs, language, and dress code. There were separatist elements in Kurdistan, and the population was generally hostile to the government, which had marginalized it for years. Unemployment was higher than anywhere else in the country, services were underfunded, investment was low, and there were often demonstrations, which were sometimes brutally put down.

But at least they were left to practice their own traditions more than people elsewhere in Iran. Sufism has always been widespread among the Kurds, and it continues to be so today.

The authorities knew who the sheikhs were, engaged in a degree of dialogue with them, and generally turned a blind eye to their communities.

So I wanted to meet this sheikh, I told Faisal, as we paid for our meal and made our way back down the path to the taxis. All I knew of him was that he spoke English and that he lived somewhere in the city of Sanandaj.

"But remember," I said as we parted, "in all likelihood we may never get to meet him at all. My acquaintance no longer had the sheikh's phone number, and no address. All he remembered was his name: Sheikh Mukhtar Hashemi."

The following day we flew to Kermanshah and hired a taxi to take us to Sanandaj, the capital of Kurdistan, a few hours away. But first we stopped at Taq-e-Bostan, on the edge of Kermanshah, to look at the cliff, which is inscribed with bas-reliefs preserved from the second great Persian empire, the Sassanian period, around A.D. 379. In fine relief, there was Shah Ardeshir II on his horse, trampling his enemy, the Roman emperor Julianus, and being crowned by the Zoroastrian god Ahura Mazda. The shah did indeed capture the Roman emperor, and enslaved another one. The Romans were never able to defeat the Persians, and the two empires skirmished along their borders for centuries.

Before setting off for Sanandaj, we went for lunch at one of the open-air restaurants nearby. Faisal, our driver, and I sat on one of the beds, an open-water channel gurgling quietly nearby. We were eating our chicken kebabs, when the driver, a handsome man in his fifties, said something to Faisal with a motion of his head to somewhere behind me. I asked Faisal what he had said.

"He said that if those three Kurdish girls sitting behind us, the ones on their own without any male accompaniment, were his daughters, he would kill them. Not literally, I think, but he means he would be furious, and would drive them out of the restaurant."

"Why?" I asked.

"Because an ocean begins with a few small drops."

The lyrical turn of phrase made his response all the more chilling. We fell silent. I turned to snatch a brief look at the girls, who were laughing and eating together, oblivious of what the driver had just said. So much for my fantasies of the new Iranian woman. Kurdistan was not Tehran. This was tribal country, and however romantic and welcoming it might appear, it was where the darker side of traditional values also held sway. Even so, those three young girls were still willing to sit in that restaurant on their own, by all accounts breaking a taboo that seemed sacrosanct to our older driver. In Kurdistan, too, it seemed, some things were beginning to change, to the displeasure of an older generation.

The driver's machismo was not restricted to his ideas on the place of women. He would not permit a single vehicle to remain in front of him, and we spent an exhausting few hours grinding in third gear behind lorries over dry hills and then roaring past them in the greener valleys, the hills gradually rising to mountains in the direction of Iraq. Bizarrely, every now and then, usually just after he had passed yet another truck on an approaching bend, he would break out with some verse or other of Hafez in a voice full of emotional intensity.

We were more than relieved to arrive at the hotel, a modern and somewhat luxurious arrangement on the edge of Sanandaj. We dumped our bags and went into town in search of a tea shop. Despite the elegant dress of the older generation—the men in baggy trousers with sharp fitted vests and exquisite headwear; the women in long fluid dresses of various colors, with white embroidered blouses, and beautiful flowing scarves—the city itself was more ragged than anything I had seen so far. Men were sitting on the sidewalk peddling trinkets, cell phones, cigarette lighters, or the customary baggy trousers. The man who gave me a shoe shine told me through Faisal that it was almost impossible to earn a living there. Food prices kept going up and few people managed to earn regular wages. Being a sidewalk entrepreneur was about the only option.

We clambered down some steep steps into the tearoom he had indicated, and found ourselves in what I could only describe as a sort of Aladdin's cave, all yellow and red and sparkling with hookahs made of cut glass. The whole basement was packed with young men sitting on daybeds, each group sharing a teapot and a hookah. On the walls were a picture of Christ crucified, one of Ahura Mazda, and, believe it or not, a cowboy hat and a pair of steer horns. The Elvis haircut had evidently reached Sanandaj. Almost everyone had one, which made me look even more conspicuous than usual.

We caused a general stir, and a great many smiles and waving hands. Faisal and I had to wait a few moments for a bed to become vacant, but then a small group ushered us over to share theirs. They left soon afterward with gracious nods, and when the owner—a young man in his twenties—came over to take our order, we asked about the wall decorations.

"It's for fun," he said. "And I also want to make everyone feel welcome, wherever they come from or whatever religion they are."

They had been closed down several times, but had been open without interruption now for a few months. Most young men in Sanandaj were out of work, and the teahouse was a good place for company with which to while away the hours. We decided on apple flavor for our hookah, and the clean infusion woke me up and sharpened my senses. I have never smoked cigarettes, and have a distaste for their smell and their smoke. But I found the hookah attractive not only for the communal ritual, the bubbling water, the overall aesthetic of the pipe, but for the water-cleaned infusion, sweet with the odor of fruit and flowers.

The water pipe is an import from Arab cultures, and was never an intrinsically Iranian pastime. But Iranian men in their twenties have taken to it in droves in recent years, and the pipe is shared by the group, the delicate flavor of apple or rose scenting the air around them. It became so popular that the regime decided to ban it the year before, and many of the teahouses that also offered hookahs, like this one in Sanandaj, were closed, as they had been in Shiraz. The resentment those laws generated only put the regime more out of touch than ever with its people. At the time of our visit, the teahouses in Sanandaj were beginning to open again.

The next day we were strolling through the bazaar when I asked Faisal if he could get someone to point us in the direction of the ceramic section. He stopped and said a few words to someone, who in turn called over a man who was passing by.

"He will show you the way," he said. And he did, to the bathroom section. When we explained we meant ceramic tiles, as in antique tiles, he laughed and motioned us to follow him farther.

"Faisal," I said on a whim, "why don't you ask him if he has heard of Sheikh Mukhtar Hashemi?"

We hadn't asked anyone that question since our arrival in Sanandaj. After all, whom would we ask? We didn't know a soul, and it seemed a little foolish and also pointless to ask a passerby on the street. The whole idea of finding the sheikh had already begun to feel like something of a fool's errand. Faisal hesitated, looking at me with a cynical glance I had almost come to grow fond of.

"Why not?" I said. "It can't do any harm to ask. And anyway, that's what we came here for!"

Faisal turned and said something to the man. He stopped in his tracks and stared at us.

"You want to meet Sheikh Hashemi?" he asked.

"Yes, we do."

"I was the first *mureed* [disciple] of the sheikh after his father died. Would you like to go to the *khaneghah* [house of worship]?"

Faisal and I looked at each other, taken aback. We forgot all about the ceramic section. Right there and then the man bundled us into a taxi and took us to a low building enclosed in a garden somewhere in the residential district. Several men were at the entrance, and when our man spoke to them, one of them pulled out his cell phone. After speaking a few sentences he handed the phone to me.

"It is the sheikh," he said.

"How refreshing to hear an English voice," a voice more English than my own said. "I would be glad to meet you. You have good timing, which is a good signal. I arrived last night from a conference in Syria, and tomorrow morning I am going to Lake Orumiyeh, not far from the border with Azerbaijan. I am a water engineer, and the national adviser on the environmental problems concerning the lake. It is one of the larger saltwater lakes in the world, you know, and its water level is diminishing at a worrying pace."

He told me he would meet us in the lobby of our hotel in two hours. First his mureed would take us to his restaurant for lunch. Ali's restaurant was a welcoming hole-in-the-wall where we had the traditional soup of crushed meat and beans. While we were eating, Ali showed us scars on his arms and legs where he had been tortured ten years before for taking part in a demonstration.

"They kicked me around on the floor and then stuck redhot skewers under my skin," he said. "They enjoyed themselves. They took in hundreds of us that time, hoping to snuff out all opposition and dissent. But it's just gone underground. Life is not easy here, but it will change. Things always change. I just hope it is in my lifetime." He was probably around forty, but was overweight and looked several years older. His life, he said, made sense because of the Sufi community and his spiritual practices.

"The sheikh is a good man," he said as he dropped us off at the hotel. "His father was a saint. His grandfather was one of the most revered saints of the last century. Even today, many people make the pilgrimage to his tomb in the mountains."

At 4:00 P.M. exactly, a youngish man with spectacles and a slight bulge at the midriff strode into the hotel lobby with two aides. He wore a long green robe and a green turban.

"Delighted to meet you," he said in Oxford English. "I thought I had better be on time for an Englishman. It's one of the good habits I learned in London."

We sat down and he immediately ordered ice cream for everyone, including the aides. He explained that his father had had to flee the country at the time of the Revolution. At first he had gone to Baghdad, because that was the original home of the founder of his order, the Sufi Qaderi. But Saddam Hussein had wanted to use him and his influence for political purposes, so he fled with his three wives and children to London. Mukhtar was eight when they arrived in England, and was thirty-seven now. He had grown up in the English education system, and had a Ph.D. in water engineering. In his twenties he was administrator and press secretary for the Muslim Council in London. Before his father died, he named Mukhtar as his successor, and said it was his duty to return to Kurdistan when the time was right.

Now he had a wife and three children, ministered to thousands of people as sheikh of the order—advising on personal problems and family affairs, giving spiritual practices and training, officiating at funerals ("not weddings, they always say it

ROGER HOUSDEN

will be too raucous for me, meaning I would not approve of the alcohol")—and had a full-time profession as a water engineer. His cell phone rang constantly, and was mostly answered by one of his aides.

"Our spiritual way is simple: love and tolerance," he said, glancing at us over his spectacles. He stopped for a moment and then took off his turban to reveal a ponytail of dark hair streaked with gray. "I am taking this off to make it more comfortable between us," he said, smiling.

Then he described what he meant by the practice of love; that for the Sufis it is known not as a good idea or ideal to live up to, but as an experience. It emerges when the noise of the habitual mind—our judgments, opinions, and expectations—gives way to the silent heart that unites everyone. Their spiritual practices are designed to facilitate this, and their community is the practical means and vehicle through which they express that love. Because real love, he said, looking first at me and then at Faisal, was active, not just a feeling.

"That sounds like a very different form of spirituality from the one we hear about in the West when the subject of Iran comes up," I said, between spoonfuls of ice cream.

"Of course, people think we are all fanatics," he said with a sigh. "But there is fundamentalism everywhere in the world, not least, dare I say, in the United States. And I have heard that even there it is an influence on government policy. Our community is respected now by the authorities here. They see we are a force for the social good, and they leave us largely alone. Though we do have problems sometimes with the Wahabi sect, which has a presence here. They are the ones from Saudi Arabia who are the literalist, fundamentalist Muslims. They think we are too accommodating, too tolerant of other views."

I asked him what it had been like to come back to Kurdistan after so long in London. It was an honor to take the role his

145

father had bestowed upon him, he said. An honor and a blessing, as well as a responsibility. And at the time he was still spending three months in England each year to continue his studies.

"No one there knows I am a Sufi sheikh," he said with a giggle. "To them I am Mukhtar the Water Engineer. They would simply never believe my life here. But I can think of no better life than one of service to others. And I have been given that blessing."

Even in our short time together, I could see him putting this into action. No call on the phone was turned away or put on hold. People were constantly asking him for something, and for him it was an honor to be able to respond. And here I was, an unknown dropping in from the sky, and on his only day in town he in turn dropped everything to come and spend time with us in a hotel lobby.

"Would you like to see something of our practices?" he asked. "As you may know, music and singing are at the heart of what we do, and I would just like you to have a taste before you leave."

Seeing our faces, he started making some phone calls, and a moment later turned to us.

"Five or six young men will meet us in half an hour at the khaneghah. You are quite fortunate. They are usually busy at this time of day, but things seem to be going your way."

When we arrived at the khaneghah the young men were already there, along with a middle-aged woman. The great majority of the community was young, the sheikh told us. The woman was the leader of the women's group, men and women meeting separately for spiritual practices. Some five hundred women met every Thursday, while around a hundred men, many in their twenties, would meet later the same evening. Sufism was growing rapidly again in popularity among the younger generations, whereas few older men had much time for it. Simply, it wasn't cool when they were young; it was again now.

The men sat down on the floor in a row, each holding a large frame drum called a *daf*. We sat opposite them, and one of them began singing, a lilting, plaintive chant that the others joined in on. Soon they added the drums, and before long they were swaying from side to side in a rhythm that was as hypnotic and evocative for me as it must have been for them. It was a beautiful sound, an expression of the longing so evident in all Iranian art forms, and I found myself swaying, too, all thought or concern submerging in an expansive warmth and tranquillity.

I don't know how long we sat there, eyes closed within moments, but eventually the singers slowed, the drumming came to rest. The sheikh turned to us, apologized for having to leave us to spend some time with his family, and assigned us a driver to take us back to the hotel. I felt grateful for the quiet, wordless place I had been brought to by the rhythm and cadence of the music and voices; but more than anything I felt grateful for the sheikh's spontaneous generosity toward two people he had never seen before. This, if anything, was spirit in action. As we parted, he said I would be welcome to return a few weeks later, when he would be more available.

"Then, God willing," he said, "you may have the opportunity to see our full community in ceremony. And it may even happen that you see things you would not have believed possible."

The next day the sheikh's driver turned up to take us back to Kermanshah. His name was Barzan. On the way we stopped for lunch at Palangan, a village rather out of our way, in the mountains, that Barzan thought we would appreciate. The inhabitants ran a fish farm installed by the government to help provide them with a livelihood other than running contraband across the Iraqi border nearby.

The village itself clung to a mountain above the river. It must be a lonely, isolated place in winter, and when Faisal said as much, Barzan replied that the village was snowed in for three or four months of the year. Though it was late November at the time, the weather was still mild, with no sign of snow yet, for which I was thankful. Chickens were clucking and scratching about, donkeys were still clip-clopping over the cobbles; the only human inhabitants we saw were all at the fish farm below.

As soon as we got out of the car, before we had even stopped for a moment to look over the village, Faisal unzipped a bag, took out a fishing rod, and attached a fly from a pocket.

"*What* are you doing?" I asked.

"I'm going to cast a line in that stream down there," he said. And without another word, he ran down the grassy slope to the bank of a fast-running river.

Perplexed, Barzan and I sat down on a carpet outside a shack as one of the villagers started grilling us some fresh trout on charcoal. Four women, all in voluminous bright dresses, with strong, open faces and bare feet, were sitting on the ground gutting a pile of fish, a large tin bowl between them. We exchanged the occasional curious glance and a mutual recognition of our foreignness. Ten minutes later Faisal appeared with a small trout and gave it to the villagers, who gutted it, too, and threw it on the grill.

"I can't help it," Faisal said. "I have to cast a line wherever I go. I take one with me everywhere. It's how I connect to the place. It's one of my oddities. It's like you and your need to sleep an hour or two longer than anyone else. We are all weird in our own way."

Over tea and fish, our driver said that most people for fifty miles around Sanandaj were in the Sufi community. There was a family nearby whose son had been murdered. Both the victim and the murderer, who was known to everyone, were in the community, and the sheikh had come out to meet with all the villagers and the victim's family. Invoking a higher law, he managed to persuade them to forgive the killer rather than demand his death.

Barzan then told us a remarkable story of a friend of his, then in his twenties, who went blind when he was ten. The doctors said his condition was incurable. The boy's parents called the sheikh's father, the earlier sheikh, in London, weeping on the phone and telling him of their boy's tragic misfortune. The sheikh told them to put the boy on the phone. He told the boy to recite a certain verse from the Koran that evening, and then to lie down on a carpet on the floor and go to sleep. When he woke up, the sheikh said, the boy would see the pattern of the carpet before his eyes. In the morning the boy awoke and could see perfectly. His eyesight had been perfect ever since, and he now ran his own stall in the bazaar.

Sufism is a gateway to the miraculous. It has always been known as such, but here in Kurdistan, the miraculous was taken as a matter of fact. For Iranians, even for those of a secular bent—of whom there are many   another dimension is always felt to be near at hand. They even have a word for it, *al ghayb,* the unseen world that can move mountains in this one. Rather than blind faith, the existence of *al ghayb* requires an imaginative leap, a leap that is willing to conceive that the world itself might turn at any moment on a different axis.

It is this kind of imagination we are in short supply of in the West, I thought as we went on our way back to Tehran, the kind of imagination that can allow for the impossible. I didn't know it at the time, but on my return to Kurdistan I would see the impossible take place before my own eyes.

CHAPTER 8

# *more than one veil*

When Faisal and I returned to the capital from Kurdistan, he went off to more hours of waiting in his lawyer's office, and I went to pay a visit to Haleh Anvari. Again, it was Toufan who had made the connection.

Haleh, she said, was a passionate questioner of the status quo. As an artist and a photographer, her main interest was to inquire into the place of women in the culture. "She's an intellectual as much as an artist. Like some of our filmmakers in a way. Artists like her voice the aspirations and conflicts of the culture they live in. They point to a deeper and wider view of being human, and in ways that transcend the merely evident and quotidian. It is artists like these that can point to possible futures."

It was because of what I had heard of her engagement with women's rights and freedoms that I wanted to meet Haleh Anvari on my return to Tehran. Here was an artist with an issue—one that raised strong emotions and opinions in the West. Several women in the United States had told me they would never go to Iran out of solidarity for the women there, who were treated so badly and had to wear the veil.

"But most Iranian women don't wear veils," Haleh was telling me over her kitchen table. "Neither do the majority of them wear black chadors, the full-length garment you see in the Western media whenever they want to portray an Iranian woman. I used to work as a fixer in Tehran for Western journalists, and no matter what story they did—the economy, politics, even Iranian caviar—the visual would always be the same, a woman in a black chador. It's an image that conveys the idea that women are oppressed by religious zealots. What the Islamic Republic hoped would be an icon of their revolution has in fact become a cliché. It is now used universally outside of Iran to signify the exact opposite of what they intended. But because it is a cliché, its use in the West also simplifies and diminishes the individuality of Iranian women."

She turned on her computer and showed me a photograph. A woman stood facing an open window, her back to the camera. Her outstretched arms held a diaphanous fold of muslin sparkling with woven red flowers that hung down her back to the floor. Haleh clearly intended the woman to be breaking a taboo, standing before the world ablaze with color like that.

All that beauty and strength, with its shades of longing. It reminded me of my mother's favorite painting, one by Salvador Dalí in which a young woman stands facing an open window. Haleh's photo was part of a performance piece, *Power of a Cliché*—part lecture, part slide show—that she had recently shown in London, but that was prohibited in Iran.

The cliché of the black chador was divisive, she was saying, because it reduced Iranian women to an anonymous stereotype. It denied them their individuality and the strength and courage with which so many of them had faced their fate in Iran as mothers and sisters. A woman in a chador may be a teacher, a lawyer, a doctor; she may be a surgeon or a professor, a liberal or a radical. Women were individuals in Iran just as they were anywhere else, but the black chador masked this; it hid individuality beneath a collective anonymity.

Haleh Anvari was silent for a moment, and used the space between thoughts to pour us more tea. She was a strong, vital presence across the table. Forty-seven years old and dressed in swaths of color, she had been educated in an English boarding school, and had gone on to a degree in politics and philosophy. Her father was one of the journalists who were imprisoned by the Shah, and like many intellectuals at the time, the family was inspired by the initial promise of the Revolution until its aspirations degenerated into violence and mayhem.

When she began speaking again, her tone was more reflective, nostalgic even. She had wanted to use color in *Power of a Cliché* to break the stereotype, to return individuality to the chador and to women. She had wanted to encourage a sense of commonality between herself and those like her, both here and in the West, with the *chadori* women. When she was growing up, the women in her family would wear a variety of beautiful chadors for different occasions, and always white in the home. For them the chador was worn not to hide from the outside world, but to enter it. Still today there was a certain respect in the culture for the chador—for its complex and contextual meanings.

"But all these are lost in the simplistic image of black. Black has no nuance, no play of light and shade. The chadors even have to be manufactured in Japan because it is so difficult to get true black. It is the most unforgiving of garments. It was only used previously for formal occasions, but then the Revolution turned it into a brand. The Islamic Republic took the black chador for their symbol of female purity and faith. It was to be an icon of the new Islamic woman, after the years of Western decadence under the Shah. In the Shah's time many traditional women would stay home because street life, with its values of materialism and exhibitionism, was considered corrupt, not only by their husbands but by the women themselves. And yet here's the irony: black is not a color recommended for women in the Koran. In fact it is rather discouraged."

One of the Shah's big mistakes had been to try to force Western values on a culture that was still highly traditional and conservative. This was why, initially, the Republic's imposition of the hijab and even the chador was seen as liberating innovations. They had allowed women to enter public life while preserving their modesty and affirming their faith.

I flashed to a memory of teaching English to Iranians in Oxford in the 1970s. Many of them had told me of abuses they or their friends had suffered at the hands of Savak, the Shah's secret police.

"I said a moment ago that most Iranian women don't wear a veil. What I mean to say is that the hijab is a scarf worn over the head, not over the face. At least some form of hijab has to be worn in public, but the black chador, though strongly encouraged in the more traditional areas of the country, was never obligatory except in government buildings."

The veil covering the face was an Arab invention, not an Iranian one. It can only be found in those areas of Iran with a significant Arab population. On the island of Qeshm, in the Persian Gulf, for instance, the women wear heavy leather masks from a young age, and are never allowed to take them off. Still today women on the island are considered the property of men, replaceable as any animal might be. Theirs is a desperate situation, and, not surprisingly, the suicide rate of women on Qeshm is high. But Qeshm is as far removed culturally from Tehran or Isfahan or Shiraz as a small town in Alaska is from New York.

I remembered then something I had noticed in the English-language newspaper that morning. The death notices for men were always accompanied by a photo, but those for women had only a written message. This suggested to me that women could be veiled or hidden from view in more ways than one.

Haleh looked up and fixed her dark eyes on me.

"This is so true. Veiling the presence of a woman, veiling your true meaning, veiling the inside from the outside—these were all ancient and intrinsic features of the culture. Veils may not be worn, as many in the West imagine they are, but there are many other veils that continue to be drawn in different ways."

Even to utter the name of the mother in a traditional household was to reveal too much. And then what did it say about the role of women when, at her wedding, the bride only said yes to the groom on the third time of asking? A woman was expected to be retiring; shyness was considered attractive. To be expressive of your opinions as a woman went against the ancient Persian notion of politesse. And in the case of a traditional home, the tall walls were in fact an adobe hijab. An old house had an inner section for family and close friends—they called it *andarooni*—and an outside section where guests and strangers were received. The traditional house had what is known as a *gooshvareh* balcony where the women could see what was going on below without being seen themselves.

I sat back and looked around me. There was certainly no gooshvareh balcony here. I was in a house that was a far cry from anything that might be called traditional. If I had been asked to imagine the kitchen of a home in Tehran, I would never have come up with anything like the one I was in now. Haleh's kitchen was the only one I had seen anywhere that included a sunken rock pool with turtles flapping around in it. Steel counters, granite floors, exposed stone, upscale accoutrements that you might take for granted on the Upper East Side, that was surprising enough to see in Tehran; but a turtle pool . . .

Haleh shared the house with her husband and teenage son in northern Tehran. Its walls were covered in contemporary Iranian art, which she collected as much to support the young art scene as to gratify her own tastes. Yet for all its sophisticated décor, the house was modest in size, enclosed in a garden and accessed through a high wooden gate.

Accepting a sugary cookie to eat with my tea, I mentioned the taxi driver who, when I was last in Tehran, had spoken to me using the most elevated, gracious forms of phrasing. I imagined it was an example of *taarof,* the polite form of speech, and I wondered if there was any connection between taarof and what Haleh was saying about veils and women and traditional households.

"A big connection. Taarof is the art of camouflaged expression. Iranians have lived in an uncertain world for centuries and have had to learn to express themselves in ways that do not immediately reveal their intentions or position. This is one of the things the West finds so hard to understand about our politics and political discourse. In fact all discourse in Iran is political, or, you might say, diplomatic. We have a horror of direct speech. Our speech is a maze, with many twists and turns of etiquette, lines of poetry, and pleasantries that create diversion and hidden corners. Taarof helps us to appear grand in public and elusive when we wish to be invisible. Rather than a cultural flaw, it is a social requirement. It's considered uncivilized to be direct."

She gave the everyday example of going to visit someone for tea. The host had to be allowed to plead for the guest to accept a cup of tea, and the guest had to decline several times before accepting—like the bride who had to be asked three times before saying yes. Everyone's sensibilities had to be honored. The host had to be permitted to demonstrate her hospitality, while the guest had to be allowed not to appear to need the food.

I was a little confused. We had just had tea, and none of that had taken place. That was because I was a foreigner, she explained. And also because she herself was the product of two worlds. And then things were changing now. Haleh acknowledged being affected by the influence of her son. The younger generation was expressing itself with a new kind of honesty. Her son, Kasra, had all the street slang, loved Persian rap, and watched Dubai 1, MBC, and all the foreign channels. Taarof was not part of his culture at all. His generation was direct, and its members voiced their opinions through pop music, art, and all the other expressions of youth culture.

Kasra came in at that moment, a tall, willowy presence with a flop of dark hair. He greeted me in perfect English with a casualness and self-confidence I assumed he had learned from his mother by osmosis. He hadn't done his homework, and Haleh spent a few moments encouraging him to go upstairs and work—as distinct from playing—on the computer. I was thinking I should move on.

"One more thought before you go," Haleh said as her son climbed the stairs to the study. "For all that I have said about the traditional role of women here—and there is no doubt that this is still the norm in the culture in general—I also have to say that women in Iran today are breaking the hijab of expression, both politically and artistically. Women are expressing themselves now in every art form in a culture where they have been taught not to reveal themselves. There are many best-selling books written today by women for women. Since the Revolution there have been as many women writers as male ones. And do you know what gave them permission? The Revolution. The Revolution created a new form of language for foreign relations that was unapologetic, angry, and direct. That had never been known in Iran before, and it has rippled through the society and had unintended results like this new willingness on the part of women to express themselves.

"Oh, and a very last thought. Would you like to join us for Yalda the day after tomorrow? It's the Zoroastrian festival of the longest night of the year, December twenty-first. It's a very family affair, lots of eating and drinking. You will enjoy it, I think.

Not many traditions still exist that go back over three thousand years."

No one is a stranger for long in Iran. I was touched by her generosity and accepted gladly. We said good-bye with the customary three pecks on the cheek, and I went down the path and out into the world beyond her garden gate.

I arrived back at Haleh's a little early the next evening. Shahriar, her husband, was in charge of the kitchen, and in the few moments we had before her other guests arrived, I asked her why she had come back to Iran after having been raised and educated in England.

She laughed a raucous laugh, head thrown back, body rippling with mirth.

"I came to forget a love affair, of course! I hadn't been here long before I was invited to a cousin's wedding and a man there asked me to lunch because he thought I might make him a possible wife. I told him straight out, 'I'm not a virgin.' I said, 'In fact I've slept with quite a few men and I'm still in love with one of them!' For a Persian man that's usually all you have to say to send them running. Although in my case it was true. The man was Shahriar, and on our third date he said, 'You were crazy to tell me that. I want to marry you all the more.' So we did. Seventeen years later we still haven't gone back to the UK, though my husband always said we would when we were married. But now we may finally make the leap, because of my son's education."

There was a knock on the door and a stream of visitors piled in. They had come for the festival of Yalda, signifying the birth of Mithra, the sun god who, in the era of the first Persian Empire, some 3,500 years ago, achieved a status almost equal to Ahura Mazda. The return of the sun after the darkest night of the year brings light, joy, and goodness back to the earth. It represents the victory of the forces of light, Ahura, over the forces of darkness, Ahriman.

In the Roman Empire of the fourth century, Mithra was a popular deity, especially among the military. Due to errors calculating leap years and dates, the birthday of Mithra was moved to December 25. Until then, Christ's birthday had been celebrated on January 6, but with the Mithraic cult still popular in Roman Europe, the Church knew to follow success, so they proclaimed December 25 as Christ's birthday, too.

The gathering included Haleh's and Shahriar's cousins and uncles, their mothers, and friends. People milled around and picked at the trays of nuts and dried fruit that have always been a feature of Yalda. There were large slices of watermelon, too, and bowls of ripe pomegranates to represent the first flush of new life.

There were perhaps fifteen of us around the table for a delectable fish curry served up by Shahriar with a sharp lemon paste from Isfahan. Shahriar's mother lived in Isfahan, and she had made the paste in her home there—lemon preparations being a feature of Isfahani cuisine.

The language of preference around the table was naturally Persian, though people broke out in English at different moments, not just in deference to my presence but because, as in upper-class homes in India, people here moved freely between their native language and the language in which most of them had been educated.

The man on my right, one of Haleh's uncles, lived between Paris and Tehran, and we communicated in French. A large man with a shock of white hair that flowed over his ears, he told me he worked in the oil and gas industry and had recently published a book on Sufism in France. Another uncle told me he had come back to Iran from Canada and Dubai a few years before, because it was easier to make money in Tehran, especially in property. It was true that the Tehran property market had blown into a bubble on a par with London's in recent years, though now, on the cusp of 2009, it had just collapsed in line with everywhere else in the world. If the uncle's fortunes had sunk along with it, you would never have guessed it from the jollity, unaided by alcohol, with which he held forth at that table.

To end the evening, everyone consulted the *Diwan of Hafez* for a verse that would give the tone of the coming year—another Yalda tradition. When my turn came, I opened to a page at random, as is the custom, and read this:

> *Hafez, I am at home.*
> *Why are you not here?*

Could that have been random? Or does the unconscious determine everything we do, down to the page we turn to in a book? I was in someone else's home, surrounded by someone else's family. Hafez was referring to another kind of home—the one as close as the jugular vein. Perhaps I had gone missing from that one, too, and not even noticed.

As I was leaving, Haleh asked me what I was doing for Christmas Day. I hadn't thought Christmas was on the calendar in Tehran.

"Why don't you join us for Christmas Day dinner at the British embassy with the ambassador and his wife, Sir Geoffrey and Lady Adams? They are good friends of ours, and I know they would love to have an English writer along. I will confirm and let you know."

I thanked her, feeling faintly ambivalent about spending Christmas in what I imagined would be the formality of the English diplomatic world. I had assumed that, being in Tehran, I would have skipped the usual Christmas frenzy altogether. The thought had rather gladdened me, but then I had already been invited to a glittering social event on Christmas Eve, so why not go the whole way and be doubly festive? Christmas in Tehran was starting to take on a far grander air than my usual experience back home. A walk along the cliff path and a reflective dinner with a few friends was what I normally understood Christmas to be. Yet if Christmas in Tehran included dinner in the very bastion of nineteenth-century colonialism, the British embassy in Tehran, then I would drink to that.

CHAPTER *9*

# *christmas in tehran*

The taxi dropped me off outside a pair of large wrought-iron gates. Before I could press the bell, a man came forward in the courtyard beyond, pressed a switch, and the gates swung open. With a flourish he ushered me toward an open door and into the home of Pari Saberi. It was Christmas Eve, and Pari Saberi was having a party.

I found myself in a room filled with people in formal evening wear. A crystal chandelier glittered from the ceiling; contemporary art hung as in a gallery on all of the walls. A large abstract sculpture took up one corner. Women in long, backless evening gowns were standing in clusters with glasses held high, one with black gloves that reached to her elbows. The men were variously dressed: one wearing a yellow bow tie and a wingtip shirt, others in black suits, and one or two in black polo-neck sweaters. I was in the one sports jacket I had with me, and my all-weather black trousers.

A large lady with a head of big auburn hair and dressed in a long, flowing gown stood up and came over to introduce herself. Pari Saberi was in her mid-seventies, with a presence that conveyed an eventful life. She was Iran's foremost theater director, and had returned to Iran from France in 1984 in order to help give Iranians some respite from the terrible war with Saddam Hussein's Iraq; to offer the message of love and beauty that art could convey.

Monet, I remembered, had been moved by the same impulse some seventy years earlier. The large-scale series of water-lily paintings in the Orangerie was intended as a healing balm for the people of Paris as World War I drew to a close.

Pari Saberi had also wanted to help sustain Iranian pride in the country's glorious literary past. Mining the rich material of the Persian classics for her stories, she drew her inspiration from Rumi, Ferdowsi, Attar, and other great Persian poets and writers.

She pointed to the man with the yellow bow tie, who was holding forth on the state of the economy. "The president of Total, the French oil company," she said.

To his left she pointed out a fashion designer, with shaven head and black wool sweater, whose career had culminated the previous year in an exhibition of his work in the Victoria and Albert Museum in London. And over there was a professor of French literature at Tehran University, in high heels and tight skirt, extolling the eagerness, intellectual curiosity, and hunger of her students.

"And that's why I would never leave, because of them," she was saying. "The more of us stay, the more change will be possible."

We sat down for a few moments in a corner of the room, tall stemmed glasses in hand. She had been brought up in France, and had enjoyed a liberal education in the rich cultural heritage of Paris. On her return to Iran she had left behind the contemporary European dramas she was used to directing in Paris, and now, twenty-five years later, she was still directing original work based on the Persian classics.

"I've been working on a production called *Flying Shams,*" Pari was saying. "I produced it a few years ago, but it has just had a rerun. It tells the story of the relationship between Rumi and his spiritual friend, the mysterious Shams of Tabriz. It is set to Rumi's poetry and a musical score, and of course it includes the Whirling Dervish dance—or ecstatic prayer, as it really is— since Rumi was the founder of the Whirling Dervishes. But what I am engrossed in now is a musical production of *Rostam's Seven Steps.* Rostam is the hero of Ferdowsi's *Shahnahmeh,* and the steps he takes are those required for ultimate knowledge, or the secret of being human. You know, of course, that the *Shahnahmeh* is part of our national identity. That's why I want to do this play now—to remind us of where we come from, of how rich our wisdom tradition is, far older than Islam."

How different our priorities are in the West. In our world, the search is always on for the new and original; the rational intellect (including the anti-intellectual) almost always eclipses the mythic and spiritual in the choice of theme. Wisdom-inspired Western contemporary art has tended to draw its inspiration from the East, as in the Zen-inspired poetry of Gary Snyder or the minimalist music of John Cage and Philip Glass. The universal, mystical element in Christianity—our equivalent of Sufism—has never been more than a marginal interest in our materialist culture.

Whereas Saberi, like many Iranian artists and filmmakers, was living and working in an environment watered by the roots of a mythic past, which drew on a living mystical tradition whose influence was still to be seen in the rituals and customs of daily life. Like the festival of Yalda I had just participated in, where the words of Hafez were consulted. Like the ecstatic chanting and prayers of the Sufis in Kurdistan. Persian literature reflected a fascination with perennial themes, the ones that never went away—birth, death, and, between these two, the journey of the hero in search of wisdom and love.

Dinner was served in an adjoining room whose length was filled with a long oak table glowing in the soft light of three silver candelabra. Two overstuffed turkeys sat on their own silver trays, and the Total man with the bow tie set about carving them with the flair of a Frenchman who had performed a similar exercise a thousand times. Dozens of vegetable dishes were lined down the center of the table.

Each place had a name tag, and mine was next to that of Pari Saberi's daughter, Maryam Shirinlou, a petite, vital woman around forty years old. My only clear memory of that Christmas dinner was of the first few minutes. For the rest of the meal, Maryam and I were deep in a conversation that soon faded out the hum of the rest of the table.

Like her mother, she was an artist, with a show in London about to open in the Xerxes Gallery, whose owner, a Persian himself, specialized in bringing the work of Iranian artists to Britain. Her work often included poems by Rumi written over her images, sometimes in cuneiform, which is similar to Sanskrit. She had never set out to be a professional artist; in the beginning, art had been more like therapy for her, a way to work through her inner chaos as a teenager. There was the turmoil of her family life and the turmoil of a revolutionary Iran at war. Her parents had divorced, and she was brought up between L.A. and Iran, with all the challenges of a young person trying to accommodate the differences between the two cultures.

"At first I identified art with my personal suffering, so I longed to grow out of the art and the suffering both. Gradually I came to realize that I could let go of the suffering and continue to paint; that art had a value in and of itself, independent of its original connection in my life with suffering.

"Now I would say that art has become a means to express my

spiritual life, whereas in my teens, my spiritual life served as a refuge from both art and suffering. The spiritual world has been important for me ever since I had a transforming experience at the age of seven. It was a moment when, for no reason, my separate identity suddenly dropped away and I was aware of being intimately and forever part of all life. There was no dividing line between myself and anyone or anything else. Now my inner questions exist alongside my awareness of a dimension which is free of struggle. Both of these realities contribute to who I am. They are all part of the work I do, and there is no contradiction."

I asked her about the process of inscribing poems in her work, and she said the poetry was mostly Rumi's. He gave voice to her deepest feelings, to a sense of union that she knew from personal experience. Hafez was more difficult for her to understand. She grew up in L.A. until she was twelve, so her Farsi was not good enough to catch the subtleties of Hafez. But in the end, she said, they all spoke the same truth. Their poems transcended tradition, including the tradition of Sufism.

Maryam returned to the States as a young adult, and had only been back in Iran ten years or so. Her whole generation, the one that came of age during the war with Iraq, lost its roots, and it's taken her a long time to find herself. On top of that, coming back from a world with other ways of thinking forced her to look for her roots even more, and she was still doing that now, to some degree. Finding her own traditions and her place in her hometown had been an important part of her development as an artist. And then she felt she had work to do here. She wanted to help bring another image of Iran and Iranians to the world.

I asked her how unusual it was to be a single woman of her age in Tehran.

"It's becoming more and more common," she answered. "The society here is changing rapidly. When I first came back to Tehran I was afraid no one would rent me an apartment, because traditionally a single woman wanting a place of her own would be suspected of prostitution. Hotels are still reluctant to give a room to a single woman. If you are single you normally live with your parents. But in fact I had no problem at all. Even traditional landlords were willing to show me their apartments."

"And what about men?" I asked.

"Ah, yes, not so easy. Men are generally very materialistic here, and not much interested in the spiritual life, which matters to me. They may look modern and open on the surface, but their underlying attitude remains the same as it has always been—men have more power than women, and their power is maintained by the law. The law gives men unconscious influence and power."

A woman I'd met a few days earlier had said that one of the most difficult challenges facing women in Iran was sexual harassment at work. She had had to resign three times because of male harassment. She thought it was impossible to stop, because it was part of the male-dominated culture to assume that a woman exists first and foremost for the pleasure of men. When she complained to the director of the company, he just shrugged. She also told me there was no respect for a woman's opinion at work, and that it was an unwritten rule that all senior positions were reserved exclusively for men.

Traditional family values only perpetuated this power structure. If a boy and a girl were arrested for kissing in the street—or even for holding hands—they were taken to the police station and the police would call the father of the girl and tell him what his daughter had been found doing. The father would feel shamed, and would ensure it didn't happen again. Shame and the importance of appearances were powerful forces in Iranian culture. So the police used family pressure in this way to reinforce the laws of the state. Many laws would be much harder to apply if they weren't implicitly supported by the prevailing family system.

So many impressions, so many strands of thought to weave in the air. We talked on, Maryam and I, so absorbed in our exchange that when the evening ended I could barely remember what I had eaten at that sumptuous, elegant table. Yet for all the stimulation, and no doubt because of it, it was a relief finally to open the door of my hotel room and to sit on the bed with Rumi again. The return to solitude was a balm, especially when I knew that another grand social event awaited me the following day. As usual, I opened the book at random, and the lines I found were these:

> Every moment and place says,
> "Put this design in your carpet!"

The next afternoon, on Christmas Day, sentries checked me in through a high wall topped with barbed wire and directed me toward a large, imposing pile in the middle of extensive lawns. The British embassy in Tehran bears some resemblance to a fortress. A wide door ushers you into the building, and that day, two uniformed staff were there to offer the house cocktail—champagne with pomegranate juice—which you duly took with you through a couple of linked rooms to the terrace at the back of the embassy.

There, the ambassador, Sir Geoffrey Adams, was holding court in a jazzy tie and without a jacket, explaining to his dozen guests that the lawn before them was where some twelve thousand *bazaris,* or merchants in the bazaar, had camped out in 1916 to demand that the Qajar shah of the time agree to the founding of a parliament. The building had been constructed in mid-Victorian times, and all the stained glass and the chandeliers had been sent from England and hauled up from the coast by camel.

Sir Geoffrey was an Oxford Arab scholar who had recently been knighted for his services to the realm in two other delicate areas of the world, Cairo and Jerusalem. He bore more than a passing resemblance to President Sarkozy of France. Though Sir Geoffrey was a good several inches taller than Sarkozy, they were both in their early fifties, with the same hairline, wiry energy, and strong jaw. From what I could see on the terrace, I imagined Sir Geoffrey to be the warmer of the two.

Haleh and her husband raised their glasses to me as I came in and, welcoming me over, introduced me to the ambassador and his wife. Several other guests I did not know, some Iranians along with one or two Englishmen, were clustered around them.

Mary Ellen, the ambassador's wife, a woman with blond hair down to her shoulders, exuded a warm, benevolent presence. She was telling an Iranian woman that the main challenge of diplomatic life was that you had to move to a different posting every three years, just as you were getting used to one place and making friends there. They had another six months to go in Tehran, and didn't yet know where they would be sent after that.

Sir Geoffrey had gone on to tell everyone how, at the beginning of each new posting, British diplomats had to have an audience with the Queen, since it was she they were technically representing abroad. Then, on arriving in Tehran, he had had to introduce himself to President Ahmadinejad, a chore that neither of them relished. When Sir Geoffrey walked into his office, the president barely acknowledged him other than to say that protocol was the only reason for admitting him.

Knowing the fondness with which Iranian men regarded children, Sir Geoffrey broke the awkward silence that followed to say how excited his two young girls were to come to Iran. Ahmadinejad immediately looked up, smiled, and asked after them. Even such a character as Ahmadinejad, Sir Geoffrey said, had a soft spot somewhere. It was the diplomat's job to find it.

A couple of cocktails later we were ushered into a large formal dining room with eminent and somber figures from the nineteenth century gazing down at us from the walls. A large Christmas tree festooned with colored lights stood in a corner with gift boxes piled around it. Four or five Iranian staff stood at the ready by a silver dining service. A long, polished oak table took up the center of the room.

With some relish, Sir Geoffrey told us that the table was the very same one that Roosevelt, Churchill, and Stalin had gathered around at the Tehran Conference in 1943. Stalin had refused to meet anywhere else. Tehran at the time was under Russian control, while the English controlled the southern half of the country. Churchill arrived via Cairo and Baghdad, a perilous journey to undertake at the time. They brought Reza Shah—the father of the last shah, Mohammed Reza—in before dinner to meet the illustrious guests, and then he was ushered out so "the adults could carry on with their conversation," as the ambassador put it, with considerable irony. It was then that they agreed to divide Poland and give half of it over to Russian control. It was at this table that they had agreed to launch the D-Day invasion.

It felt strange to be sitting in the pomp and grandeur of the old embassy after being in the smog-filled streets of the city outside, and I wondered what it must be like for the people who worked here to make that transition every day. The embassy was a symbol of old imperial power. It had been built at a time when the British Empire literally spread over half the world. Its walls breathed an implicit sense of superiority and entitlement—something I understood to be part of my own cultural inheritance, an underlying attitude that I both recognized traces of in myself and resented at the same time.

The embassy staff was all Iranian, and was apparently always having trouble with its own government. One day their passport would be confiscated, the next they would have to report to some government office, and so on—anything to make their life at the embassy as unappealing as possible. Even so, many of them had been on the staff for years.

As dinner was served, the ambassador moved lightly from guest to guest, never engaging with anyone for more than a few minutes at a time. His manner struck me as a fascinating mix of informality, affability, and guardedness—just what one might expect, perhaps, of a career diplomat. And yet the atmosphere around that venerable table, even as it groaned with the weight of history throughout our conversation, was surprisingly less formal than it had been at Pari Saberi's house the night before.

Sir Geoffrey's two children ran in and out as we made our way through dinner, pulling Christmas crackers and reading out the messages inside them with one guest after another, while we swapped stories and toasted the imminent New Year. Haleh was her usual gregarious self, while Shahriar, her husband, a businessman with factories in Mashhad, sat quietly talking to his neighbor, an Iranian poet.

There was a couple who had been friends at college in England, and had met again on the Internet after thirty years. He was English and she was Iranian, and he had left London three years before to make his home with her in Tehran. He had dropped into an unusually stimulating life, he told me, and despite the restrictions that he had to accommodate to in Tehran, he didn't miss London at all.

Even there, sitting in that grand formal dining room, a setting generally unfamiliar to me, I was aware of belonging in some way by association. This was a thread in my past, if not my future, and it aroused a jumble of feelings. I realized I enjoyed something about being in this markedly English setting. At the same time I felt a certain aversion for the assumed authority of its oak-lined walls: the colonial era's conviction that it knew what was best for others around the world, and that it would act on their behalf. As when Reza Shah was shooed out of the room in 1943. In some way, I thought, even in this new century, it was still in the genes of an Englishman to feel "to the manner born."

Geoffrey Adams appeared to be a thoroughly modern man, yet he still lived and acted in a world that seemed to me like a shell of the past. He and his family lived in embassies like this one around the globe that continued to exude the air of upper-class England with all its assumed prerogatives. (It is no accident that Virgin Airlines calls its business section Upper Class.) But I, too, am between worlds in my own way, as he is in his. Even as I inhaled with a certain pleasure the whiff of Establishment England that hung over that table, it reminded me of how glad I was for my life in America.

As we finished dessert, Mary Ellen handed out Christmas presents to everyone from the foot of the Christmas tree. I was touched to be given a gift by someone whose only connection to me was our common national history. Mine was a book I had never heard of. It turned out to be by an American, a tender, nostalgic evocation of life in a country farmhouse outside of Shiraz in the 1960s.

As the rustle of the gift wrap died down, Sir Geoffrey asked me if I would be willing to recite some poetry. He and Mary Ellen shared a passion for the English Romantics. I happened to be a fan of Wordsworth, too, and, glad to have some respite from the small talk, I recited a few lines from *The Prelude*.

Thinking we should offer poetic tribute to Iran, I followed Wordsworth with a few lines of Rumi:

> *Your eyes, when they really see*
> *A rose or an anemone, flood the*
> *Wheeling universe with tears . . .*

Sir Geoffrey knew a little of Rumi in Farsi, and he, too, recited some lines. He was followed by the Persian poet, who declaimed first Rumi and then Hafez with a passionate intensity that made the lines sing.

Others contributed their own favorite poems, the afternoon wore into evening, and by the time I left I felt grateful to Haleh for having gathered me into this privileged company; grateful, also, for the kindness of my English hosts, and for the opportunity to see that ambassadors, too, could be romantic souls.

Meanwhile, Muharram—the ten-day Shia festival of mourning commemorating the murder of Imam Hossein in A.D. 680—was about to begin in Iran, and in my taxi back to the hotel I was dreaming already of my journey the next day to Mashhad, the holy city near the border with Afghanistan.

# CHAPTER 10

# one imam and
# three wise men

Early-morning flights are a health hazard for a late riser like me.
What I needed on landing in Mashhad was not breakfast but
an hour in bed. Except that the bed in my hotel room was perfectly suited for one of the seven dwarves, and at six foot two I
do not qualify for that category. Not even close. No other room
was available, so I trundled my bag along Imam Reza Street,
Mashhad's main thoroughfare, past tawdry and ramshackle
shops and the pompous and overblown façades of new hotels.
Black flags hung all down the street in anticipation of Muharram. There would be no singing or dancing or weddings in
this city for forty days, and for all that time the television and
radio would be playing nothing but funerary music.

But there at the far end was a golden dome, as at the end of a
rainbow, while on my way down the street small sparks of life lit
up even my red eyes: a shopkeeper carefully sweeping his step;
saffron and pomegranate seeds in bulging sacks; a shoeshine

boy's smile as I gave him my foot. The golden dome announced the shrine of Imam Reza, who died in 818. Reza, the eighth Shia imam, was a man of great scholarship revered for his saintly qualities.

I found a hotel with a large lobby and restaurant, and more chrome and gold plate than I would have thought necessary. But at least I could fit into the bed. Mashhad is the second-largest city in Iran, with some three million inhabitants, and is continuing to expand because of the business and pilgrim trade that the shrine of Imam Reza brings in. Twenty million pilgrims descend on this city every year. New hotels were under construction all along Imam Reza Street, and the sidewalk was filled with people even in the early morning.

Ali the guide turned up in the hotel lobby a few hours after my arrival. Without a guide, a non-Muslim would never get within sight of the shrine itself. I also needed him to take me to the tombs of the great poets, Omar Khayyam and Attar, which were an hour or more out of the city. Ali was short and dapper, in his fifties, with slicked-back silver hair and a smart sports jacket. He lost no time in telling me his own story over tea in the hotel lobby. He spoke good English because he had spent three years in the UK during his twenties.

He had been a fitter on a ship that docked there, and after disembarking he never went back. He enrolled in an electrician's course in Plymouth and fell in love with a local girl. He brought her to Mashhad for a month to meet his parents, but they said they would disown him if he married a non-Muslim. They also said they would not speak to him anymore if he continued to live in the UK; that his place was here, in his hometown. So he returned and married a local girl suggested by his mother. He is still married to the same girl, and is now a grandfather several times over.

I liked Ali the guide, his easy manner, his acceptance of fate. But I felt the span of our cultural divide, thinking how strange it would have been for a Westerner to have done what he did, return to his hometown and marry his mother's choice. A door to another world had opened and then closed for him. While we were sitting in the lobby over tea, the woman at the next table, attractive and middle-aged, started talking to him, throwing the occasional glance my way.

"What is she saying?" I asked.

A little embarrassed, Ali told me she wanted to know if I was married, and how old I was.

"She is divorced and lives alone. She has a beautiful daughter, twenty years old. She said she is a very good cook and house-keeper. Life is not easy for a single woman here. She wants to get out of the country. She wants to marry a foreigner."

A live-in housekeeper and consort for a passport, no questions asked. I felt awkward, being propositioned for marriage by a total stranger. At the same time it was sad, a poignant reminder of how difficult life was for most women in Iran.

"Tell her I am flattered," I said. "But that I am already in a relationship with someone at home."

It was a lie, but what else could I have said? Ali exchanged a few more words with her; I smiled and made a slight bow in her direction as we got up to go—something I have never done, but it somehow felt appropriate in the circumstances, and the least I could do, as if I had stepped back a century for a moment—and then we were through the door and on our way to the shrine of Imam Reza.

The main road goes underground just before the entrance and dissolves into the vast parking lot that sprawls for acres beneath the complex. The shrine is governed by a trust set up by the government, and it has been pouring millions into development recently, including this underground car park, a mini-city that opened two or three years ago. Since it came to power in 1979, the Islamic Republic has made a point of increasing Mashhad's iconic stature in the Shiite world, both in Iran and abroad.

"Every one of those twenty million pilgrims makes a donation," Ali said as we stood on the moving staircase that took us up to the entrance. "The trust has investments all over the world, even in America."

We emerged into a great courtyard, with open arches leading to other courtyards. The golden dome was to our right, and another dome, Safavid era surely, its blue tiles glistening in the morning sun, rose up ahead of us. Minarets pierced the air to the left and right. The shrine itself was surrounded by seven great courtyards, each with their mosque, built at different times by benefactors down through the centuries, from Timurid to Safavid, Qajar, and most recently the Islamic Republic. Everyone has wanted to make their mark here; to identify themselves with the heart of Shiite faith, and with the only holy Imam to be buried in Iran.

"This reminds me of nothing more than the Vatican," I muttered to Ali as we stepped off the escalator and out into the great courtyard. "The gigantism, the smell of money and power."

Ali smiled and said nothing.

The courtyards were built for tens of thousands of people, and were strewn with large floral red carpets for the devout to kneel and send their prayers on the wind in the direction of Mecca.

We wandered past a great library and two madrasahs, through an arch, and into the courtyard of the Azim-e-Gohar Shad Mosque. Gohar Shad was the Persian wife of Tamurlane's eldest son, and it was her influence that introduced Persian art and language into Tamurlane's dynasty—just a few decades after the Mongol conqueror had sacked Isfahan, in 1387, and built a pyramid of seventy thousand Isfahani skulls. The Mongols had a fetish for skull pyramids. They built them everywhere they went.

Gohar Shad's mosque dissolved for a moment the smell of the world in a shower of color and faint odor of jasmine and roses. A rhythmic procession of arcades laced its way all around the courtyard, in the center of which was a small copy of the Dome of the Rock in Jerusalem, glowing gold. Stand anywhere in that great open space and in any direction you will be dazzled with bursts of cobalt blue, turquoise, white, green, yellow, saffron, eggplant, and black tile work, much of it renovated and added to by the Safavid and, later still, Qajar dynasties.

In the main sanctuary the Qajars installed a wooden stairway in readiness for the imminent appearance of the Twelfth Imam. The Jewish Messiah, the Shia's Twelfth Imam, the Resurrected Christ: the same figure in different guises. This Messiah with three different names is the direct descendant of the one first conceived by Zoroaster. For the return of the Redeemer at the end of time is a Zoroastrian fancy. It's a powerful and attractive idea, the restoration of heaven on earth—especially if your life is one long trial of toil and trouble.

The Jews seized on the notion while they were in captivity in Babylon, when any redeeming glimmer of light in their darkness must have seemed worth clinging to. The Christians took up the victim's standard of the returning savior when Christ had been unjustly crucified and they themselves were hiding in caves from persecution. The Shiites, too, felt unfairly victimized when their first leaders, or imams, were murdered by a rival faction in the struggle for the succession to Mohammed. So they in their turn, with the Jews and the Christians as precedents, fell upon the idea of a redeeming savior, known by them as the Twelfth Imam, who would return to save the faithful at the end times.

No one, not even the Supreme Leader, Ayatollah Khamenei, was allowed to put his foot on those stairs in the Timurid mosque by the shrine of Imam Reza. Only His feet would do, and the faithful are still waiting, patient as ever.

Robert Byron, a hard man to please and the author of the brilliant, idiosyncratic *Journey to Oxiana,* gave his rare seal of approval to Gohar Shad's courtyard: "It needs no acquaintance with other styles to acclaim this court, among the buildings now existing, as the most beautiful example of color in architecture ever devised."

Ali and I strolled across the courtyard through the milling pilgrims to the entrance of the shrine itself. Several men were ready at the entrance to take our shoes and hand us slippers.

"You never know who you are handing your shoes to here," Ali told me. "Of the seven thousand—yes, seven thousand—people working here, three thousand or so are volunteers, and for all you know it could be a bank manager or a captain of industry who gives you your slippers at the door. People from every level of society consider it an honor to put in a few hours of service a week here."

When you turn in to the shrine room you find yourself in the thick of a frenzied devotion. Every wall is mirrored with pieces of silver glass that multiply the thousand hands from all over Iran and beyond that are straining to touch the *zahir*, the protective grille around the tomb. The mirrors, like Creation itself, multiply and reflect the glory of God. People cry out, weep with abandon, recite the Koran under their breath, press water bottles against the rails to make their water holy.

Imam Reza is above all else an intercessor who pleads to God on behalf of the faithful. They beseech the Imam to grant their wishes—to heal their sick, have their debts paid, solve a family dispute, find a job, absolve their sins. The crowd heaves and sways like an ocean, backward and forward to the edge of the tomb, the impassive stone in the middle of the swell.

With the press of the bodies all around me, incapable of moving anywhere except with the tide, I wonder for an instant if, in the midst of all this hope and expectation, the Imam's presence—his *baraka*, the Sufis would call it—still lingered here, independent of the wish and mind of the crowd. I would have thought that such a presence of saintliness—the "odor of sanctity," the Catholics say—would be registered only in a mind that itself was present and quiet, no easy state to attain in a clamor like this.

The rest—the emotion, the tears, the praises and wailing—was surely a self-induced passion designed to force the Imam into granting concessions. But then I'm not a Catholic or a Shiite, and so I speak with no authority. Then, perhaps everything finally is self-induced. What I did know was that my own soul didn't quiver to this kind of beat, and I wasn't feeling anything much beyond a certain claustrophobia.

Guards with long feather dusters kept the press of the crowd circulating slowly around the tomb. At one point a tall, bony man in a ragged tunic murmured in Ali's ear, and Ali spent a few moments reassuring him. I was a Muslim in training from Croatia, he told the guard. Non-Muslims were forbidden in the shrine room, and my looks were hardly likely to ensure an automatic pass. But Ali's explanation was both ready and clever, for Croatia is both European and largely Muslim.

Out of our sight, behind a curtain, women were heaving back and forth in their own devotions. As we were moved to and fro in rhythm around in a circle, another guard asked Ali the same question, nodding sternly in my direction. This time Ali signaled me to follow him, and we gradually extricated ourselves from the mass of bodies toward the exit. He knew the shrine police, he explained as we emerged into the courtyard again, and at least for a few moments they generally turned a blind eye for a single male visitor if he was with Ali. We agreed to return to Imam Reza another day.

We rose early the following morning to go to another, quite different sanctuary, the resting place of Omar Khayyam, on the edge of the city of Nishapur. The city was on the old Silk Road, and was established by Shah Shapur I in the third century A.D. For nearly two millennia it provided the world with its supply of turquoise from the mines nearby.

A thousand years ago, when Omar Khayyaam lived here, Nishapur was one of the ten greatest cities on earth. Then the husband of Genghis Khan's daughter was murdered somewhere on its streets. She ordered the death of all 1.7 million inhabitants, and had their skulls piled into the requisite mountain—a terrifying but shockingly standard Mongol assertion of power at the time. Now no one has heard of Nishapur outside of Iran. We skirted around it, passed the new science university that had recently opened in Omar Khayyam's name, and came to a stop at the entrance to a large, tranquil garden.

. "People in the West usually think of Omar Khayyam as a poet," Ali said as we got out of his car—one of the small models that Renault had recently licensed for manufacture in Iran. "But for us he's a great scientist as well as a poet. Did you know that when Armstrong went to the moon he left a gold bar with the names of nine scientists who contributed to that flight? One of those names was Omar Khayyam."

I didn't know that.

The garden tea shop was open, with just one customer sitting in the morning sun with a hookah—*kalyan* in Farsi. We sat down at a table outside, and gazed over a well-kept garden of roses and herb beds and greenery. Someone was reciting Omar's poems to music over a loudspeaker. The café owner brought out a small brass tray with little white cups and a white teapot, between which was lodged a tiny vase of violet and yellow pansies—the smallest of gestures, a humble showing of beauty. Ali poured the saffron tea, and I ordered a kalyan scented with orange.

"It's good for me to get out of Mashhad," Ali said between sips of tea. "I love this garden. I had a heart attack last year, and I need all the clean air I can get."

"That's why I come here," the man at the next table called over in excellent English. "Life in Iran is stressful. Everything is stressful. Even breathing is stressful. And then of course people are afraid to step out of line. No wonder people have heart attacks."

This was forthcoming for an opener with strangers, but perhaps the man assumed my origins guaranteed that I would be of the same opinion. I assured them both, however, that heart attacks were the highest-ranking cause of fatality in the United States, and that life there had its fair share of stresses, too.

We sat there in the light as it turned by degrees to gold. The odor of orange curled and drifted away from the kalyan, and our small talk went the same way. The soothing voice of the reader of Omar's *Rubaiyat* lifted my feelings on its melody of minor key.

"You know what he's singing?" Ali said. "He's telling you, 'In life devote yourself to joy and love...Live as if you are already in heaven above.'"

"What do you think he means," I asked, "by 'Live as if you are in heaven above'?"

"I think we are in heaven here," Ali said. What more can one ask? Conversation, good tea, the scent of orange...

"He's saying that joy and love are timeless," our neighbor added. "And when we are beyond time we are in heaven. Mind you, easy to say, sitting here in the sun."

We laughed, and thanked our good fortune. After another round of saffron tea, we were ready to stroll over to the resting place of Omar Khayyam.

It is a strange and beautiful structure, really, planted there in the middle of a tranquil garden. It is designed to represent a tent, as *khayyam* means "tent" and Omar's father was a tentmaker. But this tent soars high rather than spreading itself wide. Eight pylons, representing the tent ropes, sustain an elongated domed roof that resembles nothing so much as a jellyfish, trailing eight tails with their tips nailed to the ground. Under the dome was the simple tomb of a man who had one of the most brilliant minds the world has ever known.

Omar Khayyam was born in Nishapur in 1048 and died in 1123. He was the greatest mathematician of the Middle Ages, as well as a philosopher, astronomer, and poet. He was the author of the most important treatise on algebra before modern times, and also devised general methods for solving cubic equations that were used for centuries after his death, all over Europe as well as in the East. He was a Renaissance polymath centuries before the Renaissance.

The ruling Seljuk sultan of the time invited him to build an observatory, and he measured the length of the solar year correctly to six decimal places. Basing his calculations on the Hindu calendar, he made reforms to the Persian calendar that are still evident today. Four hundred years before Copernicus, Omar demonstrated that the earth rotated on its axis and revolved around the sun. His equipment was a revolving platform and an arrangement of star charts lit by candles around the circular walls of a room. Word of his discovery probably seeped into Europe during the Renaissance.

Omar was a philosopher, not of the Aristotelian school of logic, but of the Socratic tradition that sees philosophy as the noble quest to know who one is. He was an exponent of the teachings of Avicenna, another great Persian philosopher, who had lived a century earlier, and Omar taught classes in Nishapur on Avicenna's ideas. Omar was a seeker after truth and knowledge— a Gnostic, we might say—who was satisfied neither by the rote explanations of religion nor by the scientific dogma of his day. He was obliged to explain his views on Islam several times to the religious authorities.

None of this is common knowledge now in the West. Cultural bias always shapes history to the advantage of the storyteller, and we automatically assign Omar's discoveries to individuals more familiar to us, like Copernicus and Kepler. (Conventional wisdom also typically overlooks Aristarchus the Greek, who made the same discovery in the third century B.C.) Omar Khayyam is generally known to the West only as the author of the *Rubaiyat,* which gained immense popularity in the nineteenth century through Edward Fitzgerald's free translation. *Rubaiyat* means "quatrain," and the *Rubaiyat* of Omar Khayyam consists of a thousand joyous and life-affirming four-line verses.

Standing there under his tent with Ali that day, I asked myself why a one-thousand-year-old Omar should matter to us in the first decade or so of the twenty-first century. Even if he was the Einstein of his time, there have been hundreds more bright stars since then. But it was not the sum of his particular achievements, impressive as they were, that moved me, but what was even more than the sum of those parts. His poetry and his science contribute to something greater still—his place in the unbroken thread of human endeavor, of human love and longing and questioning. Our world today—our achievements, our civilizations—rests on the bones of men and women like him, whether we know their names or not.

The human spirit runs like a current down the line of the generations, binding us all in a rolling wave of continuous story. In Iran, this sense of shared history is in the air, and people breathe it in as their daily bread. It nourishes them in a way that we, in our transient and disposable culture, can barely begin to imagine. And yet we, too, long for that connection, that instinctual sense of belonging.

Ali tapped my arm and suggested we walk over to the tomb of Attar, in another garden nearby.

"We have no memorials to soldiers or generals," he said. "We have our poets and saints, and each of them has his story."

"So tell me the story of Attar."

"He is a great soul," Ali began, as if we were on our way to meet Attar in person. "You know he lived to be almost a hundred years old, the whole of the twelfth century. When Rumi was still a boy, his family passed by Nishapur on their way to Konya, fleeing the Mongol invasions. Attar was near the end of his life then; perhaps it was even in the year of his death, 1220. The two met, and Attar recognized the teenage boy Rumi as a great spirit. When he saw Rumi's father walking toward him with the young man a little behind, he is reported to have said, "Here comes a sea, followed by an ocean!" To honor this insight, Attar gave Rumi his *Book of Secrets,* a collection of spiritual stories and lives of the saints he had met on his travels.

Later in life, Rumi said that "Attar has roamed the seven valleys of love while we have remained in one alley." Attar's father was a pharmacist, and the son went into the family business, prescribing drugs, perfumes, and herbal remedies for a constant stream of townspeople. One day a Sufi came into his shop and asked why he was wasting his life. Attar understood the message, and left for many years to join the Sufis and to travel the known world as far as India. He also received an excellent education in medicine, Arabic, and theosophy at the madrasah attached to the Imam Reza shrine in Mashhad.

We had arrived at a small octagon built in the fifteenth century, the Timurid era, with a blue dome that sheltered a simple tomb. As we stepped through the door, Ali bowed his head and reached out a hand to the slab of stone in the center. Then he broke into song with a voice that cut through the air and dissolved the vague fog I hadn't even realized I was in. Who would have guessed that this unassuming man had a voice and a passion that could bring me back to myself in a moment?

"I sing some verses of Attar to my family every evening," Ali said, his hand still in touch with the tomb. "What I sang just now translates something like this:

'I shall grasp the soul's skirt with my hand
And stamp on the world's head with my foot.
I shall trample Matter and Space with my horse.
Beyond all Being I shall utter a great shout,
And in that moment I shall be alone with Him.'"

I had never met a man who sang to his family each evening. I was beginning to feel a genuine appreciation for Ali the guide. He pointed to a tall stele at the head of Attar's tomb. It dated from Seljuk times, Ali said, and Attar's life story was inscribed on it.

"You know that Genghis Khan's daughter had the whole population of Nishapur massacred, even the cats and the dogs," he explained. "She only spared four hundred scientists and poets in order to have them taken east and sold for a high price. Well, Attar had returned to the city by then and was working again as a pharmacist, though by now he was also recognized as a great spiritual master. Attar was captured by a Mongol who intended to take him away for sale. Before they left, someone offered to buy him, but Attar told him to wait until a man on a horse arrived. He would give the Mongol a better price. 'When he asks you your price,' said Attar, 'ask him for his saddlebag.'

"The horseman came, and the Mongol struck the deal. But the saddlebag was full of nothing but dust and stale bread. In a fury, the Mongol killed both the horseman and Attar. But as Attar's neck was struck he continued muttering his poems, and the Mongol kept hearing them inside his head. The Mongol realized he had killed a great saint, and he immediately became Attar's follower in the Sufi way. Over the years he himself gathered many followers around him, and when he was approaching death he asked to be buried by Attar's tomb. His grave is here, unmarked, under the floor."

For poets and prophets, seers and dreamers, the world of myth is as real as this one, if not more so. Attar's story reminded me of the Greek Orpheus, whose head continued singing after it was cut off and thrown in the river. I don't know if Attar's long life ended the way this story tells it, and probably no one does. But it was clear enough in the quiet of that blue Timurid dome that Attar lives on still, through his poetry and his story.

We made our way back to Ali's little Renault and headed off to our final destination of the day. In a town called Tus, not far from Mashhad, was the resting place of Ferdowsi, the author of Iran's greatest epic, the *Shahnameh*—the Book of Kings. Like

Nishapur, Tus was one of those towns later destroyed by the Mongol hordes, though in Ferdowsi's time it was another prosperous way station along the old Silk Road.

We stopped in a busy street and joined the steady stream of visitors through gates that ushered us into a garden much larger and more formal than the one surrounding Omar Khayyam. A large pool with fountains lay before a stone structure that reminded me somehow of the tomb of Cyrus the Great outside of Shiraz, except it was far more grandiose and monolithic, a squat square bulk decorated with pillars.

Inside, carved figures, life-sized, loom out of the walls, engaged in battle all the way around the spacious underground hall. The structure was built in 1934, and the sculpted figures reminded me of the heavy limbs and stylized postures of Communist art. This was a tourist destination, and the tranquil, contemplative air of Khayyam and Attar was exchanged here for the bustle of people milling about in search of their collective past. Ferdowsi's tomb lies in the center of the hall, with verses from his *Shahnameh* inscribed on the lid.

"See this man here with his sword raised above his head," Ali said, pausing to look on a portion of the sculpted wall. "That is Rostam, our greatest hero, who like other heroes had to negotiate seven challenges on his way to full manhood. His great tragedy was that he had a son whom he never knew, called Sohrab. One day, unknown to either of them, they met in battle. With great difficulty, Rostam finally managed to kill Sohrab, and only later did he discover that he had killed his son."

How different from the Greek story, I thought, taking in Rostam with his sword raised high. Parricide was the thing for Homer, as, in psychological terms, it has continued to be for Freud and Jung in our own time. It makes sense psychologically to us that the young man has to free himself from the father figure in order to make his own way in the world. But the Persians believe the same story, in reverse.

Unwittingly or not, Rostam, their great hero, makes sure that he is not supplanted by the younger generation. The old ways and the old power structures are thereby maintained. I remember Toufan telling me in Tehran that it was her duty to call her parents first thing every morning. The honor and respect given to the older generation cut two ways. It was something that we in the West could admire and mourn the loss of in our own culture. It could also be a prison that bound people to the status quo.

A few minutes of being a tourist at the shrine of Ferdowsi was enough for me, and after my day of the tombs, I was glad to return to a quiet evening in the hotel in Mashhad. I wanted to spend some time with myself and with Rumi.

I lay down on my bed and gazed absentmindedly at the wallpaper with its yellow flowers and green branches. I had just completed a day with the saintly dead, a miniature version of the pilgrimage I had made a few years before in Turkey, the one that had culminated at the tomb of Rumi. I had never done anything like this in Europe; I had never been called to tramp around the shrines of the saints in Italy or France.

But then Omar, Attar, and even the story of Ferdowsi, whose work I had never read, had struck me more deeply than any saint. Like Rumi himself, these men seemed more fully human to me than those who spurned this world for some other, more perfect realm. They were lusty with desire and wine and song, even as their desire hooked into a deeper vein. I opened my Rumi book, and read these lines:

> *He descends into dirt*
> *and makes it majesty.*

> *Be silent now.*
> *Say fewer and fewer praise poems.*
> *Let yourself become living poetry.*

Late the next afternoon, Ali and I made our way for the last time to the shrine of Imam Reza. It was the first night of Muharram. Just as we were entering the first courtyard, a large band of Pakistani pilgrims came filing out of an archway. They were singing at the top of their voices and beating their heads and their breasts with a shocking intensity. A tall man with a long black banner was leading them around the complex. It was a powerful sight. Tears were streaming down their faces, and it felt to me as if their grief was no longer only for the death of Hussein, but that they had tapped down into the universal well of grief, the fountain of sorrows, and even I, who had no feeling for Hussein at all, felt moved in some way beyond my own comprehension.

Ali noticed my reaction and said that he once brought an Englishwoman here during Muharram and she had cried along with the pilgrims and had been sufficiently touched to make a large donation to the shrine before leaving. My own feelings did not stretch that far.

We passed a man in a white turban and a long, camel-colored gown standing ready to read the Koran to the illiterate, though no one seemed to be taking advantage of his services. As dusk fell, a group of elderly men with brooms walked through the courtyard singing. They had just finished their work, Ali informed me, and they ended each day chanting together as they filed out of the shrine.

We stayed just long enough for me to take in again the image of the golden dome and the Timurid mosque commissioned by Gohar Shad. Then, on our way back to the hotel, we came to a crossroads in the center island of which was a beautiful small building: an octagon with, of course, a dome that shimmered blue in the evening light. When Ali told me it was the tomb of a famous Sufi, Sheikh Mohammed Mohmen, I suggested we drop in for a few minutes.

It was the one haven of peace and tranquillity that I found in that grubby and sprawling city. Until recently, Ali said, the sheikh's followers had always gathered in the building across the street, continuing a tradition of four hundred years since the sheikh had died. But the government had recently ordered it closed, apparently nervous about the large crowds that gathered there. A few old men were sitting on the floor, lips moving silently in prayer, foreheads pressed intermittently against a prayer stone made of clay. I joined them for a while and felt the centuries of devotions to which this little building had been host. I picked a prayer stone from the basket and, like the others, pressed my forehead against it. As I did so, a few flakes crumbled away from the edges. Like us, it was made of mud; and like us, it would eventually return to light and air.

As we drew past the hotel later that evening, Ali and I had our final exchange. I was leaving the next day to meet an unusual man in Shiraz. I told Ali there was no need to drive all the way down the street simply to turn and drop me off at the door of the hotel. It would be easier if I got out on the side of the street we were driving down, and crossed the road to the hotel myself.

"You cannot cross the street alone," Ali replied sternly. "It would be to my everlasting shame if anything happened to you here in my city."

# the sorrow in shiraz

I arrived in Shiraz to find the city transformed by the ritual of Muharram. In every quarter of the city, tents had been set up for men to gather in rows and sing plaintive songs while striking their chests in unison. Muharram was in full swing, and "swing" they did—swing whips over their shoulders to strike their own backs—though it's much tamer now than it used to be. Before the last Shah's time the marchers were bare-chested and would use real chains. In some towns, even today, they cover themselves in mud. In Iraq, some mourners still strike their forehead with a sword.

In every quarter of Shiraz now there was a house with a black flag on the roof where people came to listen to a series of clerics recount the story of Imam Hussein—each trying to make the crowd weep more loudly than the last. A cleric would speak for twenty minutes, and if he was not getting the desired result, he would break out into song. Everyone knows that a song can pierce the heart more quickly than a lecture.

Hussein's story transcends time and continues to move millions. Even the current president of the United States bears his name. This is what happened. Hussein's father, Ali, the husband of the Prophet's daughter, Fatima, was murdered in 661. Ali was also the caliph—the successor to Mohammed and Allah's representative on earth—and on his death, his chief opponent, Muawiya, succeeded him as head of the state. At the time there was a political faction known as the Party of Ali, which supported the succession of Ali's sons, who were the only direct bloodline of the Prophet himself. This was the fledgling Shia community.

Muawiya—the usurper, the Shiites say—was succeeded by his own son, Yazid, who took control of the Ummayid kingdom of Iraq and Syria. Yazid was a tyrant and generated broad popular dissent. Hussein never accepted the Caliphate of Yazid. The Shiites would say that he always stood for a return to the religious and ethical principles of the Prophet rather than the pursuit of glory and power. When the Shiites of Kufa, a small town in Iraq, called upon Hussein to come and accept the leadership of their community and ultimately of the whole of Islam, he felt honor bound to respond, in the cause of truth and justice in the face of tyranny.

Hussein set out with a small group of followers to Kufa. The caliph Yazid, meanwhile, ordered the governor of Kufa to intercept Hussein. The evil governor, known for his merciless cruelty, surrounded Hussein's little band at Karbala, in Iraq, with four thousand men. But on the morning of the battle, the governor's chief commander, Hur, whose name means "Freedom," felt duty bound to follow his conscience and defect to the side of Hussein. Hur was one of the first to be killed, and Hussein's entire party was massacred and beheaded. This battle was the event that sealed the division between Shiite and Sunni Muslims from that time onward.

It's a great story. One of the greatest, with all the characters and plotline you need to ensure its telling and retelling down through the centuries. You have the spiritual leader wrongfully deprived of his role as the head of Islam, who is willing to accept the supreme sacrifice for the cause of truth and justice. You have the evil governor, in the shadow of the tyrant Yazid, with his vastly greater force. And then there is the moral and spiritual dilemma of Hur, who after a night of inner torment has a change of heart and decides to follow his conscience, even though it will mean certain death.

Aware of his freedom to choose, Hur represents the essence of humanity. He follows what he knows in his heart to be the honorable cause, and in so doing goes against all ties of family, society, and class. Finally, it's a story of betrayal, with Hussein responding to a call that turns out to be false. After Mecca, Hussein's mausoleum in Karbala, Iraq, is the major pilgrimage destination for Shia Muslims worldwide.

A nineteenth-century Englishman traveling in Persia is said to have seen a crowd of men marching down the road, chanting and whipping themselves. When he asked what they were doing, they told him they were mourning the death of their saint, Imam Hussein.

"When did he die?" the Englishman asked.

"A thousand years ago and more."

"News travels slowly here," the Englishman said.

Just what you'd expect an ironic Anglo-Saxon to say. But what his dry humor neglects to account for is the power of symbol—the way an event can become emblematic of subsequent events on down through history.

More than once in Iran I heard people comparing the plight of the Palestinians to that of Imam Hussein. Like Hussein, the Palestinians are besieged by a vastly superior force, while they themselves have almost nothing with which to defend themselves. The fact that Palestinians are Sunni Muslims does not diminish the power of the association for Iranians: the small guy on the right side against the big guy on the wrong side.

The martyr is never truly defeated because he has faced death willingly and without fear. His memory will live on forever through the collective ritual that celebrates it. The whole drama of Gaza is deliberately equated by the Iranian government with Hussein. The blood of the martyr, the story goes, will eventually triumph over the sword.

In the late afternoon hundreds, maybe thousands, of men and boys, black silhouettes all, are thronging the Shah Cheragh (King of the Light), the main street in Shiraz leading to the great mosque of the same name. The dome of the mosque at the end of the street seems somehow at odds with this dark and somber crowd, its blue bulk in relief against the lighter blue of a clear winter sky.

Solemn lines march in the middle of the road to the beat of a great bass drum. Three steps forward, turn to face the opposite, parallel line of marchers, flick a scourge over your shoulder, then three steps forward again, and so on. Their voices rise and fall to the beat of the drum. *Ya Hussein! Ya Hussein!* The procession moves forward to the rhythm, led at the very front by a large and riderless white horse—a graphic symbol of Hussein's martyrdom. Interspersed throughout the procession, open vehicles carry giant models of Hussein's mausoleum in Karbala, while men hoist outsized puppets of the principal characters into the air. The scene goes on for hours, well into the early morning.

Long before the end I began to feel like a voyeur, untouched and even flat in response to the solemn ritual. I felt I was watching an institutionalized street procession—which I was—rather than any spontaneous upwelling of feeling, such as I had seen on the part of the Pakistani group just the day before in Mashhad.

For a moment I even felt a kinship with the nineteenth-century Englishman.

Leaving the crowd to its sorrows, I walked back through the dark and deserted streets to my hotel. I was almost there when a policeman emerged from the shadows and asked for my identification papers. I told him the hotel had my passport, which was the only identification I had.

"What is your business in Shiraz?" he asked.

"I am here to meet Amir Mahalatti."

The policeman, a slender man in his twenties, looked up at me in surprise. His gaze softened. Everyone in Shiraz knew Amir Mahalatti.

"You should not walk the streets alone at night," he said. "It can be dangerous. I will come with you to your hotel and check your passport."

"Amir Mahalatti. You have to meet Amir Mahalatti," a friend had said as I was leaving New York for Tehran. "He leads a double life. He spends half his time teaching at the Religion Department of Oberlin College in Ohio, and half in Shiraz. He specialized in politics and international relations, and was Iran's ambassador to the United Nations for a while. But then, when his father died, he went to McGill to study religion in honor of him. His family has held the senior cleric's post there for generations, and the community begged him to return to fulfill his duties. He felt a responsibility to both the Shirazi community and his family legacy, so he worked out a compromise that allows him to live in two worlds."

That is why, the day after I had been stopped by the policeman, I was tapping as instructed on the metal door at the end of a small alley just off Zand Boulevard. A short, neat-looking man with a carefully cropped beard opened the door and ushered me into a small garden. Among some trees was a house with a fine Qajar-looking tile picture on the exterior wall. There at the door stood Amir Mahalatti, whose father, for many years the chief cleric of Shiraz, had built the house to his own design some forty years earlier.

Somewhere in his early fifties, tall, with dark hair brushed neatly to one side, he was wearing a stylish light woolen shirt buttoned all the way to its Indian collar. With his calm and dignified air, Amir gave the immediate impression of a man at ease with himself.

I followed him into the house and was shown to a seat by a low table in a reception room that opened onto a library. Amir's mother, whose home this was, sat demurely in black by his side, while a cousin from L.A. named Zeba, appropriately but fashionably dressed, sat next to her.

I asked about the library. Amir told me it had been his father's, and that it was a collection of theological and religious texts.

"You know, my father was more than a father to me, he was my closest friend. He was the kindest, most heartfelt person I have ever met. A lot of people felt like that about him. I will never forget his funeral. I was standing there in tears when I saw a huge flower crown being brought to the grave and on it was written 'From the Jewish Community.' There was a man accompanying it in tears, and he told me he was the leader of the Jewish community of Shiraz. 'You are not alone,' he wept. 'We lost our father, too, when your father died.' There was a whole group of them, and they came up to me and told me how grateful they were for all the years my father and also my grandfather had protected them. When my grandfather died, even the Jews in Tehran performed a special ceremony for him. Since then we have kept his legacy alive with a commemoration and religious rituals."

The man who had opened the gate for me came in with a tray of tea. There was a plate of small round biscuits and the usual glass cups with ornate silver handles.

Over tea, with his mother and cousin sitting quietly by, I brought up the question of Amir's life in two cultures. It must need quite an adjustment, I said, to go back and forth between one of the most liberal of liberal arts colleges in the States to a senior clerical position in the conservative city of Shiraz in Iran.

Amir laughed at the understatement. When, some years before, he had first agreed to assume the family's clerical role in Shiraz, he hadn't even known how to tie his turban. He'd had to go through a crash course in all the protocol. Now he led prayers for a few days in the main mosque when he was here, which was during his vacations from Oberlin.

"I greatly appreciate my life in two worlds," he said. "It places me in the position of an outsider, and an outsider is less constricted by the prevailing rules and conventional wisdom precisely because of his outsider status. In that sense I have a great advantage over my father. I can be more curious. I can feel free to ask questions. What is the meaning of this or that ritual? My father never questioned the custom of collective weeping, for example. He was born into a culture that considered it normal, so it never occurred to him to question its philosophical foundations. Whereas I am free to ask these questions. I don't feel imprisoned by these rituals. I'm curious about them. Perhaps living in two worlds even helps me move more toward the essence of the tradition rather than merely being content with its form. It certainly frees me to say things others wouldn't think of saying."

He had given a sermon a couple of years earlier in the mosque where his great-grandfather used to lead prayer. His family has been going there since the mid-nineteenth century. It was at the end of Ramadan. There was a *hadith* (one of the sayings of Mohammed recorded by his followers) that spoke of the right to beauty.

Amir spoke about how it was our responsibility to wear the best clothes we could afford, because we owed it to others to satisfy their right to beauty. Then he spoke about sound pollution.

Loudspeakers were always used in mosques, and the preachers would often shout into them, thereby losing not only the point of their message but also causing discomfort to the ears of their audience. He said they should be mindful of how they used their voices, both in loudspeakers and also when they prayed and spoke to each other. A follower of his grandfather hugged him afterward and thanked him for mentioning the unmentionable.

I said that I had seen the processions for Ashura the night before, and asked Amir if he had ever taken part in the flagellation ritual. He hadn't, he said, except in a symbolic sense. He always thought that hitting oneself was too extreme.

"In Islam we say you do not own your body; it is only on loan and you are meant to take good care of it. When you go on hajj to Mecca, you cannot even scratch your body, or kill a mosquito on your foot. You have no right to harm yourself or any other living thing. So I think that symbols should replace the physical act of flagellation."

He explained that historically the practice was connected with Christian flagellants. The collective ritual was certainly important for the culture, but maybe the less defined the act, the richer it could be. Everybody wept during Ashura—clerics wept, too, though they insisted on moderation now. His father was famous for weeping openly, and not only during religious rituals. Amir had seen him sobbing once while watching *Children of Heaven,* the movie by Majid Majidi in which two children shared a pair of shoes. He cried easily himself, too, and over many things. During the song "Don't Cry for Me, Argentina" in the film *Evita,* when he saw all those people crying in the streets, he couldn't help himself.

Here in Iran, collective weeping was an important ritual. If someone wept for what happened at Karbala, he got otherworldly credits, and that encouraged Iranian men to be unembarrassed to share their feelings.

It may also encourage sham expressions of feeling, I thought to myself. After all, whatever it takes to get into heaven. To be fair, though, the weeping I had seen in Mashhad, if not in Shiraz, did not look like a show to me.

Ashura, Amir said, gave people the opportunity to express their deepest feelings without shame. What many Western observers didn't understand was that it was all related to people's experience of their present life and circumstances, the sorrows and tragedies they bore in their own lives now. It was not just the daily, almost banal disappointments of everyday life or even the blows of true misfortune, but more philosophically—what we were doing here, how we have spent our lives, how we have missed opportunities. Were we good men? Did we have a clear conscience? Did we have time to make amends? All this could bring people to tears. It was a delicate, fragile moment of introspection that was usually taboo in other cultures. In Iran it was a religious virtue and not a sign of weakness, so men could weep freely without worrying about their social image.

Certainly, like Amir, I was an easy target for a poignant movie, especially when it touched aspects of my own life that were unlived or as yet unresolved, or when it touched the core issues of being human. We could weep freely in the dark, I thought, but there were few opportunities in the West beyond funerals to weep in the clear light of day in full view of others.

Our usual response to sorrow was commonly the exhortation to "get over it," though 9/11 changed that for a while. The public outpouring of grief was not only for the victims and their families, but for America's lost sense of innocence. An era of presumed invincibility had disappeared in a single morning.

But our most common outlet for public sorrow remains what it always was, the arts: cinema, music, and theater in particular. Ever since ancient Greece, theater, music, and even painting have served as an occasion for public catharsis.

I once stood in front of *The Expulsion from the Garden of Eden* in the Brancacci Chapel in Florence. There is Adam walking out of the garden, head bowed and buried in his hands. Eve is by his side, wailing, head raised in supplication to the sky. Their naked bodies are heavy with grief; they are not walking so much as trudging out of Paradise.

I stood before them for a long time. I felt the weight of my own imperfections right through to my bones—not as guilt, but as a fact of being human—just as Amir had said that Ashura was an occasion to feel inwardly how one was spending one's life. That day, I felt the sorrow of being human right alongside all the beauty and goodness that we human beings were capable of. For the anguish of the original pair had been captured in exquisite, if poignant beauty, by the Renaissance artist Masaccio.

Amir's mother murmured something and he stood up to usher me into a room with a large rubber tree soaring toward a glass roof. It was time for lunch, and when he saw the table, Amir praised his mother profusely.

"The ingredients of a meal matter, of course. But the most important aspect is the intention of the cook. And I know well what it is in my mother's case: to spread love and well-being. Now, here you have sweet chicken cooked with a local plum, and also savory chicken with pilau. This dish you probably know, *panir-sabji,* with feta, walnuts, and herbs. And these are green beans in their own sauce."

I thought about how Amir was both part and yet not part of two wildly different cultures. Did he feel like an outsider in either or both worlds? Did he ever feel at home? Perhaps this was something he shared with Hafez, the great poet of Shiraz, though in some ways Hafez was probably even more of an outsider in his own time than Amir was in his.

"It's true that Hafez was an outsider," he said, handing me a full plate. "Hafez assumed the role of the blame-taker. He did things that made polite society—court society—think he was an infidel. He would criticize court Islam, with all its hypocrisy and pretensions. He said the essence of religion was not what we claim it to be, that religious truth had no one specific form, and that organized religion was a prison for essence. We in the West assume this to be a modern position, but there have always been people who have thought like this. Hafez was an iconoclast, really—a courageous spokesperson for truth."

Hafez, said Amir, leaning back on his chair, was the collective consciousness of the Persians. His lines were very condensed, easy to memorize, and open to any one of ten interpretations. He celebrated the joys of this life in the very moment he was pointing toward transcendence. For example, the line

*Let's engage in love before we completely dissolve.*

"You can go to the house of an Iranian Jew, or an Armenian, and they will have Hafez like anyone else. Even the communists have their interpretation of Hafez. So, like any Iranian on the street, Hafez is number one for me, followed by Rumi and Saadi and then Ferdowsi. Attar isn't so well known by the population in general, but he and Rumi are very close, from the same philosophical school. Would you like to share a kalyan? If you have eaten enough, let us go back and sit in the study."

I had eaten more than enough, my eyes larger than my stomach again, and with further thanks to Amir's mother, we returned to the room we had come from. The man with the neat beard placed a water pipe on the table between us.

"Here is a kalyan story for you," Amir said as we drew in deep breaths of peach-scented tobacco. "A sheikh gave the novice the top of his water pipe and said, 'I want to smoke a good water pipe, so I need a good piece of charcoal. Please go to hell and get some for me.' The novice went, but there was no spare fire anywhere to be seen. 'I saw people burning within themselves,' he told the sheikh, 'but there is no real fire that you are thrown into. People are their own charcoal.' Saadi said, 'Lord, throw me into the fire without showing me my sins. For fire is less burning than the sweat of one's shame.' "

"*Repentance* is a word that can cause quite a stir in the West," I responded. "Not even to mention the word *sin*. They have become too loaded to be of much value. But I appreciate the original Greek term for repentance. The literal translation is 'a turning around,' or a change of heart. And then *sin* would be more acceptable to a modern sensibility in its earlier translation as 'missing the mark.' A lot gets lost in translation, wouldn't you say?"

Maybe it was the tobacco, the effects of which are heightened considerably by its passage through water, but the conversation was flowing now.

"And isn't it interesting," I continued, "how truths like the charcoal one turn up everywhere? Dante says the same thing about the souls in purgatory. That they were content—no, privileged, even—to burn in the fire of the knowledge of their sins. It's like you said about Hafez saying that spiritual truth is universal, that it's the property of no one religion."

Amir was about to respond when a man appeared at the door, slightly stooped as in a posture of humility. He was in late middle age and dressed very simply. He began speaking with what I assumed was a substantial introduction of *taarof*, the formal Iranian etiquette that would be needed in a moment like this. For the next ten minutes he and Amir engaged in conversation, and I sat back with an occasional puff of the kalyan.

"That was the local plumber, who'd heard I'd returned to Shiraz," Amir explained when the man left. "He had no concern about interrupting us because we don't have the same boundaries here as there are in the West. He wanted to tell me about his family, to hear news of me and my brother, who is a doctor in Michigan now, and to pay his respects. That's how it is here. You live in a large web of connections, and sometimes interruptions, all of which have to be honored, across all social and class levels. You have to learn to manage all this, and your privacy within it."

By contrast, in the West, most people, including Amir, had to learn to manage loneliness. One of the things he loved about his dual lifestyle was that he lived in these two domains—one of personal freedom, the other of connection—and one continually came at the cost of the other. Belonging in Iranian culture was a given, but it came at the expense of time for privacy and individuality, whereas the converse was true in the West.

I knew in my own life that personal freedom, too, came with a price, and it was precisely the loneliness Amir had mentioned. Perhaps it was this that was prompting Amir to look for a wife. Amir was unmarried and was quietly putting the word out through his family connections in Shiraz that he was looking for a suitable partner, one who was Muslim, and ideally Iranian— more important, a woman who would be able to navigate and embrace his two worlds.

"Let me give you an example of the threads that bind us together here," he went on. "My grandfather had the greatest calligrapher of the time as one of his clerical aides. Recently I met the son of this man for the first time. He was writing his will, and he wanted to bequeath everything to a charity clinic founded by my father. All he asked in return was to be buried next to his father, who was buried next to my grandfather in our family tomb, such love had there been between them. His attachment to a family friendship extended to wishing to share in the afterlife with us. The next day I went to the mosque to pray, and there before me was the calligraphy of the man's father. In that moment I felt a profound connection to this man I had barely met—a man who wanted to be buried next to his father in our family tomb."

The water pipe was taken away and we sat for a few moments in a peach-scented silence. We agreed to meet the following day at the madrasah of Amir's father, for the ongoing rituals of Muharram.

The madrasah was on the Char Sheragh, the avenue where I had first seen the Ashura procession. When I met him at the gate the next morning, Amir ushered me into a courtyard, in the center of which was an orange tree. Beneath the tree was the tomb of his father, and Amir stooped for a moment to murmur some prayers. Men and women were milling about in the courtyard and on the terrace above that looked down on it. From somewhere I could hear the rhythmic chanting of men's voices.

Amir took me down a narrow passage to the office of the leading scholar of the school. When he had introduced us, Amir went up to the second floor to listen to someone's sermon. I should join him there when I was ready, he said. The scholar and I looked at each other uncertainly, neither of us speaking the other's language. He was an imposing figure with an impressive beard, glasses perched on his nose, a white turban, and long brown cloak.

He brightened suddenly, as if struck with a good idea, and led me out to the library. All the books were in Arabic or Farsi. I felt like a fraud looking at them, with no idea what I was looking at. In a few minutes I had shaken his hand and was clambering up the stairs to the second floor, where a large pile of shoes were scattered around the entrance to a long white hall. Some cleric was recounting the story of Imam Hussein. Men were sitting all the way around the room. Some wore turbans, but most were ordinary men such as you might see on the street. One or two appeared to be beggars, here perhaps for the food that would be served at the end of the sermon.

Amir was sitting, his back erect, some way down the hall with a couple of other clerics. I listened for a while, then went out to take in the sun on the terrace. Others were doing the same, and the courtyard below was filling up. When I returned to the hall, the cleric was singing his finale, and most of the room was in tears.

"They fed four thousand people today in the madrasah," Amir told me later, back at his house. "People throng there on this day because the food is a gift from Imam Hussein."

I, too, was a guest of Hussein, via his servant Amir. We had returned to his house for another lunch, this time of chicken in some sort of korma sauce served with saffron pilau.

"You remember the orange tree in the madrasah? Well, my father acquired the madrasah property from a Jewish lady. He was told she might consider selling it, and it was perfect for his dream of building a madrasah. It is directly on the road to Char Sheragh shrine. She told him she would like to sell it, only she had to divide the proceeds between all her children, so there wouldn't be enough to buy another, smaller house for herself. 'Don't worry, I'm sure something good will come of this,' my father said. Soon afterward she was approached by members of the Baha'i faith, who offered her double the price. 'I cannot accept,' she said, 'because I have already promised it to a good man, a true man of God.' My father got to hear of this, and knew what to do. He bought a house for the lady, presented her with the keys and the deeds, and also the original price for her house.

"Just before she left, she prayed with all her heart under the orange tree in the courtyard that the madrasah would do good work and the life of the cleric would be blessed. My father saw the depth of her prayer and was profoundly moved. Twenty years later he died. The family had a famous mausoleum, but I decided to bury him under the orange tree in the place he loved so much. The hole was dug the next day, and when I went there I saw that the roots of the orange tree were cradling the coffin."

The roots of a Jewish orange tree cradling the body of a Muslim cleric in Iran: the feeling with which Amir recounted this story was not something I would have imagined being witness to in Iran. It was a feeling of love extended between the members of religions traditionally antagonistic toward each other. It was a feeling that challenged my own notions of Islam, especially Iranian Islam.

I had always assumed—and with plenty of contemporary evidence—that one of the founding principles of Islam was the jihad, the just and holy war against all unbelievers. I knew that many Muslims interpreted jihad symbolically, to mean the struggle with one's own "sins" (for want of a better word), but still, politically, on a national scale, the external interpretation was the one in the news.

Amir led me into the reception room for another kalyan.

"If only we could depoliticize religion," he sighed, lighting the charcoal and puffing away.

The reality, he said, was that the Muslim faith was inclusive. There were more verses in the Koran on Moses, Mary, Jesus, and Abraham than there were on the Prophet Mohammed. Islam believed in all these prophets. Everything depended on the interpretation of the text. It was true that in recent years the religion had been used for political purposes that had very little if anything to do with the spirit of Islam.

Early in Islamic literature the major enemy was always seen as the self. That was the true jihad. Appreciate others and examine the self—that was the core of the religion. In fact, appreciation for others and apology for one's own shortcomings, in terms of a self-accounting, was at the heart of every faith, Amir said, taking a last draw on the kalyan and passing it to me. The only divide was not between religions, but between moderates and radicals, in all traditions.

How true this was, and for politics as well as for religion. We'd only recently disposed of a radical administration in America. The rhetoric of Bush and Ahmadinejad was eerily similar, and they seemed merely to add to each other's causes. Fundamentalist Christians could sound as shrill as their Muslim counterparts, while most Christians and Muslims lived their faith without seeking to change that of others.

Before leaving, I asked Amir if he knew of anywhere I might witness a performance of *tazieh,* the street theater commemorating the story of Imam Hussein. Abbas Kiarostami had recently made a film called *Looking at Tazieh,* whose subject was not the play so much as the audience. It showed them weeping, cheering, shouting insults, laughing. I wondered if this was still a common sight. Amir said he didn't think so, that this kind of innocent identification with the story only happened now in remote rural settings. He called to his secretary and they spoke for a few moments.

"There is a performance this afternoon on the outskirts of town," he said. "We will call a taxi for you and tell him where to drop you."

I understood now why my friend back in New York had wanted me to meet Amir. He had a nobility of character such as I had rarely encountered. He struck me as an embodiment of feeling intelligence and curiosity, the finer qualities of being human. I rose to leave, and as we parted, we agreed to continue our conversation back in America.

The taxi dropped me off by a grass-covered roundabout on the edge of Shiraz. With the traffic whining all around them, a small crowd on the grass was watching some figures dressed in colorful costume and brandishing long wooden swords. There was Hussein, played by a young man in a flowing robe, and there was a doleful white horse tethered to one side. There was the evil Yazid and the noble Hur.

This, then, was the tazieh, the passion play of Imam Hussein, being performed live on a traffic circle. I remembered Pari Saberi, the theater director, telling me how the good characters always sang their parts, while the bad ones spoke theirs. Not so long ago, she had said, the man who played the villain Yazid used to fear for his life, and at the very least was pelted with eggs. The roles were passed down in the family from father to son through the generations.

That day, in Shiraz, the performance was lackluster, and it didn't hold my attention for long. Most of the audience had brought food and were making a family outing of it, with no great concern for what the characters were doing. It would doubtless have been more stirring out in the country, in some small village as yet untouched by the skepticism of the modern world. But the fact that renowned talents such as Saberi and Kiarostami were reviving the tazieh as a theme for their work seemed to suggest how meaningful these old rituals still were for the Iranian soul.

"Capturing the slightest emotions of people's lives is always a political act," Kiarostami once said in an interview about his film. "There is a natural tendency for laughing and crying in everyone, but specifically in countries where people are oppressed. Their first need is to find someone with whom they can share their deeper feelings."

"You are very lucky to live in a country where there is still such innocence," remarked the Italian filmmaker Bernardo Bertolucci, on seeing *Looking at Tazieh*.

Such innocence and such darkness, all at the same time. I knew of no other country where people felt so free to weep with each other, and on so many occasions. But then they had their reasons, plenty of them, beyond the story of Imam Hussein. That night was my last in Shiraz. The following day I would be returning to Kurdistan. I had received word from the sheikh inviting me to the Sufi ceremonies. Before turning out my light and falling asleep, I found this passage in my Rumi book:

> *I come weeping to these waters*
> *to rise free of passion and belief.*
> *Look at my face. These tears*
> *are traces of you.*

# *razor's edge*

The woman next to me on the plane was wearing high leather boots and a fine Italian leather coat. I couldn't resist.

"Nice chador," I said.

She smiled broadly. "Thank you," she said.

We were on our way to Kermanshah. I was heading back to Kurdistan for a Sufi ceremony and some more time with the sheikh. Somebody's father or uncle was waiting for me at the airport, a man somehow connected to the khaneghah in Sanandaj and sent by the sheikh. On our way there, Sheikh Mukhtar called to say he wouldn't be attending the zikr that evening, because a close family member had died unexpectedly, and there was a large wake taking place out in some distant village. But someone else, who spoke a little English, would be at the hotel, the same one I had stayed in before, to pick me up later on. It was the first Thursday in January, and my birthday.

Later that evening an elderly man with a kindly face and a

limp was waiting in the hotel lobby to take me to the khaneghah, the same place I had come some weeks before. He showed me through the door, and it seemed everyone knew to expect me, warm smiles with hand on heart all the way around, and a glass of black tea as soon as I came in, with a spoon for the foreigner to stir the sugar, the only spoon in the house, since everyone in Iran lets the sugar dissolve on its own.

There must be a hundred or so men in the room, mostly young, but ranging in age from ten to eighty, an incongruous assembly of finely wrapped turbans—some black, some blue or white—baggy trousers, and smart leather jackets. A blind man at the front is chanting the zikr—the name of God—to the beat of two dafs played by a couple of young men. People sit facing him in rows and are singing along, swaying their bodies to and fro with the rhythm.

Two more daf players stroll up and join in; the blind singer's voice, authoritative and plaintive at the same time, gathers strength, and soon the room has become a pulsing intensity. At a certain pitch they all know to stand in a circle around the edges of the room, and one man, dressed entirely in black, his hair down to his waist, moves to the center and begins jerking his head back then bending sharply from the waist to the beat of the dafs.

*Allah Hu! Allah Hu!* The cry goes up in unison around the room, the sound pressed out in short, sharp bursts. Up and down, up and down jerks the man in black with the same sharp movement. Other men, whom I'd noticed wearing hair nets, are now shaking their hair loose and stepping into the center to join the figure in black. Their hair falling to their waists, jet black, gray, or white, they, too, begin the sharp bending to the beat of the drum and the drone of the zikr.

Then the long-hairs join hands and bend in unison, while everyone else, including me, begins the same movement, each of us holding his neighbors' hands and sharply bending low together.

In minutes the whole room is a swaying mass of chanting bodies. A sort of master of ceremonies in baggy blue trousers and a wide black cummerbund, his dark beard cut trimly, watches over everyone from the center with large, warm eyes.

Now a few men, including all the long-hairs, have let go of their neighbors' hands and are jerking up and down in a world of their own, eyes rolled back, mouths loosely open. They are jumping in the air with each bend of the torso, and one, a squat man, perhaps around fifty years old, with a little white skullcap and eyes as wide as saucers, is bouncing at least three or four feet in the air, over and over again, effortlessly, as if he were on a string.

The ringmaster shepherds him away from careening into the others, while the daf players drum on until suddenly, as if on some invisible cue, they don't. As they fall silent, the intensity subsides. The blind singer trails off, the dancers stop and smile at each other as if nothing has happened. Tea is passed around as some of them start up again, and my translator tells me a few of them will probably be there until four in the morning, though some people are starting to leave now.

One long-hair in particular catches my eye. His face is deeply relaxed, his eyes glow gently as if he were in love. Maybe this is the point. The personal will seems to be replaced in these devotions by another kind of energy, soft yet strong, in which the cares of the world have no place. This man, his gray hair falling down his back, exudes a presence that seems to emerge from deep within his own body and heart. No wonder he looks at peace, fulfilled—literally filled—with that which this world can never provide. The fuel for his journey is the depth of his devotion, and for the moment at least, he has emerged shining, as if reborn.

Others did not have that kind of light. Some, it seemed, were simply in a trance, almost a stupor, and perhaps, like the jumping man in the skullcap, had been tapping into the energy reservoirs of the body that the everyday mind usually bars access to. One large man in a white jumpsuit and black cummerbund seemed to be willfully trying to push himself beyond his limits, heaving his body up and down with laborious breaths and stabbing the air with his right hand. But for a few, especially the long-hairs, the zikr was not a trial of strength or show of power, but a heartfelt, inspiring expression of their devotion to God.

Even though I had dropped in from another world, I did not for one moment feel a stranger. The dress, the music, the rituals were not anything for which I had any reference point in my daily life. Yet the underlying feeling in that room was the same as may be released anywhere when the shell of the heart is cracked open. It touched me. I felt able to join them in a quality of human experience that was not defined by its outer trappings. They took me out of my observer status and down into a shared community of the heart.

It was probably the best birthday party I had ever had.

The sheikh was still away on his funereal obligations the next day, but he had arranged for Barzan the driver and Sohrab the translator to take me to Dulah, his family retreat hideaway in the mountains near Iraq. Barzan was late, very late. But in an hour we were groaning along in low gear up stone tracks, winding our way through lonely peaks that should have been white at this time of year, but were strangely devoid of snow. The locals were worried. Really worried. They couldn't remember a time like this. No snow would mean no water in the summer months.

We came to a halt on a bend where several other cars were parked and a few donkeys were milling around. The elderly translator, who spoke perhaps a dozen more words of English than I did of Farsi, pointed to a huddle of buildings far below us in the cleft between two mountains. We clambered down a steep path of loose white rock, the translator on a donkey led by a teenager who gazed at me unblinking all the way down. A few others, mostly women, were going the same way. Twenty minutes later we were crossing the small stream that trickled past the cluster of buildings.

Sohrab led me around and up to the back of the complex, and there were the tombs of Mukhtar's father, Sheikh Hadi, and that of his father before him, draped in cloth of green. The tombs of the Sufi saints are holy for the faithful, and pilgrims would often come to this remote and beautiful spot to pay their respects and ask for blessings.

Early in the twentieth century, Mukhtar's grandfather was known as a saint in his own lifetime, renowned throughout Kurdistan for his austerities and powers. His picture hung on the wall by his tomb, fierce eyes gazing out of a handsome head framed with wild black hair and a simple turban. He once did a solitary retreat of 120 days in total darkness, without food. I could see from the picture of Mukhtar's father—a tall, distinguished man in long robe and turban—that his son resembled him.

The air was cold in this shady valley. I was ushered into a rectangular room covered with red carpets and with a stove in the middle made out of an oil drum. Someone was peering into a large kettle that was bubbling away on the stove. Thirty men and boys were sitting quietly down the length of a plastic sheet on which there were stacks of paper-thin bread rounds and plates of potato and onion. No one spoke; the mood was inwardly focused and tranquil.

I sat down and took my place in this world that must have been unchanged for centuries. This was the retreat khaneghah, where disciples came for prolonged contemplation. A man in the corner was praying, his forehead alternately pressed to the floor and raised to the heavens, his prayer beads passing rhythmically through his fingers.

As the last plates of potato were cleared away, a few of the men from the previous night's zikr appeared, including one of the younger long-hairs. Everyone knew each other, and greetings were exchanged in a warm but straightforward way, three kisses on the cheek or a hand across the heart with a slight bow of the head. These people didn't live for themselves alone, I thought, sensing the web of connections among them.

It was similar to the feeling I had had in Tehran, and more recently with Amir Mahalatti in Shiraz, where the individual was woven into a network of family ties and friendship. Here in Dulab, though, deep in the mountains, the ties were on a subtler level. More, even, than the blood family, it was the spiritual community that brought people together here. They shared a tangible but invisible bond.

The tea server, a young man with thick black hair and a low brow, had taken the kettle off the boil and was pouring the tea now from a considerable height into rows of small glasses. Every now and then he would stop between two drags on his cigarette, mutter a prayer, and shake a little, apparently half in some altered state. Altered states and ordinary reality had a thin border here, and no one but I took any notice.

Sohrab the translator led me outside to show me around, and we were accompanied by the young long-hair, who turned out to be Mukhtar's head disciple. Above the room we had just eaten in were three rooms joined by a balcony. That, Sohrab told me, was where Mukhtar's mother lived most of the time, though for the moment she was in Europe. On the death of her husband, she chose to return to Iran with Mukhtar and live by the tombs of her husband and father-in-law. She was a powerhouse, Sohrab said, the center of life in Dulab. It took a lot of energy to maintain this place during the winter, with snow on the ground for months at a time, and she was the one who made it possible. He showed me the bakery where she had installed new baking machinery, and a room where women sat weaving cloth.

We strolled around for another half hour, Sohrab and the long-hair chatting with one person and another. I looked up at the bare mountain ridges all around us and thought how incongruous it seemed, for such a tenderness of human connection to be flowering in such a wilderness. And yet for millennia human beings have sought solitude and solace in such wild places, beginning with the Christians in the deserts of the Holy Land. The Sufis had borrowed many of their practices—the repetition of God's name, breathing patterns, the periods of solitude and fasting—from the earliest Christian hermits. And here I was now in the presence of this living tradition.

As we were leaving, I felt the prayer stone from Mashhad that I still had in my pocket, and I took it out to show the head disciple; I'm not sure why. Perhaps it was to show my credentials, to assure him I was not just another foreign nonbeliever. Perhaps I wanted to belong in some way. He looked at me, expressionless.

"From the tomb of Imam Reza," I said.

He stared at me blankly, yet courteously. Then I got it, or at least I thought I did—he was a Sunni, as are all these Sufis in Kurdistan. The prayer stone and Imam Reza are Shia. I felt more of a nonbeliever than ever, and something of a fool. At that very moment Barzan came over and dabbed my forehead with musk oil.

"From Mecca," he said.

The musk oil soothed my embarrassment. I was grateful to him. Sohrab the translator, who had painful arthritis, mounted his donkey and we made our way at a leisurely pace back up the path to the car. Later that evening Sheikh Mukhtar called to say he was back and a driver would be around to bring me over to his family house in the city.

I was ushered into a reception room with pale green walls. It was bare except for the carpets and a few cushions scattered around. Mukhtar was dressed in a long gown, and was lying back talking softly on the phone. A couple of men were sipping tea by his side. Through an archway in another room some women and children were sitting on the floor, watching television. A woman in Kurdish dress moved in and out of a kitchen with glasses of tea.

"I assume you liked Dulab?" he asked when his call had finished. "I usually spend a few days a week there. It keeps me sane. Here in Sanandaj my life is for others. People come here or call me all hours of the day and night. Two nights ago a family banged on the door at one in the morning. Their daughter is mentally unstable and she was having an episode. I sat with her, recited the Koran, and sent her to Dulab for a few days to be in the presence of saints. It helps. Healing happens there; and here, too, sometimes."

Divided between Dulab and London, Sheikh Mukhtar's life reminded me of Amir's. He somehow managed to live in two different worlds, returning periodically to England to finish his Ph.D., and ministering to thousands out here in the Kurdish mountains. I asked him if he ever felt any tension between his Western education and this world of saints and miracles.

He didn't, he said. Dulab was a paradise for him, and at the same time he was very proud of his English heritage. It was half of his thinking and all of his education. Both places lived in his heart. He sat up, and looked at me over his spectacles.

"You know," he said, "I was thirteen when my father died in London. A couple of years before that, he had asked me to be his successor. He had been like a king in Kurdistan, and suddenly, in 1979, he was a refugee. I felt protective of my father somehow— sad that he had had to live this fate. I became his aide; I would accompany him everywhere, like a servant. People would come from here and other Muslim countries to pay their respects to him in London. He was an incredible writer, a mufti scholar, a sheikh. I used to read the texts with him, ask him questions.

"I was eighteen when I accepted that Sufism was my way of life. My father was told spiritually that I would be able to continue what he had done in Kurdistan, but at first I couldn't accept that. I had been only eight years old when we left Iran, and now I was an English schoolboy. But my dad gave me a whole education on Iran. He filled ten tapes with lectures on Kurdistan, educating me on the culture, how I was to behave and so on. Then we were invited back in Khatami's time, and there was no question in my mind that I should go. I always felt I had a duty toward my father, to uphold the Sufi lineage."

A young man appeared at the doorway for a moment, then came into the room, near tears. He sat down in front of Sheikh Mukhtar and began talking and crying at the same time. He had been accused of theft, and the police had said that unless he brought the goods back they would give his case to the detectives, which would mean torture. The boy was denying that he was the thief.

Mukhtar had known the boy for ten years. His father was a devout Sufi. The boy had been an addict, like so many young men in Sanandaj and elsewhere in Iran, and his wife had left him. Mukhtar had asked her to give him one last chance, which she had. But now there was this. Mukhtar picked up his phone and dialed the victims—he knew everybody—to ask them to forgive the boy. Mukhtar spoke calmly and quietly. I could hear the person on the other end of the phone losing his temper. He would not forgive the young man. Mukhtar put down the phone and told the young man. He wept profusely, then got up and ran outside. I could see him through the window, standing outside the door with his head in his hands.

There was nothing more Mukhtar could do. He suggested we go to his "sanctuary," where we would be less disturbed. As we walked through the room where the women were watching TV, they all stood as we passed. He led me up some stairs to a tiny slip of a room crammed with books and a computer and just enough room to sit down. A copy of Edward Said's *Orientalism* lay on his desk. He was also reading Roger Scruton, the neocon writer, in order, he said, to "see how the other side thinks."

He sat at his computer chair and I sat facing him on a wooden stool. His office, tumbling as it was with his world, seemed like an image of his duty-filled life. It made me wonder if he was ever able to find time for himself. In England, perhaps?

He laughed and rocked back and forth on his swivel chair. England, he said, was even more hectic than here, only in a different way. He only went there to study. He had to compress the academic year into the short time he was there. So he worked from 6:00 A.M. to midnight every day. For him, the good thing about the UK was that he could go into the supermarket without having to greet people. He could buy the cheddar cheese that he loved but couldn't get in Iran. In Sanandaj he couldn't go to any public place and not be recognized. It was a life of celebrity. The relief of being in England was that nobody expected him to behave in a certain way.

I asked him how he would distinguish Sufism from traditional Islam. Sufism *was* traditional Islam, he said. It was the true spirit of Islam. Sharia, he explained, consisted of the unchangeable Islamic principles that all Muslims believed in. But Islamic law, or jurisprudence, was how people interpreted the principles. It was the human understanding of Sharia.

Sufism arose early in Islam as a counter to the strict interpretation of the law. It was a reaction to the legalist, literalist stance, and was based on tolerance and synthesis rather than on divisiveness. The Sunni orthodox tradition actually brought Sufis and legalists together, so for a thousand years there were great Sufi sheikhs who were also great scholars. His father was one of these. Then, after the Ottoman Empire collpased early in the twentieth century, the extremist Wahabi sect began to expand out into the Arab world from its original power base in Saudi Arabia. The Wahabi said that they were the only true Islamists.

They are among the forces behind the Islamic fundamentalism we hear so much about today.

I looked at the sheikh. Surrounded by his piles of papers and books, he seemed so small in stature, so self-effacing somehow, that he almost disappeared amid the surrounding chaos. Not what you might imagine the head of a large mystical and social order to look like. I asked him what it meant for him to be a sheikh.

He looked up at me with unexpected directness. What it did not mean, he said, was the freedom to exercise power over others. The sheikh was not a policeman. He served as a witness that you had entered the path of repentance and were dedicated to the wish to grow in spirituality. The Sufi feeling for the sheikh was higher than anything. That's why the death of his father was so traumatic for him. He had lost his father, but he had also lost his sheikh.

Sufi relationships are built on love. People came to the sheikh who were Shia as well as Sunni. Military and political leaders came to him, too, because Sufism transcended sectarian as well as social divides. He had no organizational infrastructure. He kept no membership records. This was part of the Sufis' strength; people were unable to estimate their numbers. Spirituality, after all, was above any form of political ideology. The point of spiritual practice was to know our connection with the Divine.

He paused, and smiled for a moment, as if thinking of something.

"But I'm not a very good sheikh, you know. I'm not a sheikh at all, really. I'm just the servant of these people. They give me more love than I can possibly be worthy of. I do what I can to prepare people to live in an honest way, meaning at peace with themselves and with others. Then God will make peace with you. Human beings are restless. Sufism says, 'Relax—what is it that you really want? What is your relationship with others built on?' Restlessness is a symptom of greed. We want stability of mind. Peace of mind.

"That is why the heart of our practice is the zikr, remembering the name of God. God says every beautiful word flies to heaven. *Zikr* is the most beautiful word, and we are sending that word to a place where everyone is equal. Through zikr, people understand there are more important things than the harshness of life. Even if people have a disability, for example, I say, 'Look, you have an eye to see. Think of what you do have and be grateful for that.' "

The door swung open and Mukhtar's daughter ran in, a nine-year-old in need of her father's attention. There was no separation in the house between family life and the public life of the sheikh. It wasn't as if he had an office and an appointment book. And now some stranger had come and spirited her father up to his sanctuary while she hadn't seen him all day. Mukhtar held her for a few minutes, whispering in her ear and making her laugh. That was all she needed. She squirmed off his lap and skipped back out of the door, while he turned back to me.

"How did you find the zikr last night?" he asked.

I told him it was one of the best birthdays I'd had, and thanked him for the way I was so warmly welcomed. I mentioned the wide-eyed man who jumped up and down like a spring, and asked where he got his energy from.

"We let people express themselves in their own way, because everyone has a different heart. He probably sees things in the other world. He is also a singer, and communicates his feeling powerfully with his voice. I usually draw him into the middle of the circle because he needs space and I give it to him. He knows the angels and the sheikh are there to protect him. He actually has a deep connection with my father."

There was a question I had wanted to ask him since we first met. I had heard that the Sufis in Kurdistan sometimes performed extreme practices, like swallowing coals or piercing their skulls with knives. I wanted to know if these things happened in his community, and if so, what their purpose was. I had half expected to see something like this at the zikr the night before, and was half disappointed when I didn't.

"Yes, these things do happen," Sheikh Mukhtar replied, looking up at me briefly. "Every religion believes in miracles, and we see these activities as an extension of the miracles of the Prophet and the power of God. The miracle is the healing that takes place afterward, without any surgical assistance, only prayer. The person feels the pain for a night or two after, and then they are healed."

In Sufism, he said, they spoke of the seven veils or states that you had to pass through to reach the final state of union. For these extreme practices a man had to be in the state they called *hal,* an Arabic word meaning "condition." Hal was a grace that could not be acquired or retained through one's own efforts. It was a gift from God that might occur when the soul was sufficiently purified of its attachments to the material world. In this state men would see a rock as a small sugar cube. They were conscious, but they saw with different eyes. They would see hot water to be cold, or they would eat pesticide and see it as pure water. This was a characteristic of the state of hal, not a willful act of mind.

*Not a willful act of mind.* I had seen fakirs in India who had stood on one leg or lived in a tree for years at a time, and I knew of medieval Christians like Saint Simeon, who lived perched on a pillar for much of his life. The willful subjugation of the body was precisely what these Hindus and Christians had in mind. These Sufi practices, it seemed, had a different purpose. The extraordinary feats were a result, and not a cause, of the practitioner's heightened state.

In Kurdistan, in the feudal system, the local governors would stop Sufi gatherings to show that their power was greater than that of the sheikhs, who exerted a strong influence in the community. To reassure the authorities that they were only interested in spiritual and not political power, the sheikhs would allow their followers to demonstrate miraculous powers, such as walking through fire. This commonly satisfied the governors, who, convinced of a sheikh's purely spiritual intentions, would permit the Sufi gatherings to continue. So, externally, these feats had a political function. Beyond that, their purpose was to increase the faith of others by the demonstration of supernatural powers. It was also an equalizer of sorts. People respected you for your spiritual powers, whatever your station in life. There were garbage collectors in Mukhtar's community who were highly esteemed because of who they were spiritually. For the practitioner himself, these feats deepened his desire to continue the spiritual journey with renewed faith and energy.

I had to ask: Was it too late for me to witness these extraordinary practices?

Sheikh Mukhtar was silent for a moment.

"It might be possible," he said eventually. "I can ask some people; perhaps we can have a private gathering in the next day or so. It's not so easy now, because people are working the next day. This is why our zikr is always on Thursday evenings, because it is a holiday the next day. But we shall see. Of course, one can never guarantee what will actually happen in these situations. Perhaps nothing, perhaps everything. It all depends on the spiritual atmosphere. It can never be done to order. We don't like to practice these activities often because it is a burden and a pain that I and others have to bear."

His daughter ran in again and curled into his lap, gazing at me with liquid eyes like almonds. It was time for them to have some time together. We took the cue and began to go downstairs.

"One thing about last night—why do some of the men not cut their hair?"

"Because the body is part of our prayer," Mukhtar answered,

holding his daughter in his arms. "Your bodily parts are witness to your actions. My hand is a witness that I have prayed. So is my hair. The longer the hair, the more living cells can be witness to your devotions. There is a verse in the Koran that says all living things—plants, trees, vegetable life—are constantly praying to God, and they are witness to the prayers you make. So, when we pray, every cell of our body prays also, down to the tip of a single hair. Most of the prophets had long hair, including Jesus, so we say it is in the tradition of the prophets."

Two days later, the day before my flight back to Tehran, I got a call from the sheikh saying he had arranged a zikr for that evening.

"I have told a few select people what you would like to witness. No guarantees, of course, but you may have a very interesting evening."

For most of that day my mind had been on another kind of miracle: the miracle of there being no snow in Kurdistan. I was hoping this would continue for another day or so. Everyone in Kurdistan was praying for snow except me. My flight left the next day from Kermanshah, two hours away over the mountains. Toufan had arranged for me to meet Abbas Kiarostami on my return, just before he headed off for Europe later that evening. I didn't want to miss that meeting. Neither did I relish the idea of sitting for hours or even days in a little airport somewhere waiting for the snow to clear. As Barzan drew up to the khaneghah for the evening zikr, the first few snowflakes began to fall.

"I have told a few select people," Mukhtar had said. The room was packed with men from wall to wall. There must have been at least two hundred of them sitting there, the tea maker working overtime. Rows of young men and teenagers with Elvis haircuts and slick leather jackets, and all the faces I had seen a couple of nights earlier. The news must have traveled all over town. A wave of gratitude and also embarrassment washed over me. All these people had turned up here because some foreigner was curious to see their special demonstrations of faith. But then surely it promised also to be the best show in town, the cynic in me thought. Sunday night in Sanandaj: it was either this or the gym.

They were already well into the prayers and the homilies when I arrived. Sheikh Mukhtar was sitting facing the assembly with four or five daf players by his side. When I had some tea in my hand he began speaking, first in Kurdish and then an English translation for my benefit. He welcomed me as their guest, told them I was writing a book, that people in other countries were interested in their unusual practices, and that perhaps they might be able to share with strangers a little of their own faith.

The daf players started up, the blind singer began to sing, everyone else followed along, the pitch and intensity rising. *Allah Hu! Allah Hu!* As they had done the other night, they all rose at a given moment and began bowing from the waist, each holding his neighbors' hands. Mukhtar, in a long green robe, had taken off his turban and untied his hair. It was as long as any of the long-hairs'. Moving prayerfully up and down from the waist, he conducted the others now and again with the occasional gesture. The rhythm of the dafs mounted, the bowing grew more vigorous. My hands in those of my neighbors, bowing like everyone else sharply up and down, I was aware of how quickly my mind had stopped thinking; how there was simply the movement of the body, the beat of the drum, and the guttural chanting. How there was nothing at all but an open awareness, free of thoughts.

As if on cue, the men dropped their hands and began moving in their own way around the crowded room. The sheikh stood with a line of long-hairs, all of them bowing strongly still. The dafs played on, but more softly now. Then out of nowhere a large man appeared right before me with a plastic bag full of rocks. Not stones, *rocks,* each as large as the palm of your hand. He took one out and, leaning back, swallowed it with eyes blazing. Then another man came forward, and another, shaking their bodies as the rocks slid down their throats. A bull of a man knelt before me on the floor, and as his rock disappeared down his throat, he uttered a roar.

A man in his forties, black hair down his back, emerged right in front of me with a dozen razor blades fanned out and held in his lips. His eyes wide open to the heavens, he swallowed them all in one gulp without a murmur. Another man took a skewer and threaded it through both cheeks with the unruffled tranquillity of someone threading a needle. Someone else held a red-hot ladle to his tongue as if it were a communion wafer.

A fine-looking man in a brown woolen jacket whom I'd noticed standing quietly by during the heavy bowing, his attention gathered within, knelt before me and handed me two brass bullets, two inches long. He gestured to me to place them both on his tongue. He swallowed them down and followed that up with a pack of razor blades. All the while the chanting and the bowing continued. Lest I felt completely removed from modernity, cellphone cameras were flashing everywhere.

Then those who had swallowed things began to bring them up again. Not as in vomiting, but in a snakelike way, the body writhing and turning like a corkscrew. The man with long black hair who had swallowed the razor blades brought them up one at a time—one at a time—onto the side of a daf.

On and on this went for half an hour or more, until the dafs began to grow quieter, and the men who had performed these extraordinary feats sat quietly in their own world around the sides of the room, while others came up to them now and then to place a comforting hand on their arms or shoulders.

And then it was over, as suddenly as it had begun. The sheikh raised his hand to indicate the end, and in a few short moments it was as if nothing had happened. I was aware of my familiar self resuming its seat. I glanced at the windows and registered that they were covered with snow.

Everyone sat down facing the sheikh. Tea and cakes were brought, and the sheikh began to talk about the scene we had just witnessed. These practices could never be done from the ego, he said. A person could die if he was not in the right inner state, which was arrived at only after arduous prayer and practice. I told them how humbled I was by their faith and their sacrifice. And I was. These people had put themselves through a great deal on my behalf, even if it was a form of prayer.

At the same time I felt curiously nonplussed. These men had shown me that there were powers beyond the usual limitations of the physical body. They had performed feats that would be considered impossible in my own culture. But to what end? Even though the sheikh had explained the meaning of these acts and the importance of them to his faith, I still could not quite understand.

Perhaps I was undergoing some form of culture shock, with no real reference points for what I had just seen. Perhaps the whole undertaking was just too far removed from my own view and experience of the inner life; too gross a level of proof, perhaps, for my own prejudices to absorb—as if any proof of faith were needed beyond the way one lived one's daily life. And if there was anyone whose daily life was a model of faith and surrender, it was Sheikh Mukhtar's.

The sheikh stood up to signal the end of the evening, and turned to give me the customary three kisses on the cheek. We would stay in touch, we said; and who knew, maybe we would meet up in London sometime. There was no question in my mind that in Sheikh Mukhtar I had met a genuine man of the spirit. Barzan led me out into a steady and thick fall of snow. He was to drive me to Kermanshah airport the next day.

"I think we should leave half an hour earlier," I said. "Will your Paykan be okay on those hills?"

"No problem. I will be there. Paykan is fine."

That night, alone again in my hotel room, I felt my own questions about the evening's events subside in a wave of gratitude for the generosity of this community, for the way they had welcomed me, a stranger, into their midst. That lesson found its way to my heart. I turned to Rumi, and when I saw these lines I thought of Sheikh Mukhtar and his people; how there were "love dogs"— lovers of God—in his community far up in the Kurdistan mountains whose names no one would ever know:

> *Listen to the moan of a dog*
> *For its master.*
>
> *That whining is the connection.*
>
> *There are love dogs*
> *No one knows the name of.*
>
> *Give your life*
> *To be one of them.*

Barzan was not at the hotel the next morning at the time we had agreed. The snow was still falling, though more lightly now. The traffic passed the hotel at a crawl. After another half hour, Barzan's white Paykan slid into the hotel parking lot. He had brought a friend at the insistence of the sheikh. Just in case. They spent another ten minutes attaching chains to the rear wheels, and then we set off gingerly into the morning traffic. Another fifteen minutes and we stopped to tighten the chains, which had been making such a racket we couldn't hear each other speak. Not that it made much difference for me, because we didn't speak the same language.

We left Sanandaj behind at last, and I settled back to enjoy the raw beauty of the natural environment: the bulk of the mountains, white now, and even the white ribbon of road lacing its way before us. It was invigorating, after so many weeks in hotels, to feel the elemental forces so alive around us.

Except the wipers didn't work so well. In fact they barely worked at all, which was how Barzan's friend came to prove his worth. He leaned a gloved hand out of the window and methodically pushed away the mounting snow on the windshield. We stopped every twenty minutes or so to tighten the chains, when we could no longer bear the rising pitch of their flapping around the wheel.

We were sailing along finally at thirty miles an hour, both of them laughing and nattering away in the front, the snow driving into us from the bleakness all around, when Barzan started fiddling with the CD player. In an instant we were coasting into a snowdrift on the side of the road, which by this time, near the crest of the mountains, was almost indistinguishable from the land on either side. We sat stunned into silence as the engine stalled. We were in the middle of nowhere; the snow was blowing almost horizontally in a strong wind. The hood of the car was buried in snow.

We got out and weighed our predicament. The Iranians were at a loss for what to do.

"Try to back out," I said. "But take it slowly. Don't rev up." But they don't speak English. I motioned at the rear wheels and then gesticulated to signify reverse. Barzan got in the car, started the engine, and put his foot down to the floor. The wheels spun and cut deep into the snow without moving an inch. He got out, looked sheepish, and stared at the wheels. It was bitterly cold up there, and we were already caked with snow.

"Do you have a shovel?" I asked. "We will have to dig our

way out." I made a digging motion, and they shook their heads. No shovel, and I began to feel annoyed. The idea of making it to the airport in Kermanshah on time seemed increasingly remote, but it wasn't only that. The two of them had turned up late, completely unprepared. They lived here. They must have known what it would be like to cross these mountains in snow. And they had no idea how to get out of this snowdrift, never mind not getting stuck in one in the first place.

I stood in the middle of the road. A few hundred yards farther along, a truck had stopped. "Go and ask him if he has a shovel," I shouted to Barzan—isn't it strange how you tend to speak louder when a foreigner doesn't understand you? I did the shoveling motion again, and pointed to the truck. Barzan began to look like a dog with his tail between his legs, but I was beyond compassion in that moment. He got the message and hunched off down the road.

There was a metal road sign hanging loose on a pole nearby, and I ripped it off and tried to push it under one of the wheels. Miraculously, Barzan returned with a shovel, and we set about trying to free up the Paykan. I got the two of them to sit on the rear while I slowly revved the engine and we moved back a few inches. Then I got them to push from the front, and in another twenty minutes or so we had slithered out of the drift and back onto the road.

We were sailing along again, and I began to think that our luck was turning. Maybe the flight would be delayed by the weather, and it would all work out. But up ahead of us was a steep hill with trucks strewn all over it in every direction. When we reached the chaos, a lone policeman waved us back. The road was impassable. There were no snow-clearing vehicles anywhere. Snowplows did not exist here. The truck drivers were resigned to spending a night or two on that mountain in their cabs. No one seemed unduly concerned. It was the way it was. Snow happens.

This was winter in Kurdistan. Just like it always used to be. My agenda dropped away. I finally realized—once again—that I was not in control.

Barzan looked at me. I looked at him. "Sanandaj," I said. The only thing to do was to drive all the way to Tehran by the Hamadan route, which meant we had to go back the way we came. But that would be a journey of fifteen or twenty hours in this weather. "Let's get to Sanandaj and we can take it from there," I said, knowing that he at least understood the word Sanandaj.

So back we went, with a few more stops to tighten the chains, and another brief stop courtesy of a second snowdrift, until finally we came to the outskirts of the city again. There was a little airport in Sanandaj, with a daily flight to Tehran. That flight left at 1:00 P.M. It was now 12:30.

"Barzan, airport, airport! Turn in to the airport!"

I had not booked my ticket to Sanandaj airport in the first place because I was told that flights were usually canceled there because of bad weather. Then there was only one flight a day, and it was always booked. But Barzan screeched up to the door anyway and I leaped out to try my luck. The plane was ninety minutes late, and was scheduled to take off, since the weather in Sanandaj had cleared in just the last hour. And there were "probably" seats. I would have to wait until all scheduled passengers had been assigned to see if there were any no-shows. I ran to the car, got my bags, and quickly paid Barzan and thanked him and his friend over my shoulder. For all our troubles, I felt a real affection for both of them.

The airport was tiny, and there was just one little tea stand and no food. But right then, tea sounded wonderful. I called Toufan to say I would be late, and she said Kiarostami would hang on for an extra hour. The tea server, a large bald man in a white apron, looked at me and smiled.

"Khaneghah," he said with a big grin, pointing at me, then at himself. He pointed to his open mouth, and I got it: he was one of the men who had swallowed rocks in front of me the night before. We laughed an insider's laugh.

Three hours later, when I finally was able to check in, a policeman came over and took away my passport and photocopied it. It felt odd at the time—a repeat of what had happened back in Shiraz—but I began to think that this was normal routine in Iran. I didn't think any more of it. As we took off, I realized that Kiarostami was probably heading for a plane now, too, along with Toufan. My mind cleared of its expectations. I sat back and enjoyed the ride over rolling mountains glistening white now in a winter sun.

# CHAPTER 13
## politics as usual

On my first night back in Tehran, I was told that Entr'acte had burned down. Or maybe it was burned down. Either way, the café where I had met Behzad and his artist friends several weeks earlier, the one above a cinema, no longer existed. It was an ironic piece of news, learning it as I did at a private film salon.

Even more chilling was the serendipity of the film's topic. Perhaps fifty people had gathered to watch a powerful documentary on the Rex Cinema disaster, which had happened in Abadan, an important oil town on the Persian Gulf, on August 8, 1978. The cinema was filled with hundreds of people when it mysteriously burned to the ground, killing everyone inside. No one knows for sure what happened that day at the Rex, but there are strong suspicions that the revolutionaries—this was in the chaotic year before the Revolution of 1979—set fire to what they considered a symbol of Western cultural degeneracy.

August 8—coincidentally?—was the anniversary of the day

Mossadegh, the first democratically elected prime minister of Iran, was toppled by the CIA in 1953 for daring to nationalize Iran's oil industry and wrest its profits from British and American companies. To this day, the disaster remains scarred in Abadan's memory.

The film salon was a regular fixture on the calendar of Tehran intellectuals. With the venue changing every week, a film would be shown that was not allowed on public release, and the director would be on hand to talk about it. All kinds of people were there—writers, academics, businesspeople, even diplomats from several Western countries. After the film and questions to the director, people carried on their discussions over dinner; to minimize the possibility of police disruption, no alcohol was served.

The evening was sparkling with ideas, with debates over the country's possible futures, with animated discussion over how to combine the principles of Islam with reforms that would allow a return to some form of democracy. In the West we have free public space. Conversation and debate can be held anywhere—in the media, in restaurants, in lecture halls. In Iran the only space available for the free exchange of thought was private, and the pressure-cooker environment fostered a passionate intensity.

Meanwhile, the Revolutionary Guards and the Interior Ministry were watching, and we had to be careful to arrive at the salon without drawing attention. We were told to park our cars in different streets. The government was especially worried now that Obama was being inaugurated and the Iranian elections were just a few months away.

The Iranians were used to having a clear adversary, like George W. Bush, to demonize. Obama was making conciliatory overtures that were winning hearts and minds in Iran. The Islamic Republic was scrambling to decide on a response, and the hard-line faction within the government was intensifying its intimidation of ethnic minorities, journalists, nonprofit organizations, and activists in the women's movement. The office of

Shirin Ebadi, the human-rights lawyer and recipient of the Nobel Peace Prize, had been shut down while I was in Kurdistan.

There were a lot of people who wanted change in Iran, and a lot of views on what kinds of changes were needed to get the country out of its economic doldrums, restored to the global community, and more democratized while still remaining an Islamic state. In the short time I would be in Tehran, I wanted to meet Nasser Hadian. He, if anyone, could help me unravel some of the complexities of Iran's political climate.

Hadian was a leading scholar on contemporary Iranian politics and foreign affairs, and an international lecturer on political science. He was an old school friend of Ahmadinejad's, and at the same time he was close to ex-president Khatami. As a prominent reformist he had to be careful and selective in his contacts with Westerners. Meeting me, I assumed, was no threat to him, since I was affiliated with no government organization or media outlet.

I was looking forward to hearing Nasser Hadian's own view of the complex and shifting state of the country's political fortunes. Politics was the only sphere of Iranian life that we in the West ever heard anything about. One reason for my being here was to redress that balance and to tell other stories.

But I was beginning to realize at this late stage that politics was something you couldn't avoid. For much of my life I had been cynical about the whole business of it in general, and in my twenties I had even worn a badge during elections in England that said "Don't Vote: It Only Encourages Them."

The Thatcher years had only served to entrench my opinions. Then, when New Labour challenged the Tories in 1997, I was borne along on the wings of hope and voted for Tony Blair.

But I had never done in my life what I felt moved to do just before coming to Iran, in the fall of 2008, the ink on my American passport only just dry. Like millions of others, I believed that a new era was about to dawn. I flew to Ohio, a swing state, and went from door to door handing out leaflets for Barack Obama. One or two women assured me he wasn't American, and on hearing my accent they asked if I had been flown in from abroad to help him. But even they were polite enough in their American way, and I got to listen to views firsthand that I would never have heard back in San Francisco.

If politics had never excited me until that American election of 2008, I had to acknowledge all the same that it affected the lives of everyone I had met in Iran. I remembered something that Haleh Anvari had said a few weeks earlier: that Iranians had a term—*ba siasat* (*ba,* with; plus *siasat,* politics)—that was used to mean "becoming behavior."

They have had to learn, not just over the last thirty years, but over centuries, to be politic—as in tactful, cunning, and shrewd—never to give a straight answer, and to leave options open. In Iran, politics insinuates itself into everything. I ought at least to catch a glimpse of this Machiavellian world while I was here—and especially since I had the opportunity through a meeting with Nasser Hadian.

We had agreed to meet in the lobby of the old Hilton Hotel, now known as the Estaglal. The Estaglal was in North Tehran, but it could have been any international hotel anywhere. Door-men ushered you in along a red carpet through large glass doors with gold trim. Waiters in red jackets wandered about with orders for tea and desserts. Bland hotel lobby music floated over our heads.

Nasser strode in, wearing a black suit and an open-necked shirt, and sporting a trim black beard. He gave me a brisk, firm handshake and led me out to his car. His wife was making us dinner, he said, in their apartment on the city's mountain.

As we made our way north, he asked me where I had just come from, and I told him about my journey to Kurdistan, and the saga of the snowdrift.

"You were lucky," he said emphatically. "People die here all

the time in the mountains and on the ski slopes. If you have a ski
accident, you're in real trouble. The helicopter ambulance can
take several hours to arrive, if it arrives at all. It's even the same
in the middle of Tehran. If your house catches on fire, the fire
service may or may not turn up. That's one of the reasons that
people rely so heavily on their network of friends and family."

Leaning on the horn as a taxi almost sideswiped us, he asked
me how he could help me. Apart from keeping me alive, I joked,
I would appreciate a sketch of the ongoing jostle for political
power.

"Where to begin!" he said, laughing. His own mentor, whose
name was Abdol Karim Soroush, was one of the most influential
of all religious and political philosophers in Iran. Soroush's own
story, he said, was the story of the reform movement.

In the first decade of the Revolution, Soroush, who was then
a professor at Tehran University, was an ardent supporter of the
regime's cultural restrictions on the universities and its disman-
tling of dissident student organizations. He believed in the purist,
idealistic vision of the first days of the Revolution, which saw the
Islamic Republic to be the establishment of God's law on earth.
Like the regime itself, he'd used a reactionary definition of Islam
to combat political diversity and democratic pluralism.

But by the late 1980s, after a decade of religious dictatorship,
Soroush had undergone a deep change of heart. His training in
philosophy and science began to reassert itself. Now he said that
a religion today could only thrive if it embraced rationality and
the power of reason, and that the ideal political order was one
in which religious doctrine and pluralism were reconciled. Not
surprisingly, Soroush now taught in the United States, but not
before having left a large number of changed minds behind him
in Iran.

On the other side of the argument were the conservatives,
who saw the political structure of the Islamic Republic as the op-
timal way to do God's will on earth while waiting for the return

of the Twelfth Imam. Given that the principal function of the government was to enforce their interpretation of Sharia law on the people, and given that only Shia jurists had studied that law, it was only logical that all power should be invested in a Supreme Leader who was a jurist deemed worthy and knowledgeable enough to rule the people on behalf of God.

They justified their hold on power with the assertion that the populace did not have the intellectual and religious training to be able to govern itself. Democracy was a degradation. Assured of their ideological position and in command of all the powerful institutions, including the Revolutionary Guard and the Intelligence Services of the Interior Ministry, the hard-liners were not bothered by public opinion or widespread dissatisfaction.

"It was Soroush and his more mystical approach to religion that changed me," Nasser went on, swerving to avoid hitting a pedestrian who had walked into the road without looking. "We used to meet every week, a dozen of us, and Soroush would give us a reformist reading of Islam. Before then I was a radical just like Ahmadinejad. He and I went to grade school together, and at the start of the Revolution we shared the same idealism. It was an incredible time, and it was difficult to see things clearly. Anything and everything seemed possible—social justice, equality, brotherhood, prosperity—and it was only colonial arrogance and the West that had caused all our problems and prevented us from having these things. It was the West that championed the separation of church and state, and their model was corrupt in our eyes. It was a colonial relic that had to go."

But then, he said, after the first ten years of religious rule, he and others began to appreciate the dangers of mixing religion with politics. They began to look at the recent past with a critical eye, and that was when some of his colleagues gathered around Soroush. Perhaps they had been naïve, they thought. Perhaps it was not such a good idea to merge religion and state. What was the vested interest for the clerics in having all that power, they would ask. That was when Nasser began to shift away from radicalism, and whenever he and Ahmadinejad met, they would engage in harsh debate. By the mid-1990s they had arrived at totally different perspectives.

"I haven't seen him for a couple of years now, though I have met him four or five times since he became president. He is a brilliant man. At school he was always first in everything. He was even the best soccer player. Quite frankly, I am very grateful to him. If it wasn't for his protection I would be in jail now.

"Anyway," Nasser continued as we drew up to his house, "my point is that the ideas of Soroush have become very important in Iran. There are ten journals coming out of Qom just in response to his ideas—mostly from younger clerics, but also from older ones. People in the West don't realize just how much debate and discussion go on in religious circles about the relationship between Islam and the political state, and what possible directions there might be for an Islamic Republic. It's a very dynamic situation, which is one reason Iran is so difficult to categorize. The image of the fanatical mullah has very little to do with the reality on the ground."

We had driven to the far north end of the city, to an apartment block that backed on to the empty spaces of the mountain. Nasser Hadian led me through his garage up to a spacious apartment where he introduced me to his wife, a small, demure woman who was a professor of pharmacology at Tehran University, and his daughter, who was preparing an MA thesis at Oxford on women's use of film and photography to further their rights. She had recently completed her BA at Columbia University in New York.

Both women were wearing headscarves and modest dress. The wall-length living room window gave a dizzying view of the city dropping away from the lower reaches of the mountain into the far distance. It was literally the most northerly building in Tehran. A flat-screen television on the wall was tuned to CNN.

Offering me a soft drink, Nasser showed me to the sofa and went into the kitchen to speak with his family. I sat lost in my thoughts for a moment, gazing out over the city below. Who were the mysterious *they* that Nasser had referred to in the car, I wondered. In Iran there was always the feeling that the men in office were only front men for those with their hands on the real levers of power. There seemed to be rival power blocs that were forever contradicting one another, and it was often impossible to know who was in authority. There appeared to be no transparent chain of command in any form of decision-making process in the country.

A diplomat at the film salon had told me that an Iranian American woman who had been making a film on women's rights had recently been freed from prison but not allowed to leave the country until the court agreed. The court eventually did agree, but then the airport police refused to let her board her plane.

I had experienced my own small example of this confusion recently at my hotel. When I was leaving to go to Kurdistan, the assistant manager said I could keep my room until 6:00 P.M. without extra charge. But the cashier was indignant when I told him this as I was paying my bill, and made four or five phone calls in a loud voice until finally it was smiles all around and a handshake. You just never knew here how things would turn out.

Nasser returned to keep me company for a few moments until his wife called us to dinner. We sat for a moment in prayer at the table, and I realized I was getting a firsthand experience of secular Islam right there in that house: the highest levels of Western education, free thinking and speaking between the sexes, CNN on the wall, women in hijab, and prayers before dinner.

"Ritual is important for us," Nasser said after prayers. "You need both experience and ritual, because the ritual reminds us of the transcendent experience. Without ritual, you can get lost in experience. Without any personal experience of the transcendent, ritual itself will become dry."

By *ritual* he meant the Muslim practice of prayer five times a day, fasting, and public observances like Ramadan and Ashura. Ashura, he said, the collective sorrow over the death of Imam Hussein, had given him a transcendent experience that had helped him shape his life. That was the deeper purpose of ritual, to open the door to those experiences. Religion needed to be a private and a social event, not a political one.

Through all this talk of politics I was being served the most delicate and subtle Iranian food. Exquisitely tender *kofte* in Tabrizi style, along with the most succulent lamb I have ever tasted in saffron rice. Then the burned rice stuck together from the bottom of the pan, considered a great delicacy. And to finish off, real pomegranate jelly. And grape juice, rather than alcohol, with every course.

I asked Nasser what chances he thought the reform movement had in the coming presidential elections. The situation was fluid and volatile, he said. Much depended on the jockeying of the different power blocs within the ruling elite. That was as significant as the actual vote.

"Some of us are pleading with Khatami to run. We don't know yet if he will, because there are rival factions even within the reform movement. If he decides to do so, then I think the opposition has a very good chance. A large sector of the population is desperate for change."

Iranians were hungry for the freedom to express their views. Many of them wanted the secular freedoms that they could see on the Web and their television screens: freedom of speech, of assembly, of dissent, the right to democratic process.

"Pluralism, the freedom to hold different political and religious views, is the main motivation for change. You know, Soroush once gave a whole talk on religious pluralism using Hafez and Rumi as examples. Rumi says that truth is so rich that everyone has access to a different layer. Pluralism, Soroush said, was justified by the sheer richness of truth that Rumi refers to. Hafez took the opposite stance to Rumi, though both their views justified pluralism. Hafez said God had to make so many nations because none of them could see the truth as it was. Our incapability of seeing the truth was what led to the rule of kings and the idea of rule by divine right."

But the conservative clerics knew Hafez and Rumi as well as anybody. I didn't understand how they could love these poets and at the same time hold such rigid views of religion and faith. They interpreted the poets according to their own perspective, Nasser said. Everything lay in the interpretation—not only of the poets, but of the Koran itself. The conservative clerics didn't want to accept the idea of pluralism because for them only Shiism was the path to salvation—not even Islam in general.

The meal had finished, and Nasser reached for a book on a side table. It was the *Diwan of Hafez,* and he began reading from it in his passionate, melodious voice. I understood nothing, of course, but once again I caught the flavor and tone of the old poet through the beauty of the Persian language. Even in the home of a politician, the poets were always on hand.

When I told Nasser that I had brought Rumi with me on my journey, he asked me to recite something, and I remembered these lines:

> *The roses open their shirts.*
> *It is not right to stay closed*
> *When the time of divulging comes.*

> *No more holding back. Be reckless.*
> *Tell your love to everybody.*

It was time for me to leave. The next morning I was flying to the city of Ahwaz in Mesopotamia and then on to a final visit to Isfahan before my visa ran out. Nasser and I shook hands, a genuine warmth between us.

On my way back to the Estaglal Hotel, the obvious dawned on me: politics was not just an Iranian preoccupation. It touched everyone, everywhere, all the time. It was a consequence of living in society, and was implicit in everything we did and did not do.

Art itself was a political act. This book I was writing, whether I saw it that way or not, was necessarily a political act. It expressed a point of view that was intended as a contribution to the community of ideas. Any point of view has political implications, in the same way that any form of art does. "Capturing the slightest emotions of people's lives is always a political act," Kiarostami had said.

CHAPTER *14*

# *in mesopotamia*

The city of Ahwaz spreads out from the banks of a river and is surrounded by oil wells, farmland, and industrial pall. A million people live there, many of them Arabs, since it is on the edge of Mesopotamia, near the Persian Gulf and a short ride to Basra in Iraq. In Ahwaz, the plateau that makes up most of Iran drops away toward the coast, leaving a land of palm trees and muggy heat. The Elamite ziggurat is nearby. A journey to this region, I'd heard, was like traveling back six thousand years.

On the flight from Tehran I sat by a man whom I had first imagined to be a diplomat. I had noticed him in the departure lounge, a tall, distinguished gentleman with Iranian good looks; silvery hair brushed back on the sides of his tanned, bald crown, wearing slacks and a well-cut sports jacket. His unassuming dignity stood out in the lackluster crowd. The only other person I noticed in that dowdy lounge was a mullah with a white turban and a white beard sitting impassively a few seats away. He never moved, except to register what I interpreted to be faint disdain when a woman draped in a gray chador plopped down beside him.

The diplomat sat in the seat next to me, and I discovered he was in fact a chartered accountant. After the Revolution, accountants fell out of favor, not only because they were associated with usury and profit from capital—officially inimical to the new Islamic regime—but also because the new administration wanted to keep its own books (one for itself, one for the auditors, and one for the government). So he switched to selling Persian carpets to Liberty's, the upscale furniture store in London's West End. He sent his family to London and went back and forth from Iran until ten years ago, when he retired because tastes had changed and carpets had fallen out of fashion in England.

The three men in the row in front of us were all wearing white, with shaved heads and white skullcaps.

The accountant leaned forward to say something to them, and then turned to me.

"They are hajjis," he explained. "They have just completed the pilgrimage to Mecca. Simple farmers from Ahwaz. Good people."

One of the farmers turned around and handed us a fistful of rose petals from Mecca. Handing the petals to me, the accountant said he was sympathetic to religious beliefs, but not a believer himself.

"But even so, I find the mullahs interesting," he said. "Don't think they are all religious fanatics. They span the whole political spectrum, like any other segment of the population. Many are scholars of mysticism as well as orthodoxy."

Sure enough, when I reached the baggage carousel in Ahwaz, there was the accountant chatting to the mullah who had seemed so impassive to me in Tehran. Now the same man was shaking with laughter as the accountant leaned over to relate something to him. I sidled up to them, and the mullah and I were introduced. He had come from the holy city of Qom, home to Iran's most influential theological schools and its most prestigious ayatollahs, and was in Ahwaz to meet a relative.

"Please, won't you give us a few verses of Hafez?" the accountant asked him as we waited for our bags to arrive. "Our friend here appreciates Iranian poetry."

The mullah raised himself to his full height, which was not much, and with a sonorous baritone voice, wide eyes shifting between me and the accountant, he launched into his recitation with a naturalness that was utterly disarming. The lilt of that sibilant language, the rise and fall of his voice, his bodily presence, communicated to me the feeling not so much of Hafez, but of this man himself—his warmth, his ease, his evident delight in the verses. As we parted, I noted how wrong I had been about both of them. How my assumptions follow me everywhere and shape my world until events turn up to correct them.

My hotel was by the river, and I spent that afternoon strolling the riverbank, along with a steady stream of Iranians who were doing the same. It was a Friday, a holiday. Groups of men were playing chess. Self-conscious lovers were ambling along by each other's side without holding hands. A gaggle of young army recruits pushed and shoved one another along, laughing and looking back at the foreigner, who was probably a rare sight in these parts. In the distance, plumes of red flame shot into the air, symbol of the city's oil wealth.

A crowd of men stood by the riverbank with long fishing lines out in the current, barely a word spoken between them, but a tangible sense of kinship even so. Like fishermen all over the world. Others were using battered boats to fish farther out in midstream. I thought of Faisal, how he had flung his line into the river in Kurdistan, how he would have rushed to join these men now.

Back in the hotel room I turned on the television, and there was the usual hall of earnest young men sitting in rapt attention listening to some man with a turban and beard. It was like this nearly all day, every day, on Iranian public television. It was either the mullahs or the official Iranian version of the news. The BBC and CNN were routinely scrambled. So who watched this unrelenting propaganda? More people than I thought, probably; but I couldn't help thinking that the only viewers were refugees like me, trapped in a hotel room without a satellite dish.

Ahwaz was the nearest airport to the ancient city of Susa, where writing was first invented, and where the tomb of the Jewish prophet Daniel was venerated to this day by local Muslims. Before leaving Iran, I wanted to see this unusual place. It reminded me of the religious pluralism Nasser Hadian had said was an aspiration for the reformists.

Someone in Tehran had given me the number of a man who worked for the Cultural Heritage Organization of Khuzestan. Ismael might be able to help me with my trip, I had been told. When I called him, he said in halting English that he was sorry he could not accompany me, but that he would arrange for a driver to take me to Susa, a couple of hours north. It would be an honor, he said, in somewhat exaggerated style, to invite me for dinner on my return.

The next morning an affable driver by the name of Farroukh turned up at the hotel, and we set off for Shush, or Susa, as it was known six thousand years before our era. Just beyond the hotel we passed a huge billboard angled to the road along the river. "Modesty for a lady makes her the pearl in the shell," it said. A little farther on there was another one: "The strength of Iran lies in its martyrs."

Leaving the city behind, we rolled along for a couple of hours through a plain of farmland that stretched away to the horizon, our view broken now and then only by the occasional clump of palm trees. As the outskirts of the modern town of Shush came

245

into view, my driver pointed to a castle that reared up on a hill to our left.

"Chateau de Morgan. French fort."

It was straight out of *Lawrence of Arabia,* all crenellated sandstone, built by the French Archaeological Service in the late 1890s on the site of an Elamite acropolis, to protect their researchers from raids by the local tribesmen, Arab and Lurish. Lurish! We weren't far from Lorestan, in the mountains to the east of Ahwaz, where Zizou in Isfahan came from. It was his forefathers who had stormed this fort. *Inshallah,* I would be back in Isfahan in a couple of days, and I would have to tell him how close I had come to his beloved homeland.

Even in January the sun was strong in this part of the world. It was noon and few people were in the streets. Farroukh and I had lunch at his favorite restaurant, evidently the favorite of every other driver on the road—long metal tables with plates of heaped rice and kebabs—and then we drove over to the ruins of Susa, spread out in silence below the French fort.

Susa today looks like the archaeological site that it is: a maze of low sandstone walls, never more than two or three feet high, that traces the lives and living of people over thousands of years. One of the oldest cities in the world, Susa was founded in 4200 B.C. as the capital of the Elamite Empire. The Great Pyramid of Khufu in Egypt would not be built for another fifteen hundred years; nor would Stonehenge.

If you were a slave or a priest in Khufu's Egypt, then Susa's beginnings would be almost as far back in time from you as the fall of the Roman Empire is from us today. In the era of Khufu, Sargon the Great presided over Susa. He absorbed the Elamite capital into his Akkadian Empire, though the Elamites won it back a hundred years later.

Susa's history was a cascade of riches and brutality, glories and tragedies that stretched back through the entire length of recorded history. And here it lay now, deathly silent but for the wind that whipped in sudden blasts over its stunted walls, the French fort staring grandly down at it from the most recent colonial age. And here I was, a lone Anglo-American, following my shadow among the ruins in the shadow of another old European power.

In 1175 B.C. the Elamites plundered the original stele bearing the Code of Hammurabi from Babylon. Hammurabi was Babylon's first emperor, and his Code, inscribed in rock around 1790 B.C., was the first primitive form of a constitution. Among the 282 laws on the stele are these:

*If anyone steals a minor son of another, he shall be put to death.*

*If a man takes a woman to be his wife but has no intercourse with her, this woman is no wife to him.*

Fifty years after the Elamites had stolen his city's famous stele, Nebuchadnezzar I of Babylon plundered the city in retribution, though it seems the whereabouts of the stele escaped him. Then Cyrus the Great of Persia took the city in 574 B.C. Later, Darius the Great rebuilt the city and evidently considered it his favorite residence—which was no small compliment when you consider that he also had Pasargadae and Persepolis to fall back on. Then Susa's fortunes fell once more when the Muslim armies first conquered Persia and destroyed the city all over again. In 1218 the Mongols delivered the final death blow when they completely destroyed the entire place, after which it was gradually abandoned.

It was in 1901 that Jacques de Morgan's French expedition discovered the stele of Hammurabai's Code in Susa. He brought the stele to Europe, where it has been on display in the Louvre Museum ever since.

All we had to contemplate now were these abandoned and battered stone walls, and the images and names in our imagination. Ambling along the paved streets that still laced their way through what used to be a great capital city, I tried to imagine the dramatic life of Esther, of the Old Testament's *Book of Esther*. Like Daniel, she lived in Susa during the Babylonian captivity of Judah in the sixth century B.C. It is to her that the Jews owe their festival of Purim.

The story goes that the king at the time, Xerxes I of Persia—the one who defeated the Greeks at the famous battle of Thermopylae—wanted to stage 180 days of festivities in Susa to demonstrate the wealth of his kingdom and the splendor of his majesty. He ordered his queen, Vashti, to display her beauty by appearing before the assembly wearing her crown.

But the women's movement started long before most of us realize: Vashti refused, saying she was not the king's lapdog. So Xerxes banished his queen—or put her to death, we don't really know—and ordered beautiful women to be brought to the palace from every province. They all became part of the king's harem, and from among them Xerxes chose Esther for his wife and queen, for her beauty and her intelligence. He did not know she was a Jew.

Esther had a cousin named Mordecai, and one day he overheard a plot to kill the king. He told Esther, who told the king, and the conspirators were arrested and executed. Xerxes ordered that Mordecai's name should be recorded in history. Soon afterward, Esther heard of a plot by a prominent prince of the realm to have all the Jews massacred. She told the king and at the same time revealed her Jewish ethnicity. The prince was hanged. Mordecai was made the king's prime minister, and the Jews were given the right to defend themselves against any enemy. The Jews established the annual feast of Purim in memory of their deliverance.

But despite her story, it was not easy to summon Esther's presence there on the main street of Susa. Just too much had happened before and since. The one thing that did stir me was the realization that Susa was the birthplace of writing. I had the Elamite invention of cuneiform six thousand years ago to thank for my profession. And I did thank them. I thanked the spirits of those ingenious minds of so long ago who were the source of the written word.

I climbed up to the fort for a few moments, its great wooden door barred and shut with a soldier standing by. The modern town of Shush, a quiet backwater of some forty thousand people, lay below me. There in the near distance was the tomb of Daniel the Prophet, recognizable by its conical spire, and when I had taken in the panorama, I went down to explore it.

Through the entrance gate was a small courtyard, as in a mosque, with half a dozen carpets laid out around the central fountain for teenagers to chatter on, older men to pray on, and for me to sit on and watch the devout pass by. After a few moments of watching men trickle into the shrine out of the afternoon sun, I followed them, leaving my shoes at the door.

It was a small place, with marble floors and golden interior with the tomb itself taking up most of the space. A man sat in a corner mumbling some prayers. The other visitors, including my driver, caressed and kissed its silver pillars and rubbed their cheeks like affectionate cats against the protective grille. One or two let a banknote flutter through the grille toward the tomb inside. Who knew what boon they were asking for? Or perhaps their offerings were from sheer devotion, without expectation of any reward. The devotion of Muslims to a Jewish prophet.

Daniel was born into Jewish nobility, but was carried off to Babylon as a youth and was trained in the service of the court of Nebuchadnezzar. He became famous for his interpretations of the emperor's dreams and rose to become one of the most important figures of his time, which was a long time indeed: he lived to be a hundred years old.

Toward the end of his life, by which time the Persians had conquered Babylon, he was influential in Cyrus's decision to restore the Jews to their homeland, although he himself did not return. At one point, despite his high rank at cour,t, Daniel was thrown into a lion's den because of his fervent adherence to his own God and denial of pagan deities. But he was miraculously delivered, upon which Cyrus issued a decree requiring reverence for the God of Daniel.

Miracles could make a difference, as the Sufis in Kurdistan knew. I went outside and absorbed a little longer the tranquillity of the courtyard and the trickle of the fountain in its octagonal pool. Farroukh joined me and, kneeling back, offered a few prayers into the unmoving air. It was indeed a contemplative place, the tomb of Daniel, and I was glad to while away time there.

Eventually Farroukh beckoned me to follow him to the car. We were to stop off at the ziggurat on our way back to Ahwaz. I had always associated ziggurats with Babylon and the Tower of Babel, but one of the biggest of all time was right here, in Elamite country, where it had stood for over three thousand years.

It was called Choqa Zanbil, and we found it a few miles down a side road, soaring up out of an arid plain. It was a good time to come, the sun lower now, the shadows longer, and no one around. It was the largest and best preserved ziggurat, or stepped pyramid, anywhere. Surrounding it were the remains of a town where the priests and the servants of the complex had lived, evident now by sporadic mounds and some royal tombs that I discovered were better left to themselves, their function having altered to become unofficial latrines.

A ceremonial stairway led up to the summit of the massive structure, which was built entirely of red brick. The mud bricks, all perfectly aligned and glowing darkly in the afternoon light, rose five stories high to a platform on which once stood the holy of holies, the temple in honor of the bull god of Susa. Only the elect of the culture could enter the temple, and still today all access to the summit was barred.

We're always trying to build a stairway to heaven, I thought, gazing up at the stern yet beautiful structure. As if we want to reach the gods or to become them ourselves. The Elamites with their ziggurats, the Christians with their steeples, the Muslims with their minarets, and today's skyscrapers and office blocks: the same old longing to become more than ourselves, only in another guise.

The impetus has become secular now, a vanity display by alpha males of their supremacy in the world of money and power. But at root it was surely the same motive, however distorted it may have become: to join hands with the divine, like Michaelangelo's Adam. We and the Elamites weren't so very different under our skin, the thousands of years between us just the blink of an eye. Farroukh and I wandered around the lonely mound for a few moments, gathered brown dust on our shoes, and headed back for Ahwaz.

When Ismael called early that evening and invited me to dinner, I quickly agreed. I was grateful to him for sparing me the chore of haggling with a local driver, and Farroukh had been easy company. We met in a restaurant—a shack, really—with large windows overlooking the river. The place was full of Ahwazi families digging in to the usual fare, saffron rice and kebabs, with ice cream as dessert.

Ismael's English was halting and slow, almost voluptuously so. His manner was exaggeratedly Iranian, so deferential that I felt myself squirming. He had never met a Westerner before, which was why he wanted to see me. He wanted to know if life in the United States was as bad as they were saying on Iranian television, what with the economic crisis and people losing their homes. And he wanted to know if it was true that Obama had secretly ordered the Israeli invasion of Palestine that had just taken place. Even though he was not officially in office yet? And even though he was about to be president of the United States, not of Israel?

I had heard this sort of thing before. For years now the Iranian government had carried on a relentless campaign to blame all its troubles on foreign interference, especially on Britain and America. As we knew in America only too well, negative propaganda worked, especially when the population was as committed to conspiracy theories as it was in Iran. A large section of the Iranian population, including Ismael, apparently *did* watch the official Iranian nightly news after all. They genuinely believed that foreign meddling lay behind all their woes. History had given them good grounds for suspicion, but many of Ismael's ideas were pure fantasy.

I assured Ismael that Obama was not responsible for Palestine's latest trial by fire, but I knew it was pointless to insist. I waited for him to finish his ice cream, and then made excuses to leave, because, after all, I had one of those early-morning flights to catch the next day. Even so, I didn't get out of that restaurant without posing for a photograph with my new friend. As we left, he made to pay the bill. I tried hard to intervene, knowing that as a public servant he would be earning a salary that barely gave him enough to reach the end of the month. But there was no stopping Iranian hospitality, not to mention Iranian pride.

*CHAPTER 15*

# return to beauty

A thing of beauty is a joy for ever:
Its loveliness increases; it will never
Pass into nothingness; in spite of all,
Some shape of beauty moves away the pall
From our dark spirits.

— JOHN KEATS, "ENDYMION"

I was in Isfahan the day after my dinner with Ismael. A journey like this was like life: it got faster and faster nearer the end. I took a taxi from Isfahan airport to the Ali Qapu Hotel, and the driver was so delighted to speak English that he refused any suggestion of a fare or tip. He was a student, he said. He drove a taxi to pay for his studies. I hoped I was the only English-speaking passenger he had that day.

This time I was staying on Chahar Bagh, the grand avenue that, in the time of Shah Abbas, had been graced with gardens on each side and rose hedges and jasmine from end to end. Now it was a dusty and busy thoroughfare with scooters whining in all directions and stores selling everything from jeans to flat-screen televisions and gold watches. Even so, trees still lined the divider, and a narrow water channel trickled there.

I checked in to the Ali Qapu and strolled the short distance down the Chahar Bagh to the Khaju Bridge, which spans the Zayandeh River. The bridge, another masterpiece conceived by Shah Abbas, was a favorite strolling place for Isfahanis. For pedestrians only, it joins the main city with the Armenian and Zoroastrian suburbs on the other side of the river. Girls wandered hand in hand along the wide causeway, and small groups of men lounged in the shade of the arches that laced along on either side, gossiping as the river flowed by. A lone woman stood in the first arch as if gazing out to sea. She had a bright scarf on the back of her head, and a fitted manteau over jeans. Who or what was she expecting, I wondered.

I, too, sat down in one of those twenty-three arches that lace their way across the river, and watched the current slip by. Watched its passing, the passing of my weeks in Iran, even my own passing. All of it, myself included, slipping under the bridge and away into the endless stream of human stories. How many stories had this bridge been witness to, these last four hundred years? How could I have known that in less than six months, just days after the presidential election—the election that people here were finally beginning to anticipate—how could I ever dream that the tranquil scene I was part of now would in a single stroke be turned to blood?

But I knew nothing of this then, sitting there in my own arch on that beautiful bridge whose stones were the color of honey. I began seeing all the people I had met over the previous few weeks, passing as if in some ghostly parade behind my eyes; how, despite the repression of the current times, they embodied the creative, humanist spirit of an ancient culture. I thought of the places—Shiraz, Yazd, Mashhad, Tehran, Kurdistan—that had, each in its own way, confirmed the reality of those images of Iran I had carried down through a lifetime.

And here I was now in the city that had more than lived up to my dreams. The blue dome of the Imam Mosque was the magnet that had drawn me here, and it had been a kind of ecstasy to sit in the shadow of its splendor. But Isfahan had more treasures besides than I ever imagined. This bridge was one of them. The Lotfollah Mosque was another.

Yet another was the Pavilion of the Eight Paradises. I got to my feet and strolled back up the grand avenue to the entrance of the Bagh-e-Bulbul, the "Garden of Nightingales." As in any park, families were scattered here and there on the grass with their picnics, while others were sprawled in the scant shade of tall pines and silver birches. In the garden stood an elegant pavilion with a long pool stretching away before it. This was the Hasht Behesht, the Eight Paradises, one of two surviving Safavid pavilions in Isfahan.

The name refers to a type of palace building with eight octagonal rooms around a central domed space. Each room was a separate paradise for the delight of the shah, open to the garden beyond. Beneath the dome was a fountain, and the presence of water in the building itself, along with the large open porches on all four sides, connected it even more emphatically with the garden outside.

I walked around it, and then stood and gazed up at it. The pavilion seemed to be made of space more than form, and like the domes of the great mosque it floated somehow, barely seeming to touch the ground. Two tall slender pillars of cedar sustained the largest porch, on the north side, in the middle of which was a marble pool.

The Garden of Nightingales was no more than a park now, but once there had been fountains and reflecting pools in every direction, fine walkways and riding paths, and clouds of roses and jasmine. Hasht Behesht today still had its honeycombed ceilings, and ornamentation applied later during the Qajar period, but Jean Chardin saw it days after it was completed and wrote (in his *Travelogues of Chardin*):

*Regarding the decoration and ornamentation, one cannot place value on all this intertwined glory and delicacy; the entire place is covered with gold and lapis lazuli...Various kinds of colorful marble and other stones, large Venetian glass mirrors framed in tortoiseshell, paintings by renowned artists hung behind Venetian glass, the treatment of walls with glitter. The doors have been made using woods with unique grains and the wooden surfaces are covered with gold leaf.*

I passed along the length of the one remaining pool and out and across a street that led me to Imam Square, the centerpiece of the city. I had only been there for a few days some weeks before, but on entering the square I felt the fondness of familiarity. There were the great domes, the fountains playing, the two-story parade of arches on every side.

I wandered over to the carpet shop, and there was Zizou, hunched as ever over a game of backgammon, though with his hair sticking out in every direction now, as if the hairdresser had simply plugged him in for a minute. By his side was a tattered paperback of *Pride and Prejudice*.

"For my English. There was a CD, too, but the postal service confiscated it. It's not cricket, is it?" he said, shaking my hand with a rueful smile. "You say that in England, right?"

We do.

A strange world, this, where a young man took it as a matter of course that the national post office would confiscate his CD. They frequently did the same thing with books from abroad. We played three games of backgammon and I finally won the last one. The conversation skirted the edges of religion and politics, and at one point Zizou assured me he was religiously inclined— he prayed every day, he said.

"But religion and politics should be separate. Look at the

trouble it causes otherwise. And people should be free to worship as they wish. That's what I think, anyway."

That's what I thought, too. And I thought about what Nasser Hadian had said in Tehran, that this was the most secular country in the region. Perhaps it was, yet here was a young man with spiky hair and all the opinions you would expect to go with it, and yet he prayed every day. The picture was never clear-cut in Iran.

Winning my token backgammon game was the signal to move on; on to the Jameh Mosque. I hadn't gotten there on my last visit, and I wanted to be sure not to miss this Seljuk masterpiece, remnant of the town that was here long before Shah Abbas arrived. The Seljuks were the Turkish lords of Persia from the eleventh to the fourteenth centuries. They recognized the refinement of the civilization they had conquered, and quickly assumed for themselves both the Persian culture and language.

A brisk walk through the bazaar for twenty minutes, and you see the brick domes of the Jameh Mosque peeking over the streets. The Jameh in Isfahan is one of the oldest mosques in Iran, and every passing ruler has left his mark on it. But the Seljuk original was what I was there for. You pass through a small Seljuk forest of thick brick pillars, and you find yourself beneath a magnificent brick dome with a pentagram picked out in its center. The entire masterpiece is in brickwork. I was awed by the rigorous simplicity of the whole: the arches, the pillars, the intricate squinches, the perfect dome.

The place conveyed a subtle sobriety in a hundred shades of brown. It reminded me of the atmosphere of a Romanesque church, so common all over Europe in the same eleventh century. The Romanesque arch was round, its pillars thick and sturdy, the church low and dark, the mood infused with humility and unknowing. We bow low; we pray in the mystery and the silence. Whereas the Gothic, with its high pointed arches and glorious stained glass, was all music and light; it urged us to rise to our full stature as human beings, to become co-creators with the living God.

In this Seljuk mosque, on the other hand, I was reminded of my origins in the earth, which was also the origin of brick. The Seljuks were closer to the ground than the Safavid glories of Shah Abbas. No brilliant blues, no swirling tendrils here; though the echo of nature was evident still in the honeycomb stucco, and in the half-light of this cave. For it dawned on me then: this mosque was a man-made cave, an echo of the sort of place where the first religions began.

I lingered for a while, not wanting to return too soon to the daylight world of the courtyard and the Safavid blues, which, in another mood, I responded to with such delight. Then, in the way contraries impress themselves, I decided to walk back to the Lotfollah Mosque, which I had not spent enough time in when I was here before, and let myself feel the difference.

First, though, I headed off for a brief lunch with Zizou in a restaurant he had assured me was four hundred years old. It was down an alley in a corner of the bazaar near Imam Square. We walked into a long room with Qajar-era tiles, stained-glass partitions, and an immensity of bric-a-brac hanging on the walls—old photographs, dervish begging bowls, drums, pistols—it could have doubled as an antiques shop. The back room, behind the partition, was thick with the smoke of a dozen kalyans. We sat down on a daybed, and through Zizou I ordered chicken stew and a plate of mixed and crushed peas and beans.

Zizou was not in the best of spirits. He had not made any progress on the Lorestan project since I last saw him. Or maybe it was that things weren't so good at home. He was the only one working, and he didn't work much. But when I told him I had just come from Ahwaz, he nearly leaped off the bed.

"You should have called me," he cried. "I could have come up and taken you into the mountains. Oh, there you would have seen an Iran that very few people—not even Iranians—get to see. The nomads in their tents, the women weaving carpets, the men dancing in the evening."

It would have to be for another time. I had only a couple of days left on my visa, and my mind and heart were full already. Zizou nudged me and looked in the direction of some young women in the smoking section. There were four of them, all smoking a kalyan.

"That is not good," he said, glowering. "They shouldn't be doing that. It's not a good advertisement for Iran. Only prostitutes do that sort of thing."

Zizou had the mind of a philosopher and explorer. He was his own man in many ways, and certainly not, as far as I could determine, a conservative Muslim. Yet here he was associating a woman smoking a kalyan with immorality. It sounded like the prejudice of a country boy, and in that moment I realized he was that, too.

I had seen women in Tehran and Shiraz smoking with impunity without anyone casting a second glance their way. Whom would he vote for, I found myself wondering, in the upcoming presidential election? I had assumed that all the young people I met would be for the reformist candidate, whoever he turned out to be—just a few months away, and they still hadn't declared themselves. But now I was not so sure.

We parted with a vigorous handshake and a promise on my part to look him up if ever I came to Isfahan again—which I fully expected I would, for I knew I had fallen in love with the place, and not just a little. As he hurried away to his carpet shop, I gazed fondly at his disappearing figure until it merged with the crowd in the lane of the bazaar. Where, within the narrow limits of Iranian life, would his journey take him, I wondered.

I walked over to the Lotfollah Mosque and went through the peculiar entranceway that turned sharply in the middle at ninety degrees. Coming upon the dome, I made my way to a corner and sat on the floor for a few minutes to take it all in. Then I lay down and gazed up. A melody of light played through the latticed arches. At the dome's center was a magnificent yellow sunburst, a bewildering forest of tendrils and blossoms, which, as I continued resting my eyes on it, revealed itself to consist of nine concentric circles, an explosion of light radiating out from deep within the small turquoise octagon at the very center. I began to see shapes within shapes, and to feel that I was being showered not only with beauty but with wisdom; for the intelligence inherent in the design and proportions was as tangible as the effect of the rain of color.

Streaming out from the central sun to the dome's base were spiraling showers of blue lemon shapes, each one filled with intricate and delicate white designs. Numerology is an important symbolic language in Islam, with every letter having its numerical equivalent, and it was no accident that the number of those lozenges was the exact numerical total of the letters in the words *God the Merciful.* The lozenges ended with a thin line of white flowers that ringed the entire base of the dome, and the number of those flowers was the numerical equivalent of the word *nur,* meaning "light." But what struck me more than the knowledge was the tangible experience of blessing with which I felt showered under that dome.

Its beauty humbled me, shattered my mind with its color and light, undid the threads of my thinking with its spiraling turquoise columns, like twisted ropes, and running Arabic script all in white against the deepest of lapis blue. Unlike any exercise in prettiness or mere display, beauty of this order is at the same time devastating and our salvation. Devastating in the sense of emptying us of self, of thought, of ordinary feeling, and our general notion of identity; salvation in that this emptying opens the way for the divine presence, the incursion, the downpouring of grace. This process of emptying and filling is at the heart of Islam, whose meaning is "surrender."

In these mosques of Isfahan—in the tilework, the brick-work, the domes, everywhere—I began to see the same repeating themes: the swirling tendrils and blossoms and foliage of nature; the geometric and abstract designs of the rational intellect; and the constant refrain of the Word, the creative breath that infuses life into everything. We humans are the three in one: animal, instinctual nature; reasoning mind; and the inspired Creative Spirit of the Word. These mosques mirrored our human nature and showed what was possible for us: the integration of these parts into one harmonious whole, just as they were displayed as a glorious, organic whole over this dome and around the walls.

For several moments even the guard disappeared and I was alone. The building seemed to breathe in the silence. In any event, the magnificence was so overwhelming that it drew me down into silence, inner silence, whether I wished it or not.

Finally a little girl with bangs and a sort of basin haircut and huge black eyes ran into the sanctuary ahead of her mother and, seeing me, immediately flitted over and shot out her hand. I took it in mine, and we broke into broad smiles.

The girl ran off again to her mother, and I stood up and walked slowly over to the mihrab, the niche that points to Mecca. Again, spiraling around the mihrab was a dizziness of vines in yellow on blue, and immediately above the niche was a latticed arch whose pattern was two winding vines embracing and weaving in and out of each other like lovers—which is exactly what they represented, the union of lover with beloved, the same motif that ran through all of Persian mystical poetry. In the center of the lattice, the heart of it, embraced by both vines, was a stylized version of the ancient motif of the winged man, with its echoes of Persepolis and Zoroaster. And finally, there in the very center of the mihrab, I noticed the turquoise shape of a dervish begging bowl.

We are beggars, all of us, before the Mystery. I took my time and wandered eventually out of the sanctuary, back into the dim passageway and out into the full light of day.

I stopped for a moment at the entrance portal again. Looking back up at the stalactite marvel above the door, I felt a wave of gratitude for the Lotfollah Mosque. It had clarified me, and revived my pride in the human race.

An old man was sitting stooped with a cane on the ledge by the door. He beckoned me toward him with a smile. I sat down by him and he said, with a toothless grin, "Are you happy with your life?"

"I am," I said, both surprised and delighted by the simple intimacy of the question; aware even as I answered of conditions that I would perhaps like to be different, but that did not at root impinge on the happiness I felt—especially in that moment, having emerged from the most radiantly beautiful building I had ever set foot in.

"Thank you," he said, with a broad grin. "Thank you! I am happy with my life, too. My son lives in Michigan."

The word *Michigan* dissolved in the wind. Both of us sat there in the sun, looking out in silence over the square beyond.

I felt full to the brim that night, back in my room in the Ali Qapu Hotel. It was time for me to leave this poignant, sad, and beautiful country for my own. There was a Rumi poem that voiced my feelings exactly, and I turned to it and read it out loud.

> *Late and starting to rain,*
> *it's time to go home ...*

CHAPTER 16

# interrogation, with room service

We've seen enough beautiful places
with signs on them saying
This is God's House. That's seeing the
grain like the ants do,
without the work of harvesting.
Let's leave grazing to cows and go
where we know what everyone really intends,
where we can walk around without clothes on.

— RUMI, OPEN SECRET (TRANSLATED

BY COLEMAN BARKS)

I arrived back in Tehran just in time to watch Obama's inauguration on CNN with Pari Saberi, her daughter Maryam Shirinlou, and a few of their friends. They were not especially excited. Hopeful, perhaps, but cautious about the prospect of a change of American president helping to change anything in their country anytime soon.

The following evening was my last in Iran, and a friend from the Swiss embassy had offered to hold a party at her apartment for all the people I had come to know in Tehran in the preceding weeks. Mary Ellen, the British ambassador's wife, was there, along with Pari Saberi; Maryam; Mania Akbari; Khosrow; Haleh Anvari and her husband, Shahriar; Mahsa and Atabak Vahdat; and several more. Only Toufan, who was in Switzerland with Kiarostami, and Nasser Hadian, were absent. Mahsa sang some poems of Rumi, with Atabak accompanying her on the setar. I recited some poems, and both Khosrow and I had more to drink than we should have. It was an evening rich with the warmth of good company.

As I was leaving, Elizabeth, my Swiss friend, said, "You know, Roger, I'm worried about you. You have met a lot of highly visible people. You need to be careful. Would you like to take the diplomatic car to the airport tomorrow? Just to give you some sort of official sanction."

A diplomatic car would be better than a Tehran taxi any day, though I wasn't sure what protection it could give me once I entered the airport. But why not? Elizabeth told me the driver would accompany me to the security gate and wait until I was past customs. I could signal the all-clear to him from the other side.

This all sounded rather dramatic. It was the first time the suggestion had been raised that I might be in any danger. After the first few days, when I had indulged in the fancy that my masseur could be a government plant, I had assumed there was nothing to fear. Everyone was so friendly, courteous, and welcoming. And anyway, I was not involved in politics. Elizabeth was being motherly, I concluded, which was kind of her; even so, I saw no reason not to accept her offer.

So the next afternoon I was driven to the airport by Merdad, her driver, who I discovered on the way just happened to be the all-Asia martial arts champion. Snow was threatening, and visibility was low, but the airport seemed fully functional. I went through security to check in, but for some reason my flight to

Dubai was delayed. Bad weather, they said. Maybe we will start check-in in an hour or so. I went over to security, where Merdad was waiting, and told him. He called Elizabeth, who said he should leave me there. We shook hands and I went back to wait. It seemed strange that our flight should be delayed by bad weather when none of the others were.

But finally the airline staff arrived, and I checked in and went to passport control, breathing easier now. As I approached the kiosk, an airport official came out of an office, spoke a few words to the passport officer, and pointed to me. When I got to the window he put my passport to one side and told me to wait by the kiosk while he continued to process other passengers. I waited, not unduly concerned, expecting they were doing some checks on me that would prove negative, since I had nothing to hide. Fifteen minutes passed and I began to wonder what was taking them so long.

Eventually the policeman returned and escorted me to an office in a corridor nearby. I walked in, and there were two men sitting there facing an empty chair. I was told to sit down. The one opposite me sat motionless behind a pair of wraparound dark glasses. He was a small, almost winsome presence. On his right was a nondescript-looking man with strands of hair combed over his balding head. He was behind a desk, and fiddling with a pen. It all seemed so ordinary, but I registered that it was not ordinary at all. Yet now that it was happening, it all felt curiously inevitable, even scripted somehow.

"We understand you have a problem, Mr. Roger," Baldy said, in heavily accented English. "We want to help you solve your problem and leave Iran on your flight."

At that moment a third man came in, in his late twenties, in a checked sports jacket and neat blue shirt. He found another chair and sat by my side.

"I am your translator," he said. "Just be calm and don't get angry. I told them I didn't want to do this. I am just a translator. I am too emotional for this kind of work, but they said I had to. So please, cooperate and make it as easy as possible for both of us."

"Tell us, Mr. Roger, why did you come to Iran?"

"I came to write a book to show people in the West that Iran is not what they think. To show the soul of Iran."

"And what else?"

"That's it. Nothing else."

Shades shook his head slowly from side to side.

"Please," said Translator. "Please, give them the right answers. It will be better."

"We do not believe you," said Baldy. "Who sent you here?"

"Nobody sent me here. I am here to research a book."

"Peter from Scotland says hi," Translator said out of nowhere.

"Your friend in New York—why did he tell you to meet with Nasser Hadian?"

As he spoke, I realized my life had been an open book for these men. They must have hacked into my e-mail account. They must know everyone I have seen and everything I have said on e-mail. Shades sat there impassive as stone all the while. His presence was shadowy, unsettling, even though he did nothing and said nothing. He was like a prop, an extra whose presence in a scene sets the whole tone.

"Who are you working for, Mr. Roger?" Baldy let fly his question like a bullet.

"I've already told you. I work for myself, and I'm working on a book. It's commissioned by Random House in New York. If you look back at my e-mails, you will see my correspondence with them."

Did I want to leave Iran? Baldy spoke softly now, barely

looking at me. I was not helping them to solve my problem. I didn't know I'd had had a problem until now. Why was I always changing hotels, he asked. And why did I want to meet Mr. Kiarostami?

They knew everything. All my phone calls as well as my emails.

Did I know that my friend in New York was an agent for the CIA? He was using me, Baldy said. Did I work for the State Department or for a philanthropic foundation? Western nonprofits and philanthropic foundations came here all the time under the pretense of doing good work and then served as a cover for Western intelligence. They were part of the Velvet Revolution.

"We know you know this, Mr. Roger. They try to spread a liberal agenda. But we don't want a liberal agenda in Iran. Do you understand?

I did understand, I said. But I was sure that my friend in New York did not work for the CIA or any other government organization. And neither did I. Nor did I work for the State Department or any philanthropic foundation. I was a freelance writer. It was as simple as that.

They all shook their heads, even Translator, who I was coming to realize was not just a translator after all.

"You are not helping us to solve your problem. I'm sorry." Baldy was looking at his fingers and almost mumbling to me from across the room, as if he'd lost interest. "You give us no choice. We are going to have to take you somewhere else for further questioning. Somewhere comfortable. Somewhere you know."

"I would like to exercise my right to call my embassy."

Baldy and Translator laughed and shifted positions on their chairs. "You have no rights. You are in Iran."

Shades sat as impassive as ever.

Just then there was a knock at the door, and a man walked in with my baggage. They must have asked the airline for it before

I had even sat down in their office. So then their questions were merely a charade. This was all leading to some foregone conclusion, whatever that might be.

"Please come with us now, Mr. Roger. We will go back to Tehran." Translator was curt now in his directive.

They stood up, and with two behind me and one in front, they walked me out of the airport to their car. I was not afraid. I don't know why, but I felt strangely calm, as if this were a play I had landed a part in a long time ago and now the curtain was finally rising.

We drove for an hour back into Tehran. Watching the dark streets fly by, I wondered what would happen next. I felt genuinely curious, interested in the story I had walked into, and apprehensive at the same time, embarking as I was on an unexpected adventure not of my conscious choosing. If I ever needed some wisdom from Rumi, it was now. I tried, but with only partial success, to feel the truth in some lines that I knew by heart:

> *Be grateful for whatever comes*
> *because each has been sent*
> *as a guide from beyond.*

We came to a stop finally at the rear door of the very hotel I had left earlier that afternoon, the Estaglal. We took a service elevator to the fourteenth floor and they ushered me into a suite with a king-size bed, a couple of sofas, and a spectacular view of the city. They ordered tea, then dinner for me, and continued with their questions, frequently returning to the same ones over and over.

They took out a sheaf of papers and told me to write down my answers to the questions.

"Why did you try to contact Jamal Ardogian? Surely you realize he is a particularly sensitive case?"

My New York friend had also given me the e-mail of Ardogian, who was once a senior official in the Iranian government, but was now under close scrutiny. I had e-mailed him, but he'd never replied.

"If you are just a writer, Mr. Roger, why did you have Christmas dinner with Sir Geoffrey Adams, and why did Elizabeth Bucher of the Swiss embassy throw a party for you? You know she is director of the Office of Foreign Affairs, responsible for American interests in Iran. Why was it so easy for you to meet all these people?"

It was true, I could see that it didn't look good from their point of view. Nor did I have a good answer when they asked me why I had arrived at the airport in a diplomatic car. It had all been serendipity, one contact leading to another, and none of it was planned. But from where they were standing, that would be hard to believe.

Over the next few hours I felt for the first time in my life the peculiar sensation that arises when you tell the truth as you know it over and over, and the people listening continue to shake their heads because you are not giving them the answers they want. They already know what the answers should be, according to their version of reality.

"How many times did you meet Hadian?"

"Twice."

"But you said once the first time we asked. Why did you change your answer?"

"Because I was concerned you would read more into it than there actually was."

"Beautiful answer!" Translator chimed in. "This is the first true answer you have given us."

"You are not helping us, Mr. Roger," Baldy murmured. "If we are unable to help you solve your problem, we shall have to hand you over to the security services. They will be much harder. Do you know what an Iranian jail is like? Have you heard of Evin Prison?"

I had. I didn't like what I had heard. It was near midnight now. We had been at it for several hours. Same questions, same answers. Baldy had had enough entertainment for the night, and wanted to go home to his wife and kids.

"You are tired. We will continue in the morning. Good night, Mr. Roger."

Beneath the veneer of civility was always a tangible under-belly of threat. Baldy left for the night, but Shades and Translator stayed. They would sleep on the sofas, they said. I slept fitfully that night, but sleep I did. In the morning I awoke to find my legs trembling. The shivering would start, then stop, then start again; even though I wasn't aware of being afraid. I sat there in bed as my two guards busied themselves with the bathroom. I wanted to stay in bed. It was warm there, a protective womb. I was no longer curious. I had become aware that this might all end rather badly. This was not a story in a Boy's Own adventure series. Yet still my innocence—no, my naïveté—gave me faith that the truth would ultimately prevail.

We sat around the table and ate breakfast together. Translator recited some poetry for me, Hafez and Rumi. The whole scene was tinged with unreality. Eating hard-boiled eggs with a security agent reciting spiritual love poetry. Then he called for my full attention and recited this:

> *I am a supplicant for a goblet of wine*
> *From the hand of the sweetheart.*
> *In whom can I confide this secret of mine,*
> *Where can I take this sorrow?*

"You know who wrote that?" he said. "Not Rumi, nor Hafez. That is one of the poems of Ayatollah Khomeini."

Khomeini, who could hand out death sentences like confetti. Even now, in the midst of an interrogation session, the strangeness of Iran, its divided psyche, both stunned and fascinated me. Where else in the world would you have a ruthless leader writing poems like that? Even more strange, perhaps, where would you find a member of the security services reciting poetry to a detainee?

Translator would alternately blow hot and cold: one minute menacing, the next, my friend. Every now and then he would ask me for clarification on an English phrase. I quipped that I should be charging him for English lessons. One part of me was able to joke; another was increasingly aware all the while of the gravity of my situation.

Baldy returned and we got back to work. Same questions, same answers, plus a few new questions.

"Why did you go to Kurdistan? It's a separatist area, and tourists do not generally go there."

"Yes, we know all about Sheikh Mukhtar Hashemi, but what else were you doing there?"

"Why did you want to meet Iranian Jews in Shiraz?"

"Why did you meet Amir Mahalatti?"

"Write down the names of everyone you met in Iran."

"But you already know the names of everyone I have met. You have read all the e-mails and listened to all my calls."

"Never mind. Write the names down anyway."

By noon Baldy was getting restless.

"You are not helping us," he said in that menacingly quiet and reasonable voice, honey laced with poison. "We have been courteous to you. You are older than us, and in Iranian society elders are treated with respect. But I'm sorry, we have done all we can to help you. We don't believe you. Many people come here using the cover of artistic activities for intelligence purposes. Foundations like Soros, Woodrow Wilson, Aspen—they are all covers for influencing the social context, introducing a liberal agenda.

We view your activities in the same way. We have done all we can. We will leave now, and in a short while the security services will come and take over. I'm sorry."

The stage direction must have been written into this moment. They all stood up at the same time and, without another word, went out of the room and left me alone. I went to the balcony to look at the city spread out before me. I looked down the fourteen floors to see if there was any remote chance of getting out of there. There wasn't, of course. I went back into the room and sat on the bed. The shivering started up again. Every bone in my body knew that my life was at a turning point.

Two men in baggy black suits walked in. One was bigger than I was, with gray hair, in his late fifties, a bulky, glowering presence. The other was shorter and younger, intense eyes staring sharply at me from behind spectacles.

"Sit down over here," said the short one curtly. "Three rules: Never interrupt. Don't ask to repeat the question. Answer succinctly. He's the boss, you listen to him."

The boss spoke a few sentences of Farsi.

"I know you understand Farsi. Do you recognize me?"

"I don't speak Farsi and I do not recognize you."

He was a threatening, looming presence.

"You have seen me before. Now tell me, who are you working for? Which State Department?"

I repeated the same answers I had given to the others. They were not amused. (If these two were from the security services, then *who* were the others?) The short one peered at me over his glasses, and then nodded toward the boss.

"Look, he is getting angry. I've seen him get angry before."

The boss started to crack his knuckles.

I almost laughed. This was deadly serious, I knew; but surely they had been watching too many late-night spy movies.

"Why did you come to the airport in a diplomatic car?"

I understood that it might look suspicious to them, I said, but I was telling the truth when I said that my friend at the embassy simply offered it to me for my convenience.

Then they asked me why I came to Iran on my English passport rather than my American one. I told them I knew that American passport holders had to have a guide with them at all times. I wanted to feel free to do my research on my own, so I came on my English one.

Shorty was holding my English passport. He threw it across the room.

"This is worthless. Do you realize you could disappear today and no one will ever know?"

I did realize that. In that moment, it became all too clear. It was starting to sink in that this was the direction this drama might well be taking.

"With the charges we can make against you according to Iranian law, you will spend several years in jail."

He nodded again in the direction of the boss.

"Everything is up to him. He has told me he will give you one last chance. We will give you five minutes to decide. You have the choice of going to Evin Prison or working for him."

I sat there for a few seconds in total astonishment. This was one outcome I had not even dreamed of. And then the words were out of my mouth: "What does working for him involve?"

"We want you to give us information on philanthropic foundations that are active in Iran. We want the names of the Iranians involved. We want information on other nonprofit foundations. What Harvard is doing in relation to Iran, for example. And foundations in the UK as well. You will meet your boss anywhere in the world that he tells you. We will draw up a contract and give you a salary. We have many Americans on our payroll."

I looked from one to the other, and then never gave my answer a second thought. I didn't need five minutes to decide. I would work for them, I said. And in that moment I actually meant it. I would be glad to work for them if it meant avoiding a prison sentence. But I didn't need a salary or a contract. I was in a good position to do what they wanted without much effort, and I earned my living as a writer. I felt horror at the idea of entering into a contract with them; though for all I knew, if the pressure mounted I would probably have been ready to sign anything.

"Now, write this down," Shorty said. " 'I admit I have made a mistake in collecting negative information and opinions about Iran, and I am ready to work for the Iranian Security Services by giving information on nonprofits and foundations in the arts. I will meet with the boss at designated locations.' Now sign it."

I couldn't say that I had collected negative information, I muttered, because I hadn't. That would contradict the whole point of my book.

"Then put 'negative and positive.' "

"Good. You will be able to come to Iran whenever you want. But what guarantees do we have that you will do what you say?"

The same question had crossed my own mind. I didn't know what guarantees I could give them.

Shorty adjusted his glasses and told me to stand up next to the boss. He brought out a camera and told me to smile at my boss and shake his hand. We posed for him with false smiles, and Shorty took a couple of photographs.

"We can cause trouble for you with this photo," he said. "Be sure you follow through. The other team will be here in a few minutes to take you to the airport and put you on a flight later tonight. When you reach passport control, you will be given your passport. In it will be a slip of paper with our e-mail address on it. We will e-mail you in a week."

Then they left as abruptly as they had come. I waited. Ten minutes passed, and no one appeared. Half an hour passed. I went out and stood on the balcony. I could not believe that I might actually go free. They were probably playing with my mind. For all I knew, I could be somewhere in this city for years. Maybe this was it for my life. Maybe it would end here.

But then, would it really make a great deal of difference if I never got out of here? My book would not happen; the rent on my apartment would not be paid; my life as I knew it would come to an end. But I had had a rich and eventful life. I had loved and been loved. Was there anything I would be leaving undone? I didn't think so. Nothing except the book I had come here to write. The one that had gotten me into this trouble in the first place. I did want to finish that. But if I didn't, I didn't. And if I ever did, it would have a different ending now.

Though I had many dear friends, I had no special somebody who would be devastated by my disappearance. Nobody who needed my song to go on playing. I remembered a friend telling me that she chose life when on the brink of suicide because of the love she felt for her dog. There was no one I wanted to live for with that intensity. I gazed over the city as dusk fell, the mountain looming behind, the lights twinkling on. If I ever get out of here, I thought, the one thing I would like for my life is someone to love again. If there was one thing I was certain of on that balcony, it was that love was the one thing above all that was worth living for.

An hour had passed since the two men had left. In that hour I came to know three things. First, I knew that even as I was part of a web of loving relationships that I cherished, I was at the same time utterly alone in this life. Existentially, essentially alone, as when one dies. As one may be upon hearing a diagnosis of cancer, or upon surviving a car crash. No one could share this turn of events in Tehran with me. No one could even know where I was.

But then the second thing I knew beyond all doubt was that the narrative I had assumed to be my identity was a fabrication, a fiction spun out of my neurons. Roger the traveler, the writer, the romantic, even Roger the lover of Rumi, was a provisional reality. My memories, too, were shifting and subject to change. On that balcony, all my usual reference points had drifted away. The familiar story of my life meant nothing in my present circumstances.

And yet, and yet, the very absence of my well-worn identity felt like a sudden breath of freedom; like taking off a tight-fitting suit that I had not even realized I was wearing. Now I understood that line of Rumi's, where he said we can walk around without clothes on! Now I could see that this freedom from my own cherished narrative was what I had been hankering for all along without knowing it.

Even terms like *alone* and *not alone, free* and *unfree, English* or *American* didn't make sense without my usual identity. Yet in this nakedness, not knowing anything about my life from here on in, something essential continued to palpitate, to throb beneath my skin. I am! Whatever happens, I realized then, I am. I felt the essence of who I was to be a fact independent of the apparent events and dramas of my life. Feeling this in that hotel room in Tehran was the greatest freedom I had known. *This* was my true home, a home without walls. In that moment it felt like the most spacious home of all.

Whether or not I love again; whether or not I ever write this book; even whether I live or die: whatever happens, I am—I saw and felt it as clear as day. None of this was a thought; it was a felt sensation. I felt intensely, intensely alive. Not with excitement, no, it was quite different from that. I was alive with a deep and solid and sober peace.

My curiosity emerged again. I wondered what the next chapter in the story would be. There would always be a story until there wasn't; even though I knew now with visceral certainty that however the story turned out, it didn't define who I was in essence, ungraspable, that home without walls.

It's not that I didn't have preferences. Of course I wanted my freedom. Really wanted it. But I could also feel a calm and sober detachment about whatever might happen next. The story from here on in might well not be the story I thought I was going to live. And in some inexplicable way, even that would be all right. I would continue to be, whatever happened.

A door opened in the room behind me, and Translator and Shades walked in. Shades had replaced his sunglasses with a pair of regular ones.

"We are going to the airport at 10:00 P.M.," Translator said, in a markedly gentler tone. "We need $250 to pay for your ticket. We will order you dinner and be back later."

An hour later I was outside of the room, in the ordinary world, passing through the lobby and on into their car. Everything tilted almost to normal.

We walked into the airport, and almost immediately someone shot out a hand to greet me.

"Hey, Roger, what happened?" It was Merdad, the Swiss embassy driver!

I briefly grasped his hand as Translator and Shades whisked me on through the crowd and around a corner.

"Who's that?" Translator was serious again, and worried.

"The Swiss embassy driver. It's his job to pick people up from the airport."

I waited with Shades while Translator ran back to see what Merdad was doing.

"He's running around looking for you," Translator said breathlessly when he returned. "I'm sorry, this could mean trouble for you. He's probably called the embassy."

But we went on up some stairs into an official part of the terminal. Translator and I sat down on some chairs while Shades would still see if he could get my ticket. Merdad, it seemed, had stopped worrying about me and was looking for the arrivals from a Swiss flight. We sat for a couple of hours. There was a flight to Dubai at 1:30 A.M., but Shades did not reappear, and that flight left without me.

Translator began quoting poetry again, both ancient and modern, and went on to inform me there were four kinds of knowledge: revelation, reason, scientific knowledge, and the knowledge of the mystical heart. Words, he said, were as close as we could come to the essence of truth, but they were only ever the shadow of truth. This security agent was also a philosopher.

"The trouble with your culture is that the Enlightenment separated you from spirituality and ethics. Our culture still has these deep roots, which is why it will eventually take over the world."

So he expected the *ummah,* the community of Muslims, to take over the world. Perhaps that was why the Islamic Republic was continuing to export its revolution to Lebanon and Palestine. As he spoke, I felt he was probably mouthing the official line of Ayatollah Yazdi, the powerful cleric who was the spiritual mentor of Ahmadinejad. He was certainly giving voice to what most of his colleagues in the Security Services and the Revolutionary Guard were hoping for.

"Mr. Roger, excuse me for asking, but do you live alone?"

"Yes, I do."

"We can never understand how people in the West live alone. I have heard that millions there live alone. We value family and community. This is why we don't want the global culture to wear away our traditions. And why we don't like these liberal foundations."

"Do you have a wife?" I asked.

"No, I live with my parents."

I was trying not to say too much, unsure of whether he was merely engaging me in conversation or still trying to elicit some sort of confession of "negative" beliefs from me. At the same time, this was a unique opportunity to put questions to a representative of the conservative faction.

I asked him what he thought of Ahmadinejad.

He was a man of the people, Translator said. He had been fortunate enough to shake Ahmadinejad's hand in the street. He was the first politician to use postmodern language. The Israelis spoke of a Holocaust, and he made the opposite argument in order to cast the whole subject into the realm of relative truth.

When I asked Translator if he thought Ahmadinejad would win the upcoming election, he said he thought so; though if he ran, Khatami would have a chance, too.

"But Ahmadinejad made economic promises that haven't materialized," I said. "Surely that will make a difference?"

Translator looked at me fiercely and crossed his legs.

"What the West will never understand is that in Iran only the elite care about the economy. The poor care only for the Shiite martyrs. And as for his foreign policy, I think that President Ahmadinejad has been a great success. Because of him, three countries, including Bolivia and Venezuela, withdrew their ambassadors from Israel after the recent assault on Gaza."

Just then a woman passed by, clothed in black from head to foot.

"But what do you think about the chador?" he asked me.

I hesitated for a second, and then I decided to speak my mind. "I think it makes men and women unequal. You can choose to wear your sports jacket, but she cannot choose what she wears. Individual choice is an intrinsic right in my culture." Then I could contain myself no longer. "Why are you doing this work?" I asked. "You are young, you are thoughtful, intelligent, and you speak good English. Surely you could do all sorts of things. Why did you choose this line of work?

"I am only a translator," Translator replied, almost apologetically, as if to laugh off the moment when he had admitted he was not just a translator. "Maybe in a year or two I will do something else. In the university maybe. I shouldn't be telling you this, but I'm a literature graduate." He smiled self-consciously, almost proudly. "But you see, the Intelligence Services are the protectors of truth and are in its service. It is a noble calling," he said. "It is also difficult to get work here, and this pays quite well."

I realized as he was speaking that I had learned something else. Something obvious, but that I had never had to confront so directly in my life before. There was a darkness in this world that was probably in all people, but that was certainly active in some. Zoroaster may have been right. Perhaps we are all involved, knowingly or not, in an eternal struggle between the light and the dark.

The darkness was a fact in my life now, and not just an item on the daily news. I had encountered it; it had clipped my wings, shown me that my freedom had limits like anyone else. I had lived all my life in a liberal democracy. I had traversed through the events and circumstances of my life with a large degree of good fortune. I had tended to assume that most things were possible, given the right motive and opportunity. But now I knew for a certainty that I had no special pass—that everything could be taken away from me at any moment. That knowledge gave me a weight, a humility and a gravity that I had not possessed before.

While we had been talking, Shades—who was barely noticeable, almost pathetic, without his sunglasses—had been running up and down stairs in the apparently complicated quest to find me a ticket. Finally he stood in front of us with a ticket for a flight at 4:10 A.M., which wasn't far off. Our little airport charade had been going on for hours.

We went to the passport control, and I watched as my passport was handed back and forth among several officials. Apparently there were confusions in the chains of command here, too, and some people had still to be convinced that I had the green light to leave. And then it happened. Shades gave me my ticket and passport and my cell phone. I told him how grateful I was for all his running about on my behalf, and I meant it.

He said something to Translator, who said, "He doesn't believe you."

They didn't believe me; even in this moment they didn't believe me. But it was true, and I said so again. I had just spent thirty-six hours with these two characters. Despite their ideology, I felt their humanity and even a certain fondness for them. We were all human beings doing our part. We shook hands and they left me to walk through to the departure gate.

Only when the plane lifted off the ground did I feel I was finally free. Until that moment I was half expecting to be apprehended again. But now an immense relief washed over me. Yet I still felt compromised, even unclean in some way. I had told them I would work for them. I had lied my way to freedom—though I couldn't help thinking they knew that would be the case all along. Perhaps their offer to me was a way for them to let me go without losing face. I would never know. I pushed back my seat and took the warm towel the flight attendant handed me. Then I remembered what the baggy black suit had said about my passport. I took it out, and there indeed was a piece of paper folded in the back. On it was scrawled "Shadowoftruth@gmail.com."

One February morning in 2009, a few days after landing back in New York, I opened my inbox and there was an e-mail from Tehran. It said,

> *Dear Roger,*
>
> *So glad to have spent time with you in Estaglal Hotel. We are ready to send a contract as per our agreement and we look forward to working with you. You will be welcome in Iran whenever you wish and we will do all we can to help you with your so-called book. Please reply as soon as possible.*
>
> *Sohrevad Sohrevardi*

So it was not over yet. Though there were friends close by, I felt my aloneness again. Even in New York I was not beyond my interrogators' reach. Their irony, their cynicism, had flashed over the Web to greet me that morning: Sohrevardi was the name of one of Iran's great philosophers and teachers of mysticism, and he was a martyr in the cause of the national culture of Iran in the eleventh century. "The Intelligence Services are the protectors of truth and are in its service," Translator had said.

My friend in New York had already arranged for me to talk to the State Department and to debrief with the FBI in Washington, but right then, sitting there with their message on the screen, his concern was small consolation. I immediately changed my e-mail address and took the old one out of service. I bundled myself up against the winter cold and walked down Seventh Avenue to a store where I could change my cell phone number.

Everything was normal; the people hunching by, the horns of the taxis, the street signs and lights. Yet I was conscious now in a way I had never been that there were invisible layers, other worlds, that lay hidden within consensus reality. I wondered if I might be followed. Surely not; but somewhere in this city there were agents from countries all over the world who were following someone or other. Then there were the criminals who were tailing their prey, and detectives who were tailing them in their turn. This world of everyday appearances masked a great web, not only of illicit but also of covert activity that had simply not existed for me before. I had never read a spy or detective novel in my life. For all I knew, these invisible hands and eyes exerted more influence on the events in the daily news than I would have dreamed possible. More than once that morning, I found myself looking over my shoulder.

I took the Acela Express the next day for D.C. On the way south I got a call on my new number from someone in the State Department. He couldn't be certain, of course, but he thought I should have no cause for concern over here. However, I would be advised not to travel to any country that was a close ally of

Iran's. My one regret, I realized, was that I would never be able to return to Iran, and would never see my friends there again.

"We are arranging for you to meet someone from the FBI," he said. "Just to debrief."

The man on the phone told me to go straight to my hotel room and an FBI officer would meet me there later. My room had a large window that opened onto an exterior terrace, and other guests would occasionally walk past. When the FBI officer arrived—an inconspicuous individual in a gray suit, a white shirt with a button-down collar, and a blue tie—he first inspected the terrace before entering my room. Then he came in and closed the curtain, giving a final peek outside as he did so. He asked me if I knew any of the guests farther along the walkway. I had the feeling that I was in a movie again, just as I had back in Tehran.

For several hours he questioned me in a soft and unassuming voice, sometimes asking the same question in different ways, trying to draw out every nuance of my story. I had been here before; he and my spy team back in Tehran inhabited the same world. Finally, when I had brought him up to date and showed him the e-mail I had just received, he paused for a moment, and wrote some more notes. Then he looked up with those emotionless, almost vacant eyes, and said, "Would you consider answering the e-mail they sent you? You know, play along with them for a while? It could be very helpful to us."

I looked at him, partly in astonishment, but at the same time realizing that I had half expected this all along. He was asking me to be a double agent. The thought flashed through my mind that it might seem suspicious if I refused, or perhaps unpatriotic. But I couldn't restrain myself.

"I would make a terrible spy, no matter who it was for," I blurted out. "I can't keep secrets, and I'd find it an intolerable strain, trying to pretend to be what I'm not. As I told them in

Iran, I'm a writer, not a spy. If I'm going to be of any use to my country at all, it will have to be through writing."

He nodded, stood up, and clasped my hand. Then he was gone, and I was alone in a hotel bedroom somewhere in D.C. I went out into the day, glad for the air, and wandered up Pennsylvania Avenue, sensing the looming might of the country that had become my adopted home. One of the buildings I passed was the headquarters of the FBI. Whatever covert networks the Iranians may have, the United States has a thousand times over. The Iranians and others are right to suspect our actions and motives. They're probably right to think that our eyes were watching them in every corner of their own country.

My own eyes, however, were not among that number. Nor are those of hundreds of others who continue to languish without trial in the jails of Iran. As Haleh Anvari had said, everything in Iran is political, *ba siasat,* "with politics." Truth and justice don't come into it. I later discovered that I was detained a few days before Roxana Saberi, who was not as lucky as I was. She spent several months in Evin Prison on similar charges, before being freed in response to the pressure of an international outcry. Filmmakers, journalists, women's rights activists, three students from Berkeley, and many others continue to suffer imprisonment and even torture there now, on charges doubtless as unfounded as those laid against me.

When I returned to San Francisco, I changed my phone numbers there, too. It was a small but important precaution to take, the FBI agent had said. Even in my familiar surroundings, I continued for a while to have the occasional feeling I was being watched or followed. Some weeks after my return, I heard through official sources that the Iranians did not believe I was who I said I was. They told people in New York that I had met with Israeli agents in Iran.

Zoroaster's name for evil was the Lie. The Lie is a web of lies in official Iran today. The truth is reversed even to the point of claiming that Neda Soltan, the young woman who was murdered by the Basiji on the streets of Tehran just after the elections of June 2009, was in fact the victim of an assassin hired by a BBC reporter.

As the world now knows, Ahmadinejad's faction stole that election and Iran was plunged into darkness again. Since then he and his allies in the Republican Guard have strengthened their grip on the country. They have marginalized not only the reformists but even the conservative group that represents the lineage of the founder of the Revolution, Ayatollah Khomeini. Ahmadinejad and his friends are themselves an extremist group within the Iranian power structure that is acting, so they believe, in the service of the Twelfth, or Hidden, Imam, who is expected any time now. Their job, as they see it, is to smooth the way for his arrival.

Their tactics, unfortunately, have been anything but smooth. Yet for all the brutality employed by Ahmadinejad's men, the human spirit I had witnessed during my time in Iran was more evident in the demonstrations following the election than anyone in the West could ever have expected. Even though that spirit has now been suppressed and swept from the streets—even though it has no political party attached to it, or even a leader—people's minds have changed. Iranians can no longer give their assent to the status quo. We do not know what the future holds, but one thing is certain: the Islamic Republic will never be the same after the deceit and violence that its government has heaped upon its own people. Change is inevitable in Iran. We just don't know the timeline or the direction it will take.

The American view of Iran will never be the same again either. The rantings of Bush about the Axis of Evil are already from another era. We have seen on our television screens that these are people like us. *If you prick us, do we not bleed?* What was true for Shylock the Jew in Shakespeare's *Merchant of Venice* remains as true today for the Iranians as it does for us: we are all flesh and blood and easily frightened.

A large proportion of Iranians want civil liberties like ours, freedom of speech as we have, equality between men and women, and the freedom to vote fairly. They no longer want to be isolated. They want to belong in the global community. None of these is a religiously inspired goal.

For the first time, the change that is being sought in a modern Muslim country is not ideological but secular in impetus. Unlike us, Iranians are no longer complacent. They know how precious freedom is, because they live under its opposite. They have become so desperate they are willing to die for what they feel to be their rights in a global world.

Iran always surprises. It is a remarkable, deeply human, and complex culture. It inspired and surprised me constantly when I was there, and it will surprise us all in the future. Like a Shakespeare play, you might say. Or better, a Ferdowsi saga.

Both Ferdowsi and Shakespeare celebrate the complexity of human nature. The dual forces that Zoroaster named are somewhere in all of us. Even my interrogators thought they were in the service of the Good. We all are convinced that there is a right side and that we are on it. Perhaps the best we can say is that we humans fall easily under the spell of our own convictions.

Ultimately, beyond the notions of right and wrong, self and other, good and evil, it is through love that we know our common ground. It is love that transcends national as well as personal boundaries, that sees through and beyond race and creed to the essential humanity that we share.

Rumi, my faithful guide of souls, says it better than I ever could:

> *Out beyond ideas of wrongdoing and rightdoing*
> *There is a field. I'll meet you there.*
> *When the soul lies down in that grass*
> *The world is too full to talk about.*
> *Ideas, language, even the phrase each other*
> *Doesn't make any sense.*

## ACKNOWLEDGMENTS

First and foremost, my deepest thanks and appreciation is due to every person in Iran who was willing to discuss his or her life and work with me, and who facilitated my meeting with so many other creative individuals besides themselves. Many of these people are named in my book, while some names I have changed for security reasons. Among this large number, I especially want to thank Haleh Anvari, Toufan Garekani, Nasser Hadian, Amir Mahalatti, and Sheikh Mukhtar Hashemi. Without their support, this book would not have seen the light of day.

I owe an unending debt of gratitude to Shaye Areheart, my publisher, who took a risk on commissioning this book in the first place and who stood by it in the darkest of times. And to my editor, Kate Kennedy, whose careful reading and comments unquestionably contributed to whatever virtue the book has now. Also to my agent, Joy Harris, who is always a great asset to have in my corner, and to Gabriela Pfenninger, who provided invaluable love and support and also insightful critical feedback during the writing process. Even a book, as solitary a work as it may seem, takes a village.

My sincere gratitude is also due to the Fetzer Institute for its financial support for my journey to Iran.

Finally, my heartfelt gratitude goes to Coleman Barks and Daniel Ladinsky, whose translations of Rumi and Hafez add a further poetic dimension to the book.

Roger Housden is the author of twenty books, including *Ten Poems to Change Your Life; Ten Poems to Open Your Heart; Ten Poems to Set You Free; Ten Poems to Last a Lifetime; How Rembrandt Reveals Your Beautiful, Imperfect Self; Seven Sins for a Life Worth Living;* and the novella *Chasing Rumi.* He also is the editor of *Risking Everything: 110 Poems of Love and Revelation.* Born in England, he is now an Anglo-American and lives in Sausalito, California.